AF473802

CANADIAN PHOTOGRAPHS

CANA

PHOTO

INTERVIEW BY PETER GALASSI

DIAN

GEOFFREY JAMES

GRAPHS

Figure.1

Vancouver / Toronto / Berkeley

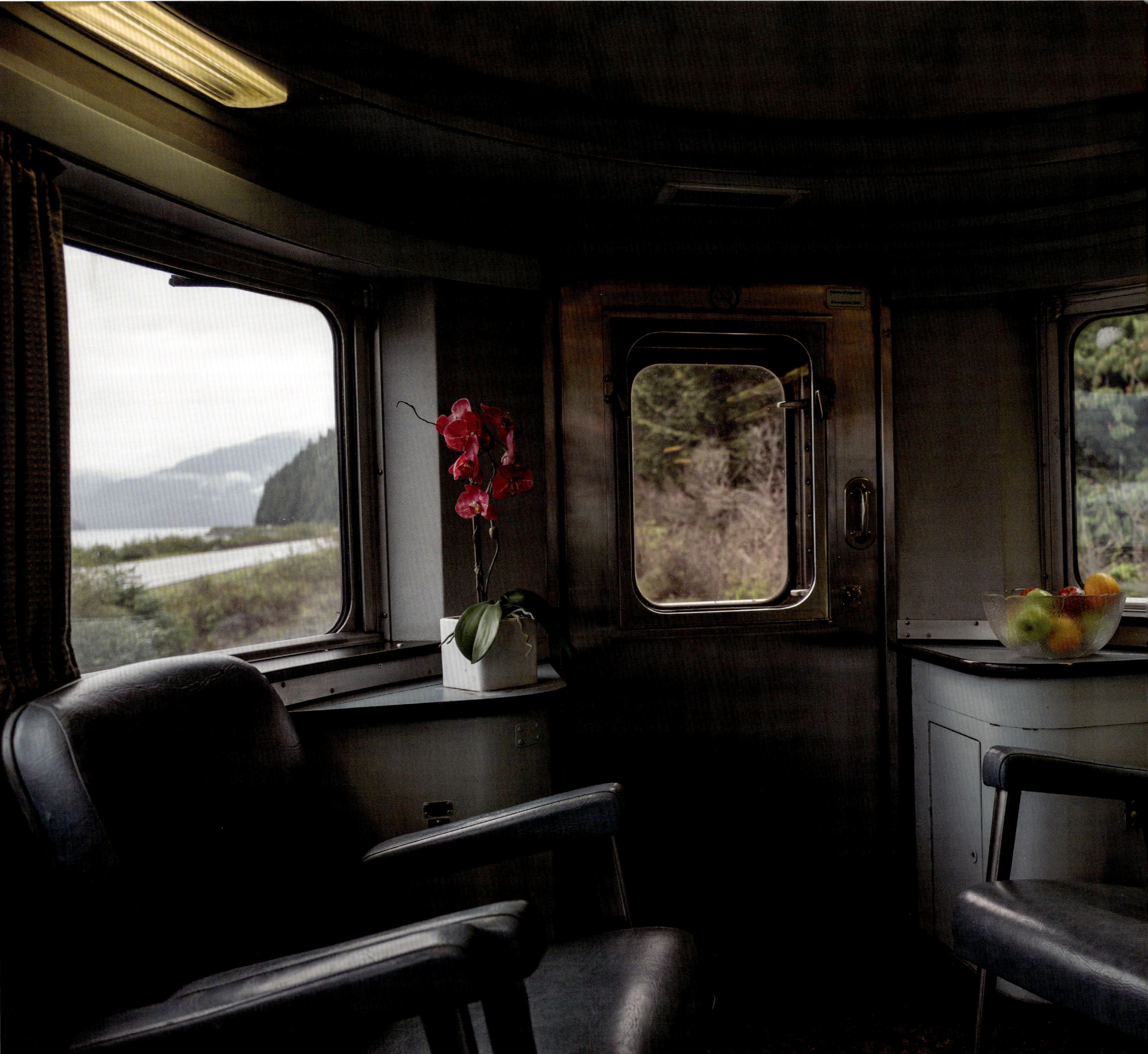

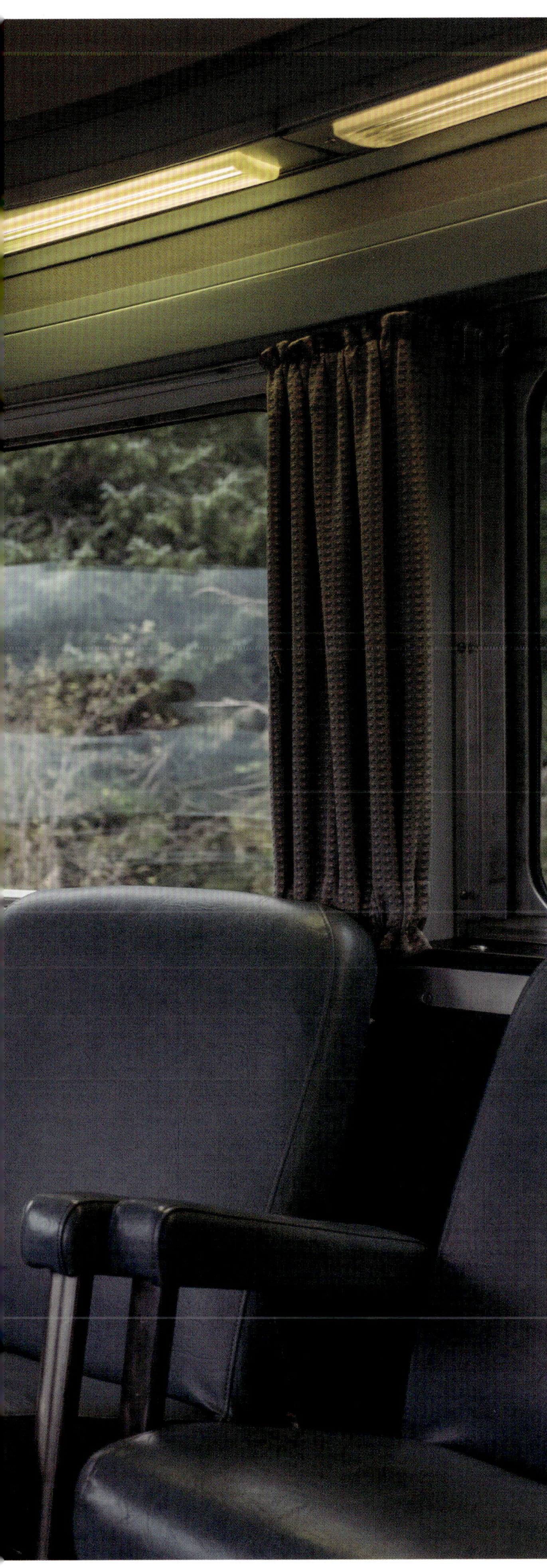

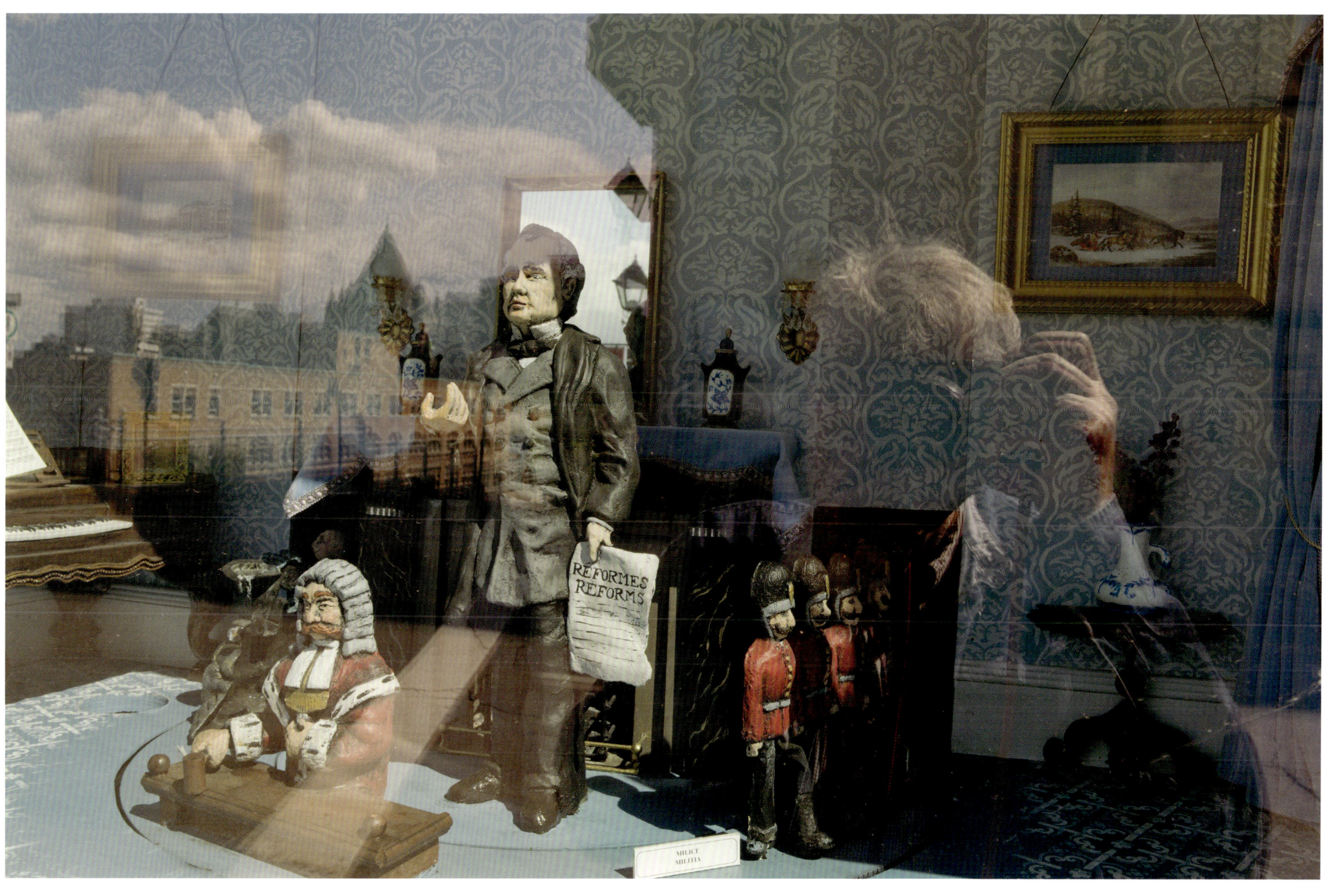
RÉFORMES
REFORMS
MILICE
MILITIA

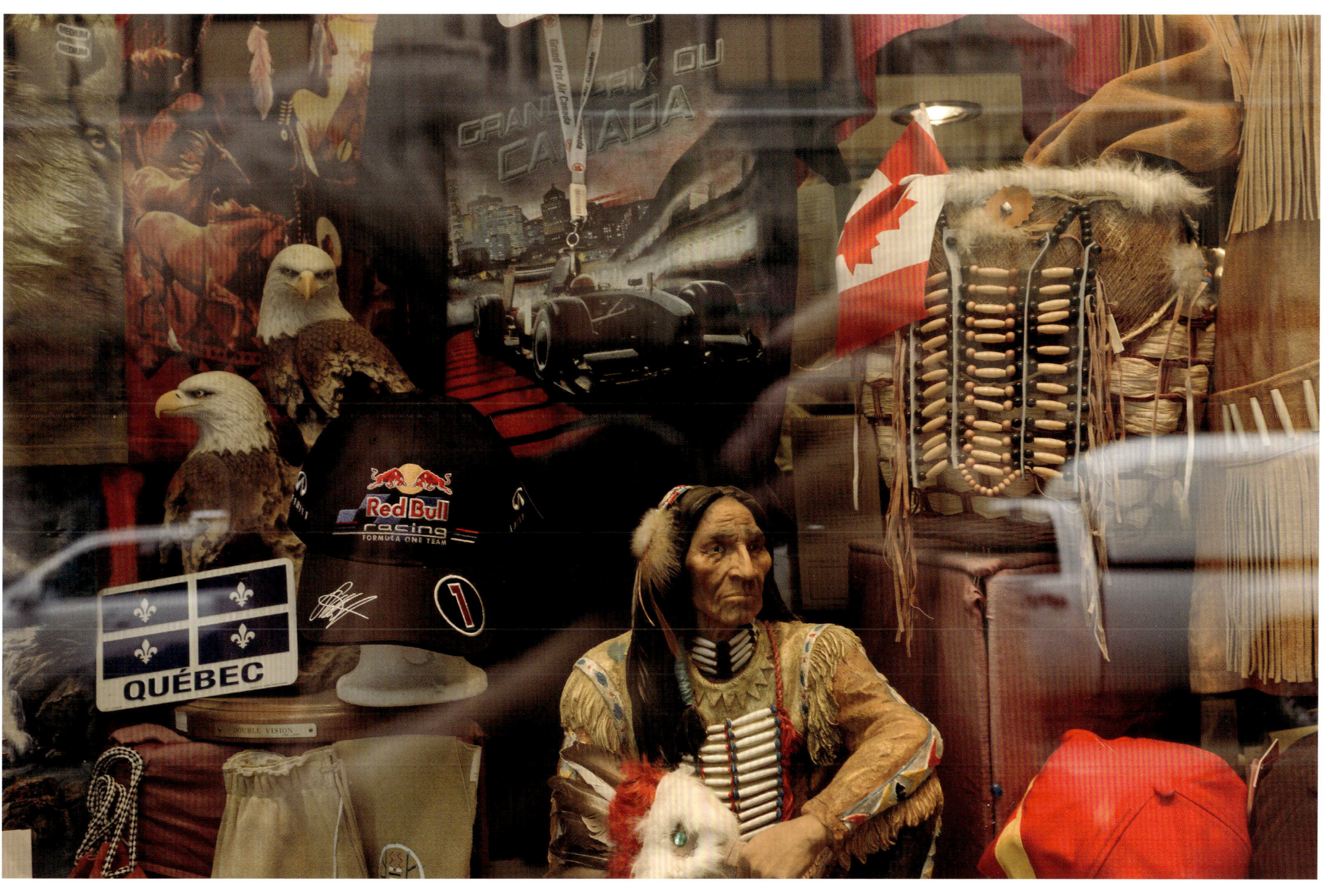
Red Bull
racing
FORMULA ONE TEAM
QUÉBEC
DOUBLE VISION

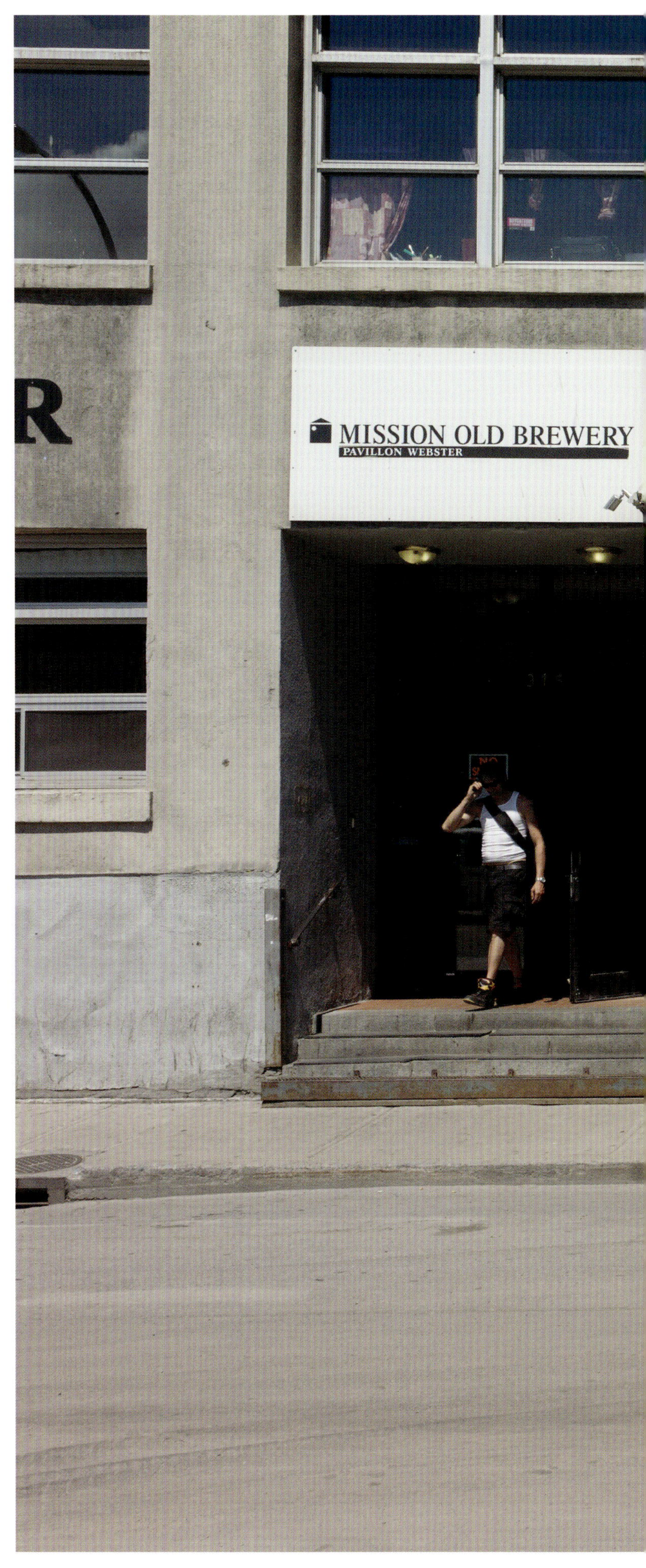
MISSION OLD BREWERY
PAVILLON WEBSTER

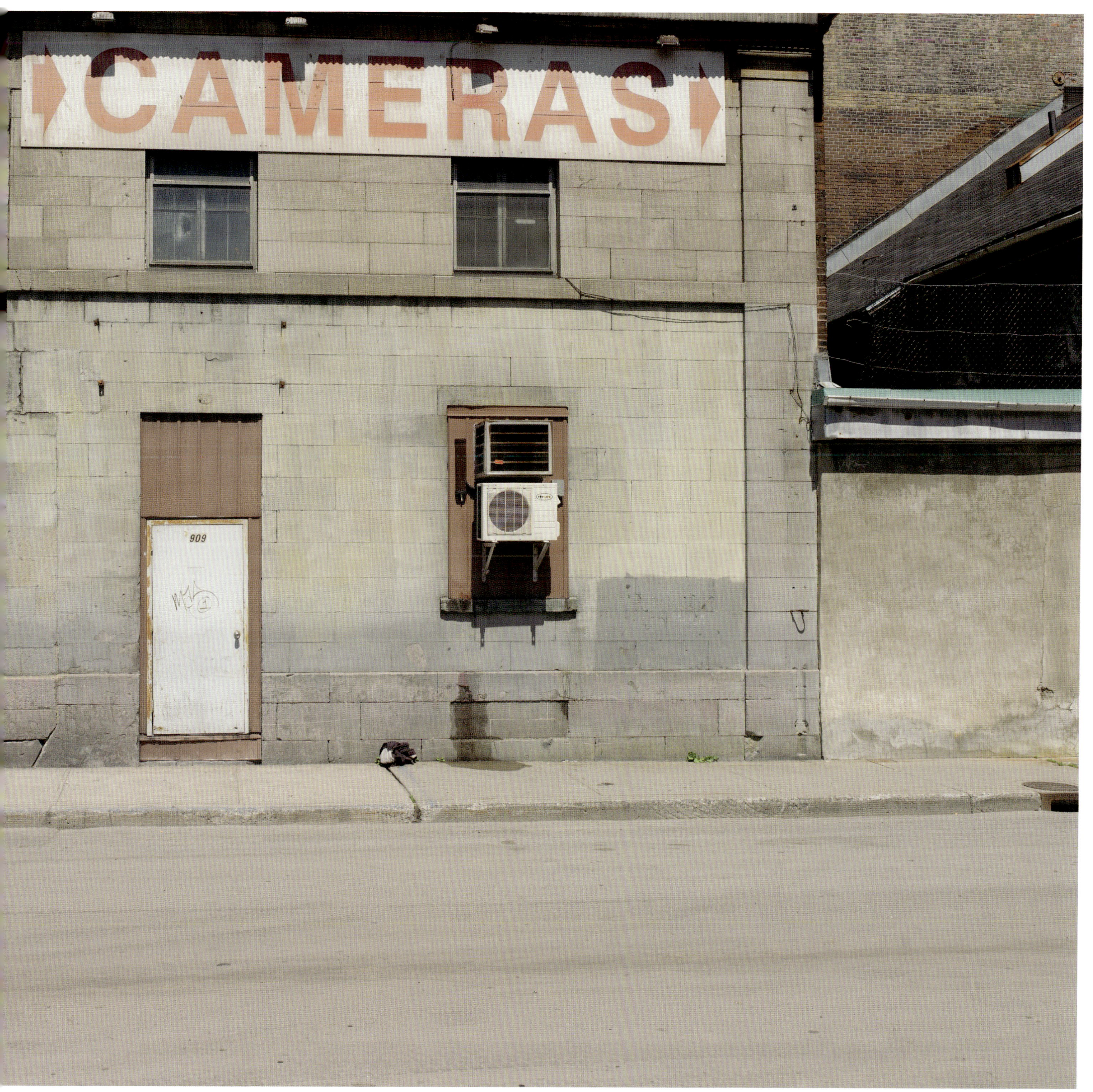
CAMERAS
909

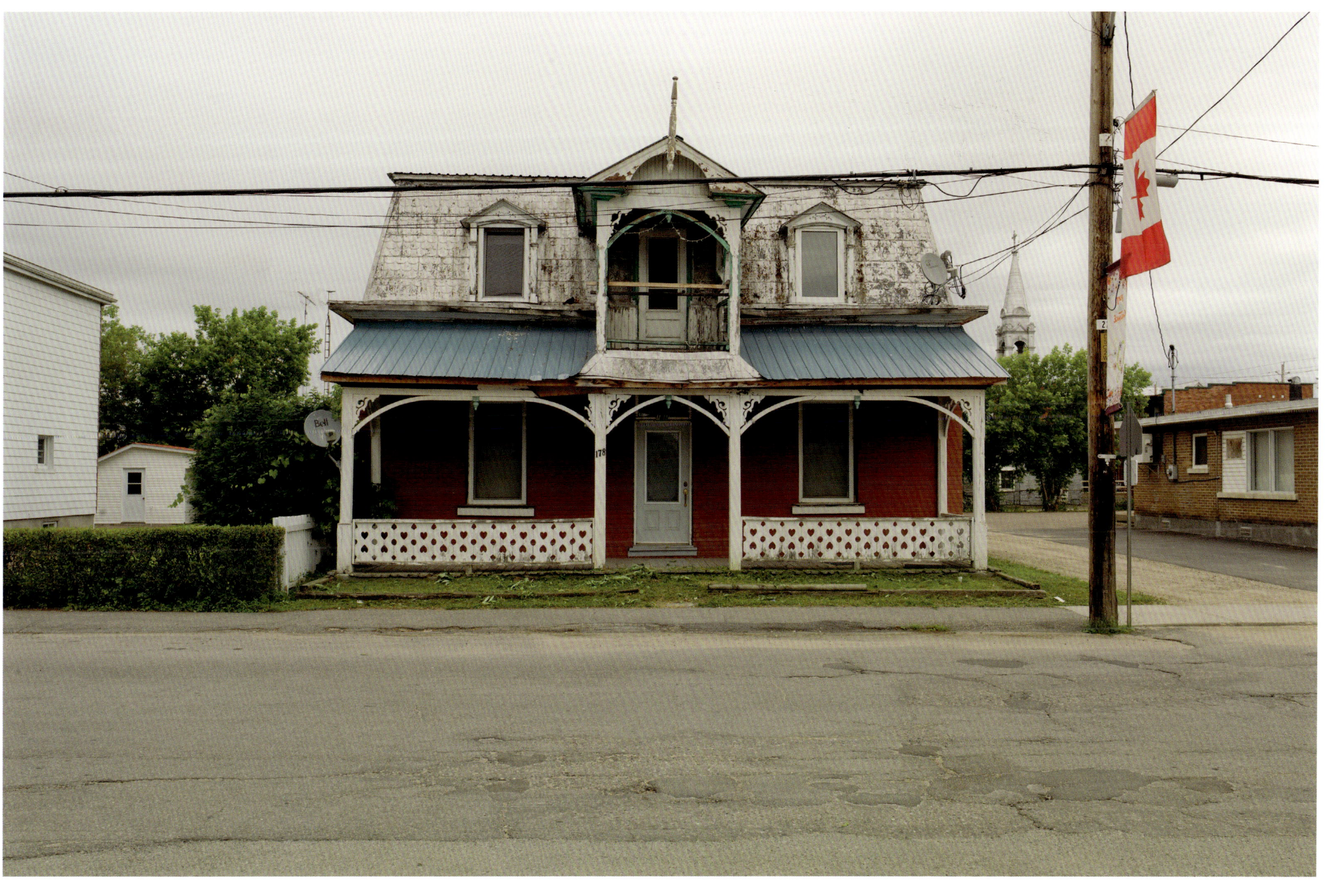
Bell
178

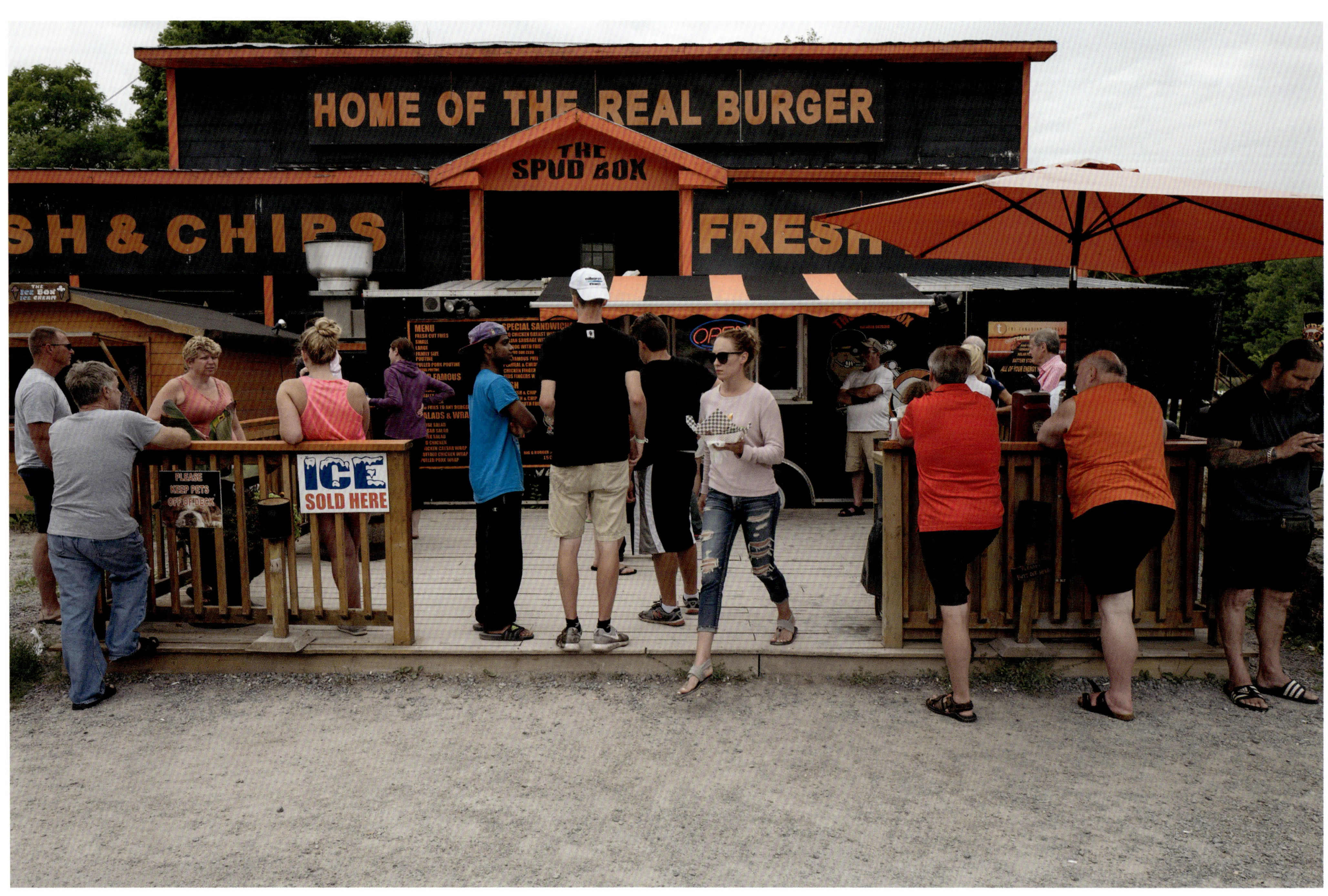
HOME OF THE REAL BURGER
THE
SPUD BOX
SH & CHIPS
FRESH
ICE
SOLD HERE
PLEASE
KEEP PETS
MENU
SPECIAL SANDWICH

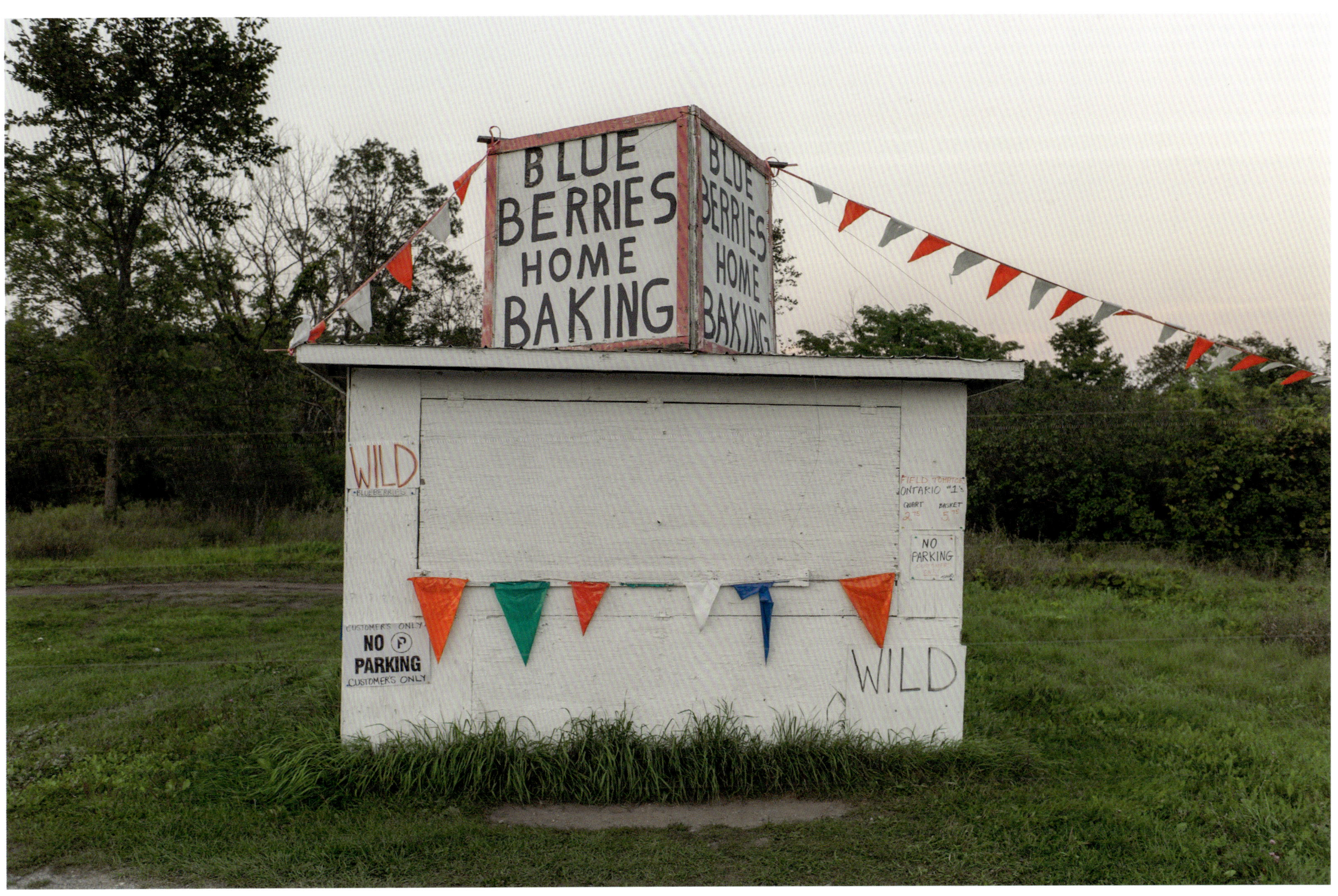
BLUE
BERRIES
HOME
BAKING
BLUE
BERRIES
HOME
BAKING
WILD
NO
PARKING
CUSTOMER'S ONLY
NO
PARKING
CUSTOMER'S ONLY
WILD

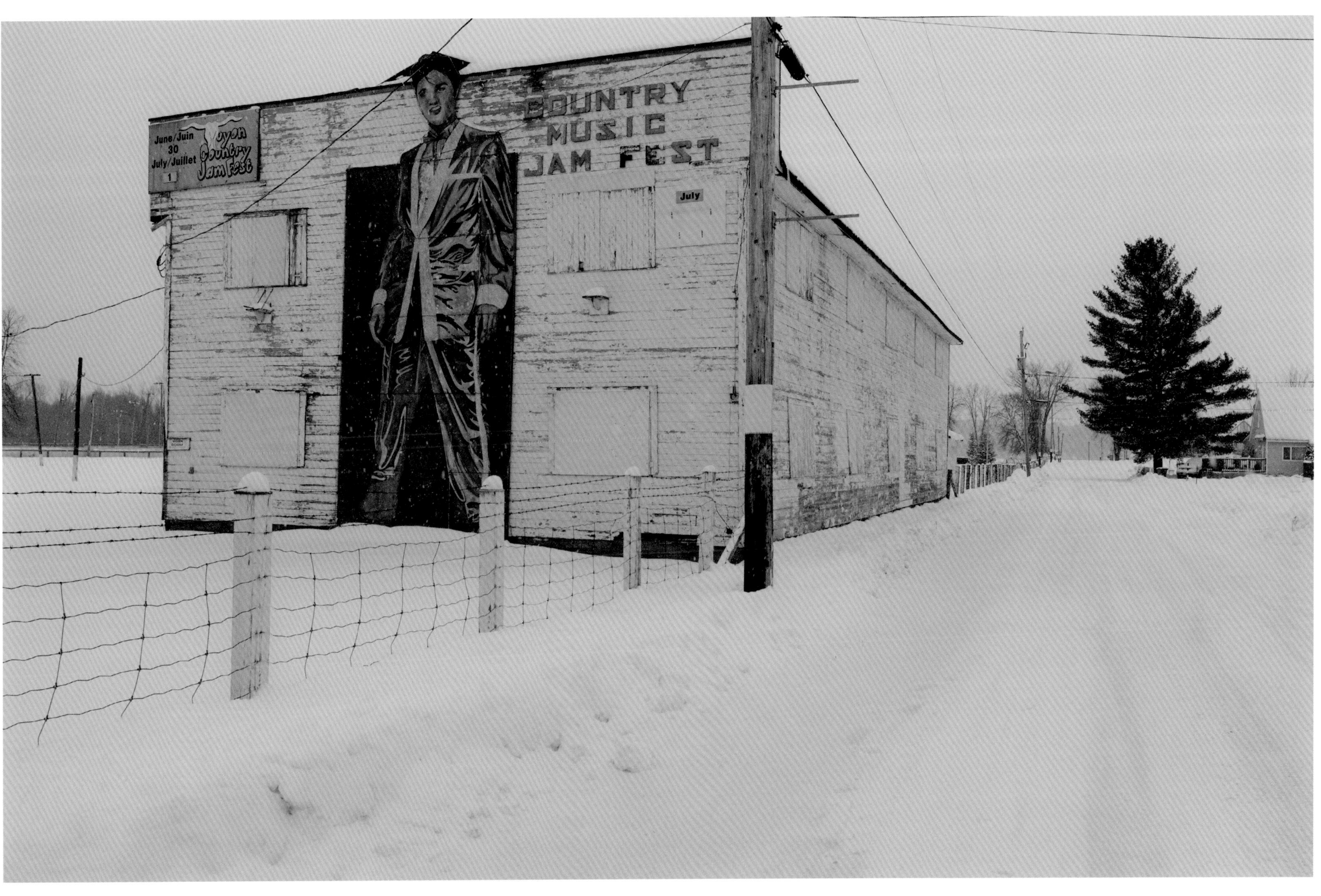
June/Juin
30
July/Juillet
1
Country
Jam Fest
COUNTRY
MUSIC
JAM FEST
July

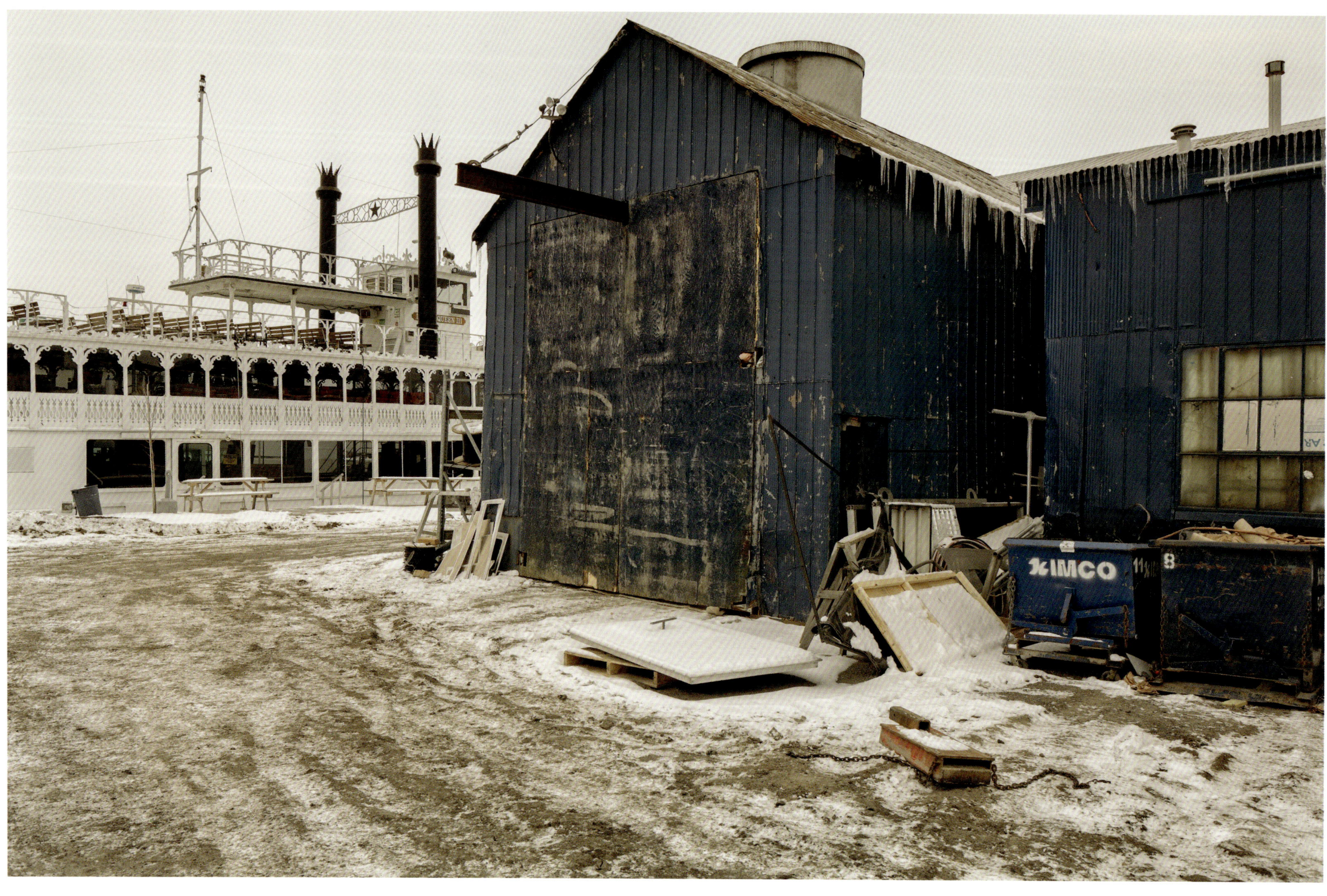
KIMCO

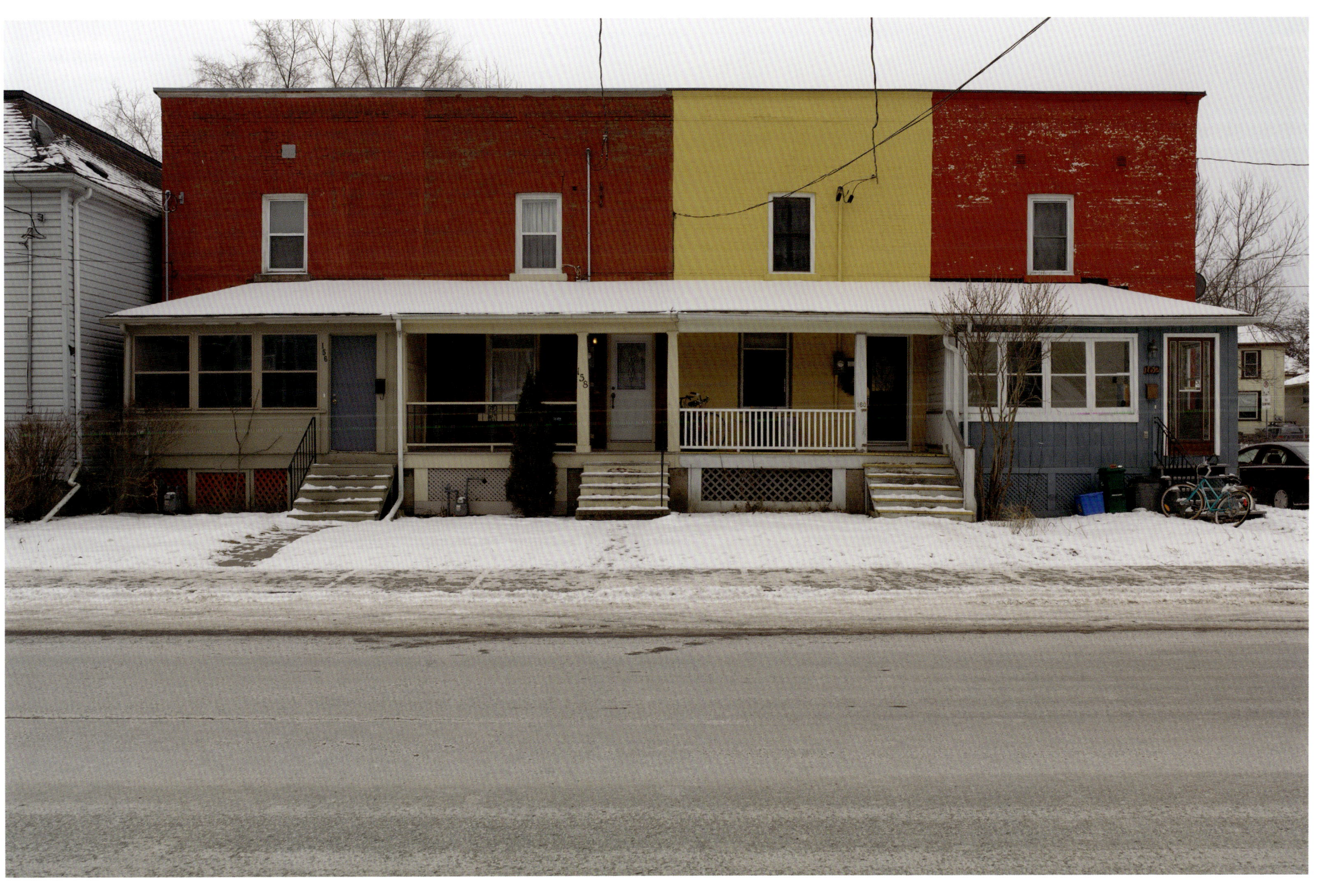

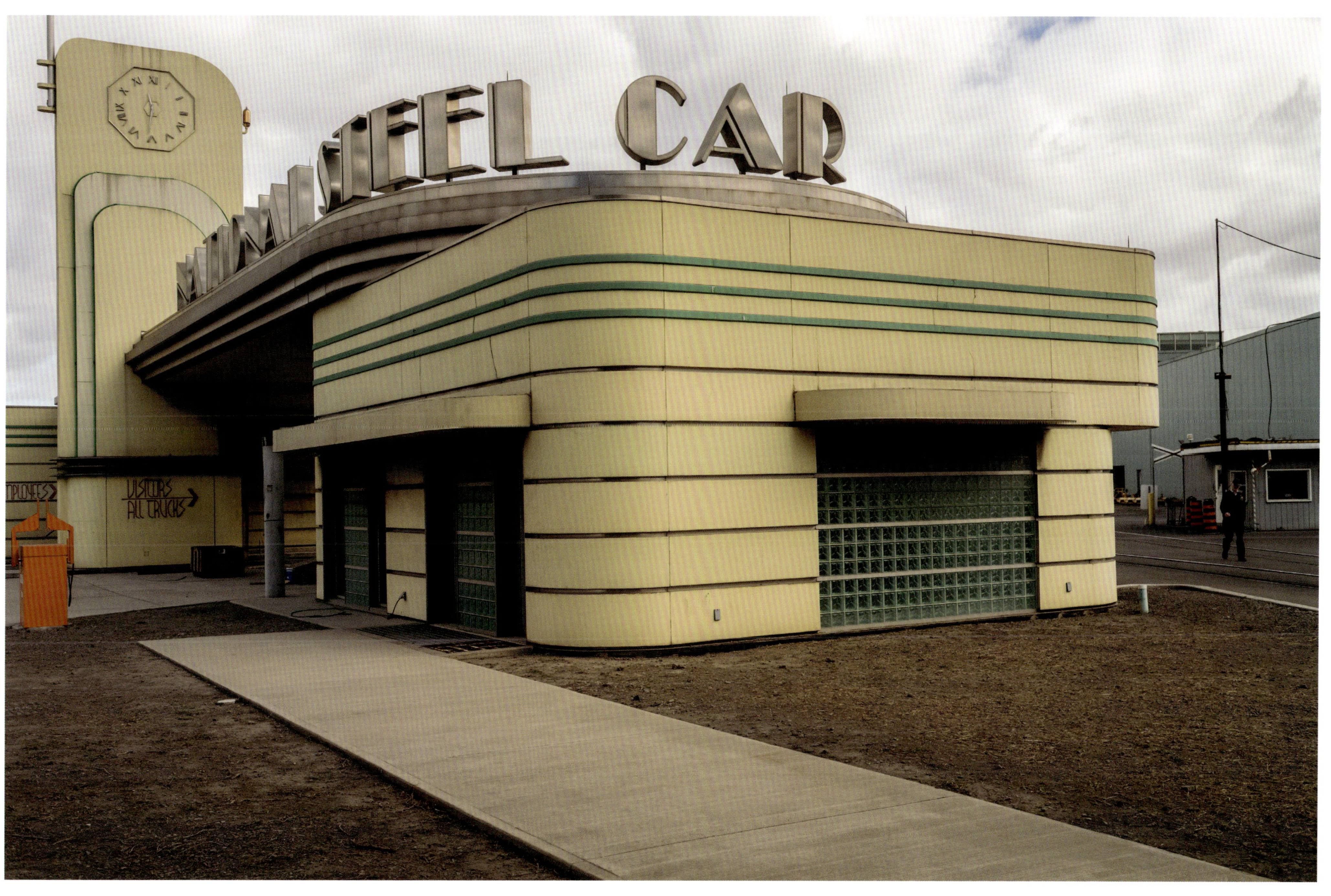
STEEL CAR
VISITORS
ALL TRUCKS

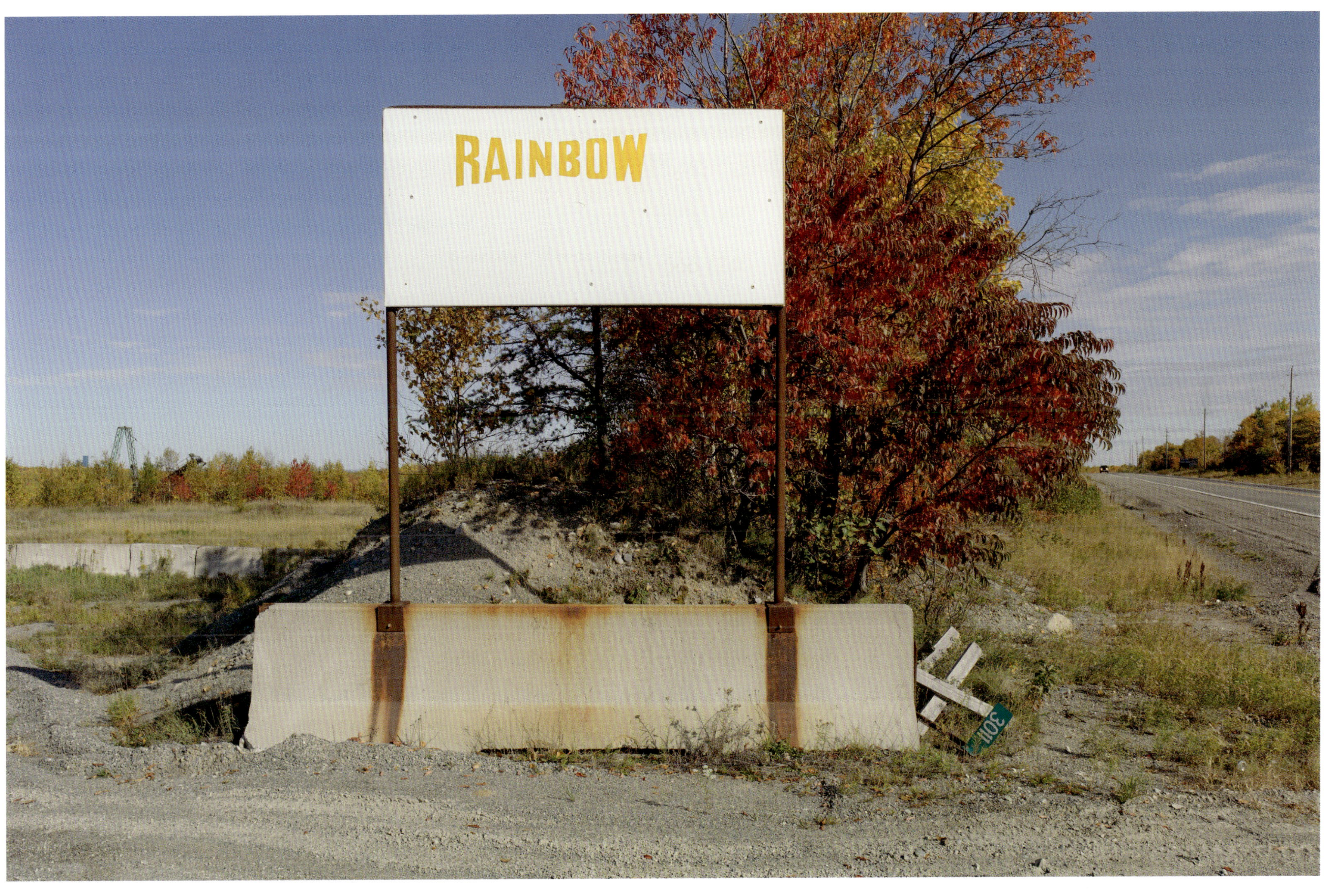
RAINBOW

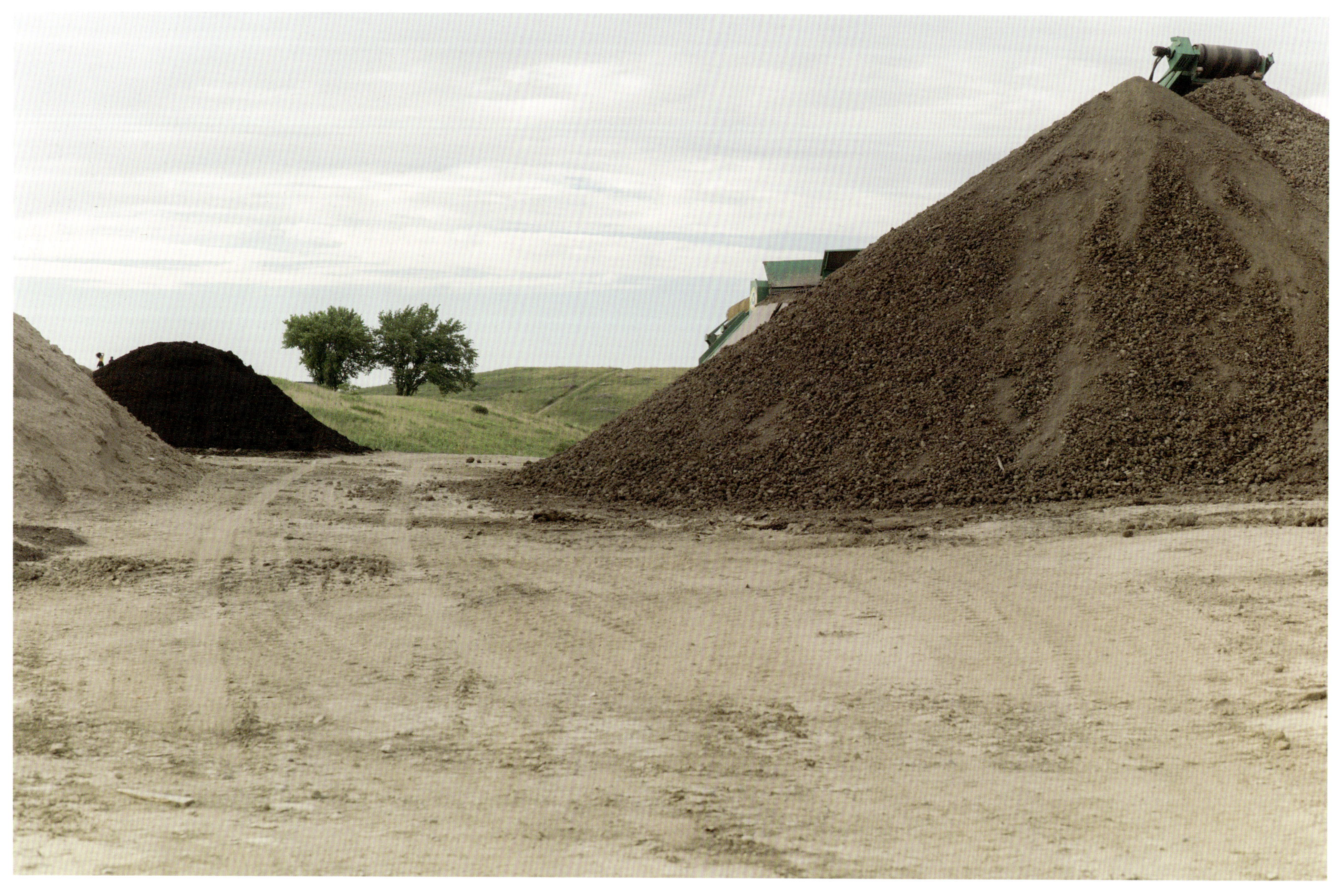

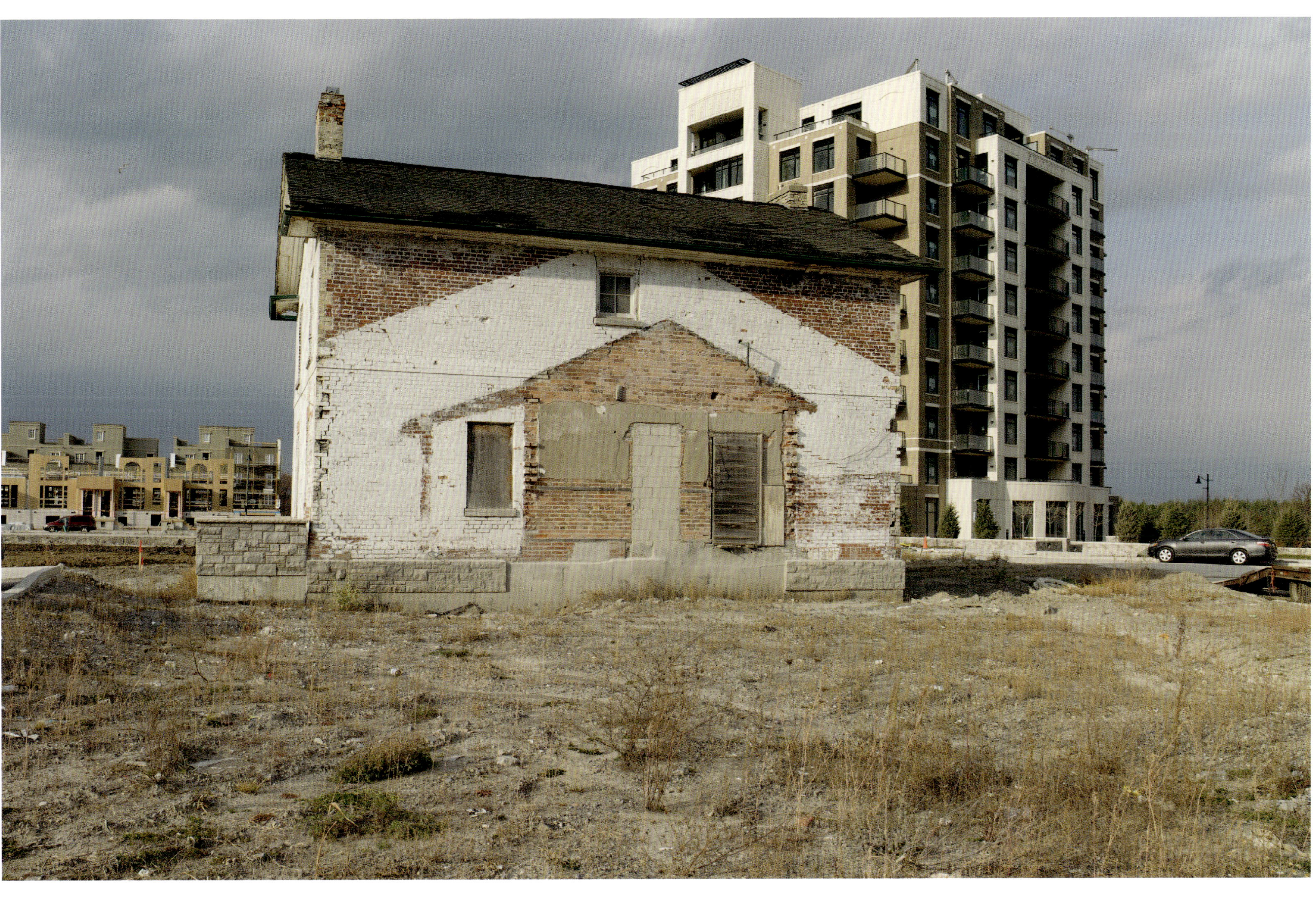

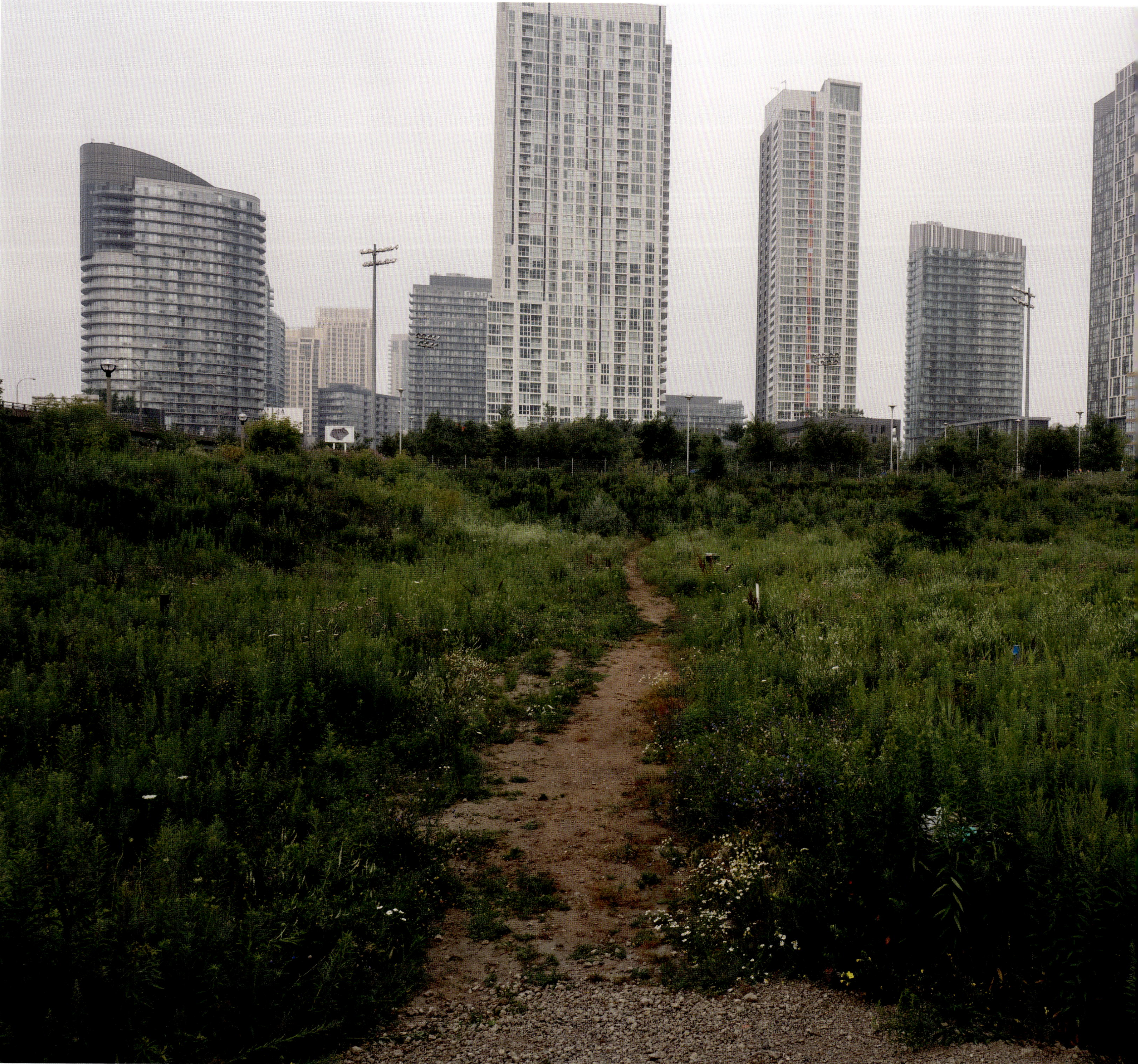

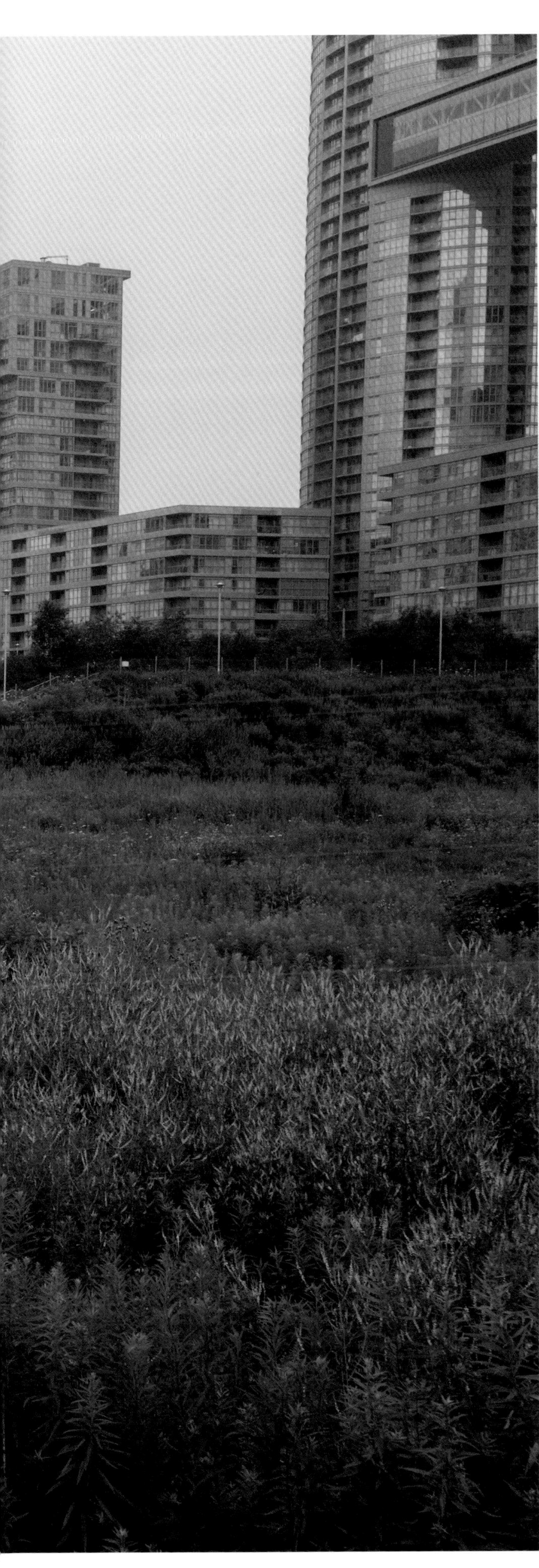

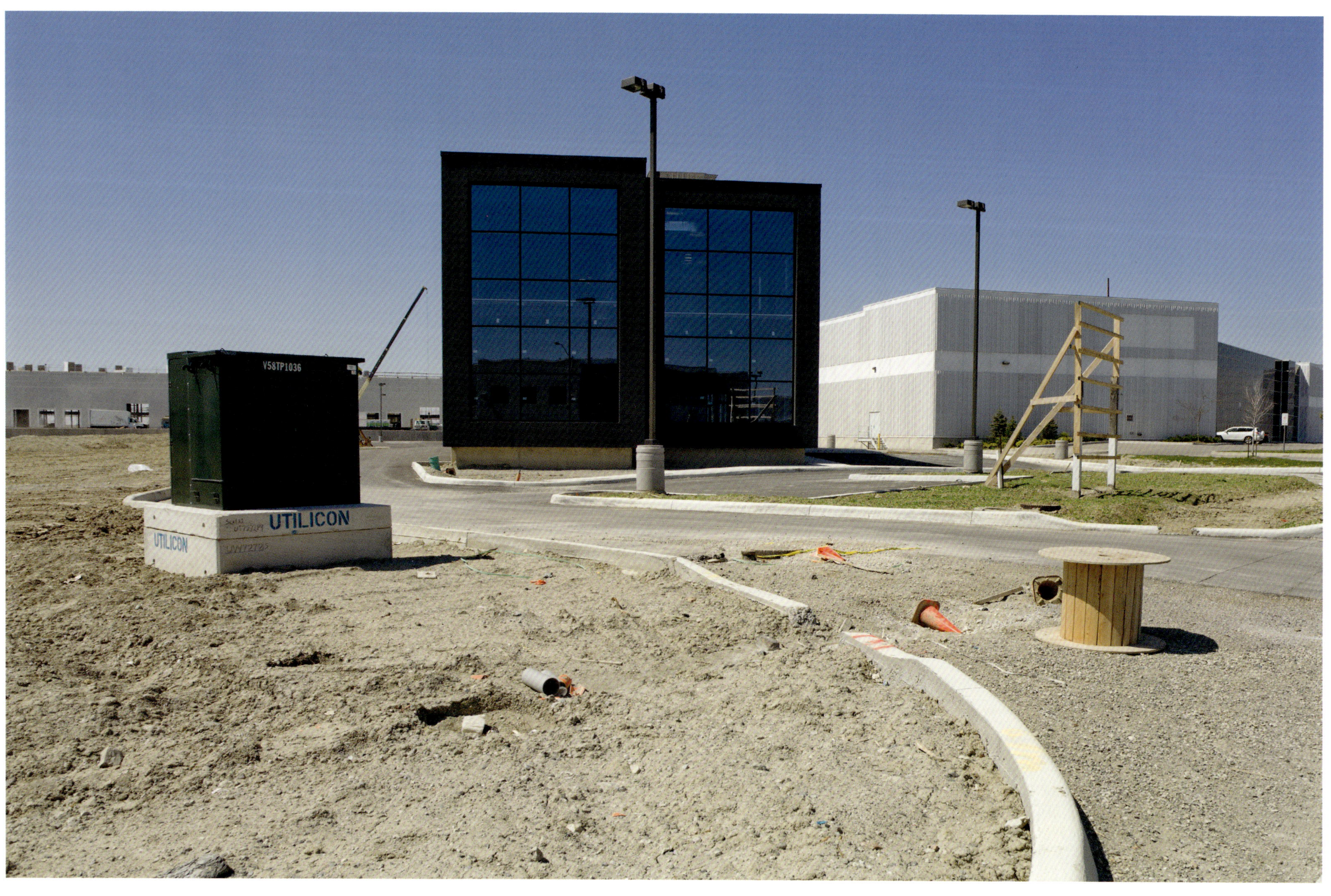
V58TP1036
UTILICON
UTILICON

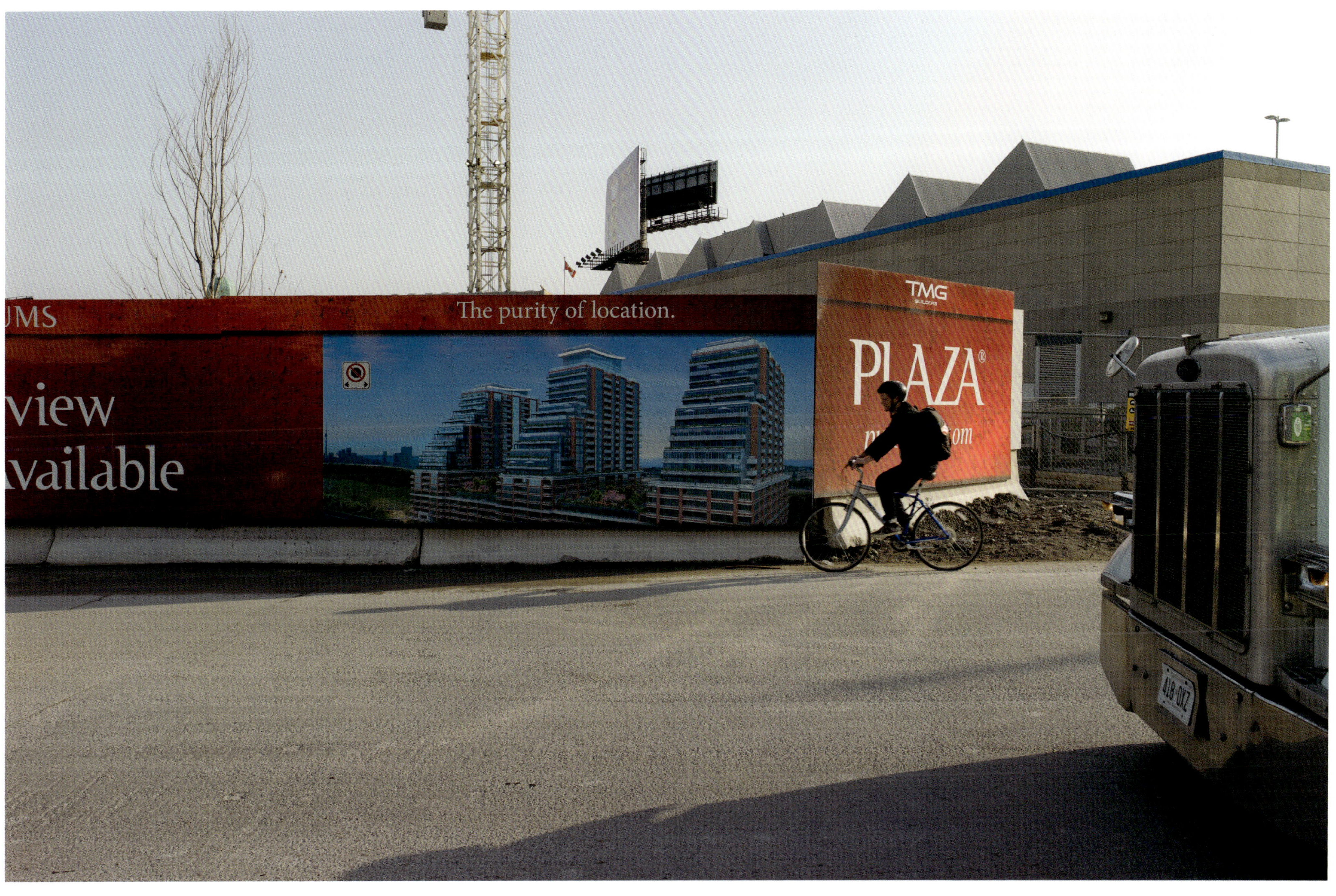
UMS
The purity of location.
view
vailable
TMG
PLAZA®

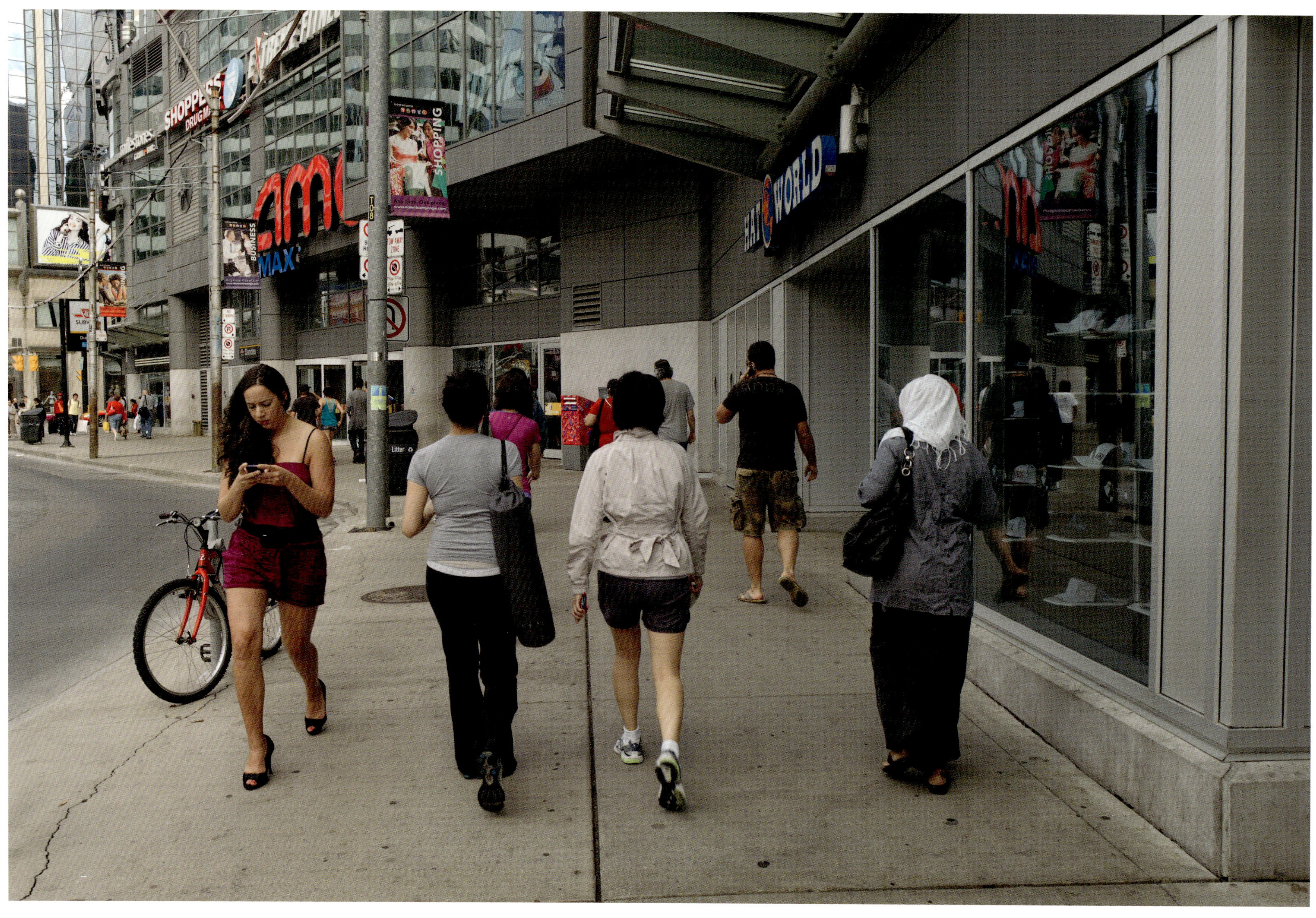
HAT WORLD
SHOPPING
BUSINESS
Litter

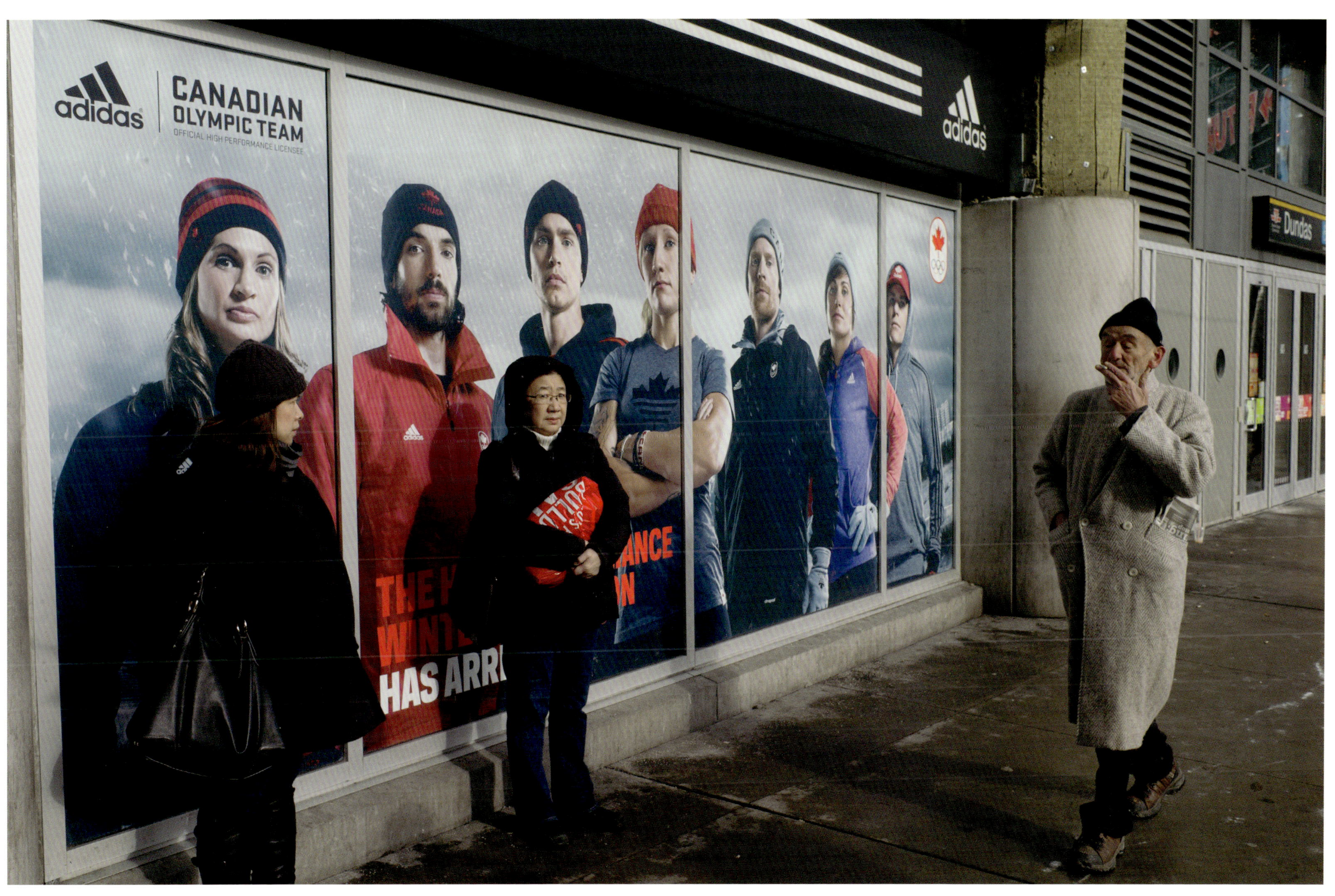
adidas
CANADIAN OLYMPIC TEAM
OFFICIAL HIGH PERFORMANCE LICENSEE
adidas
Dundas

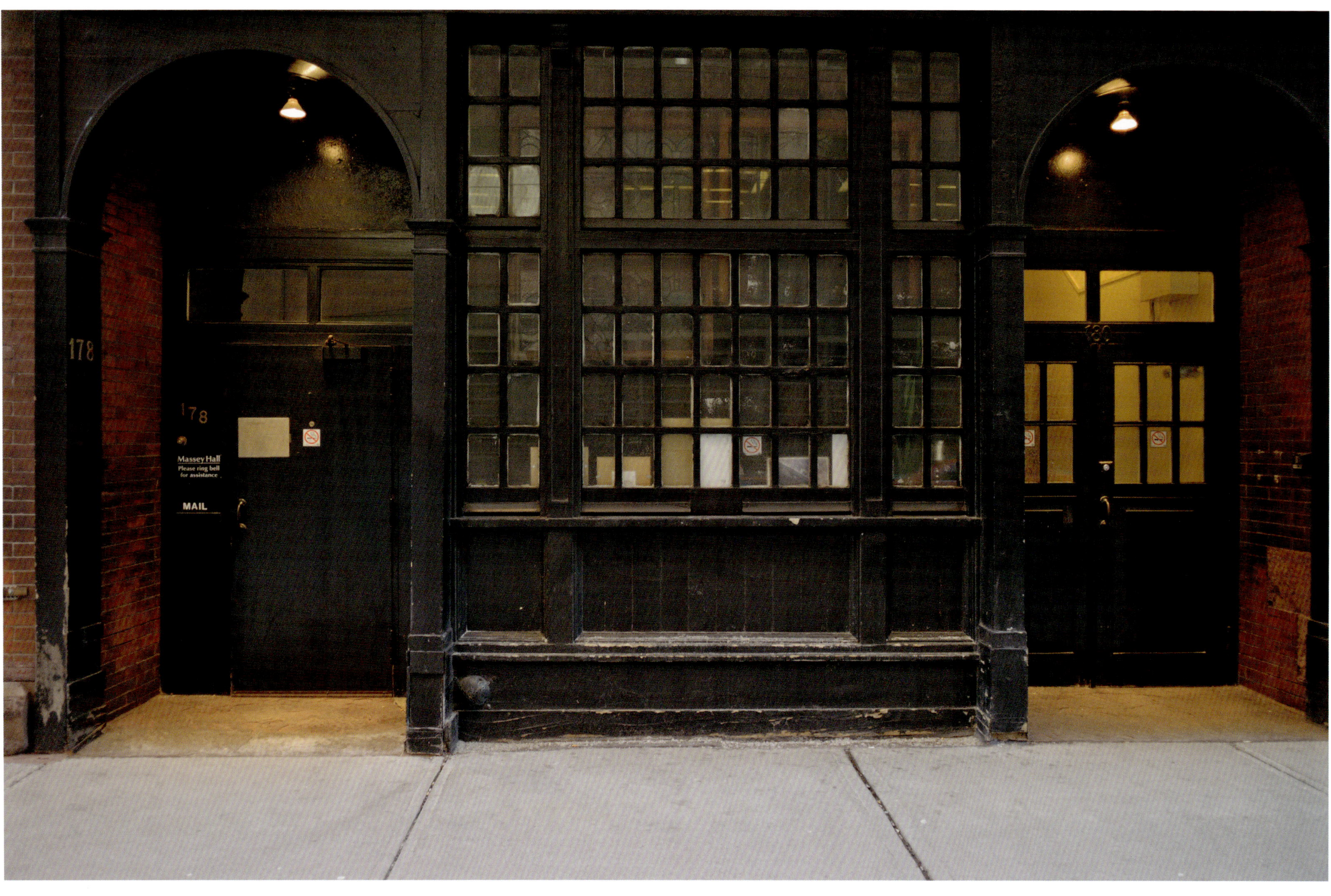
178
178
Massey Hall
Please ring bell
for assistance
MAIL

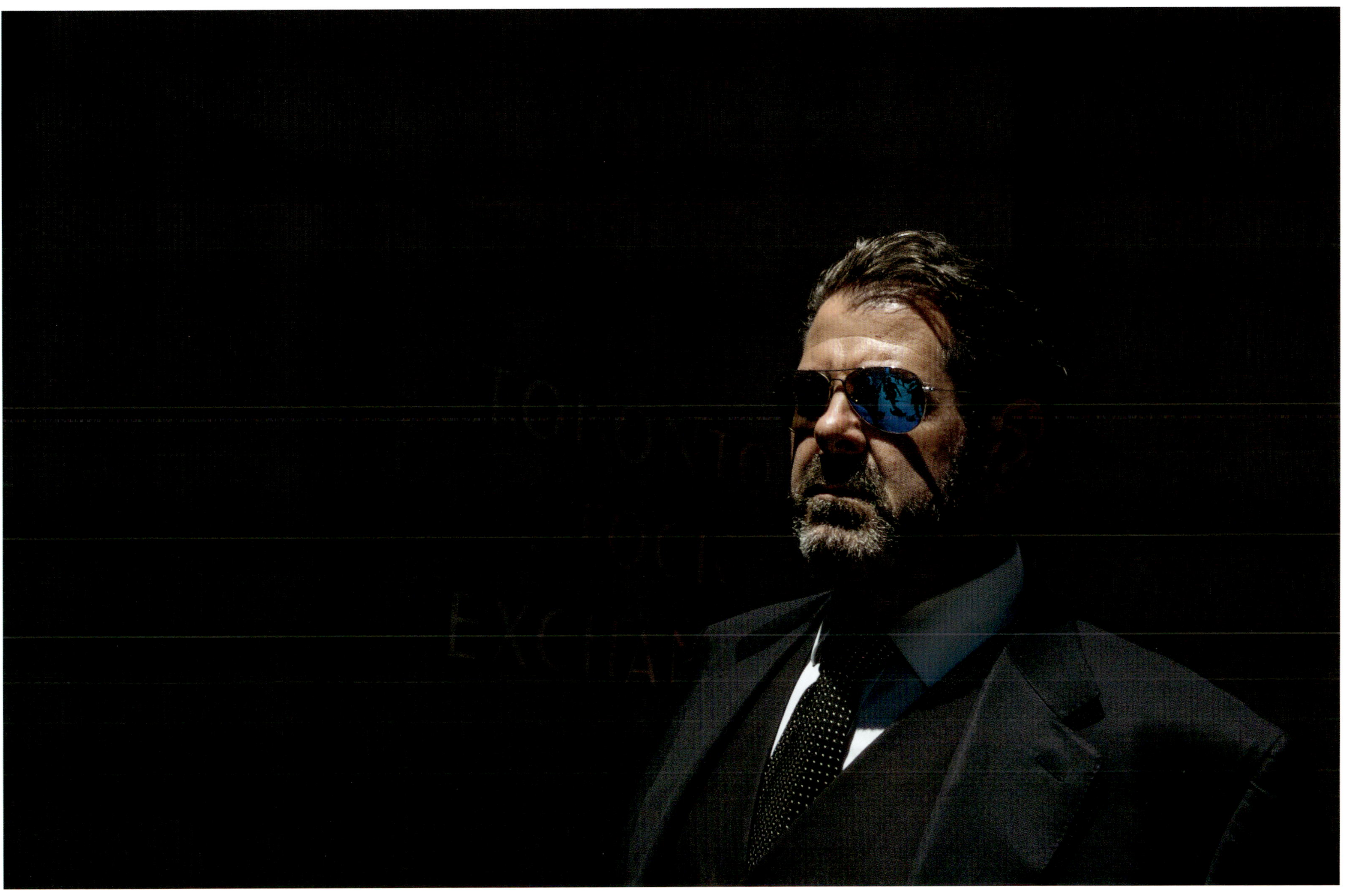

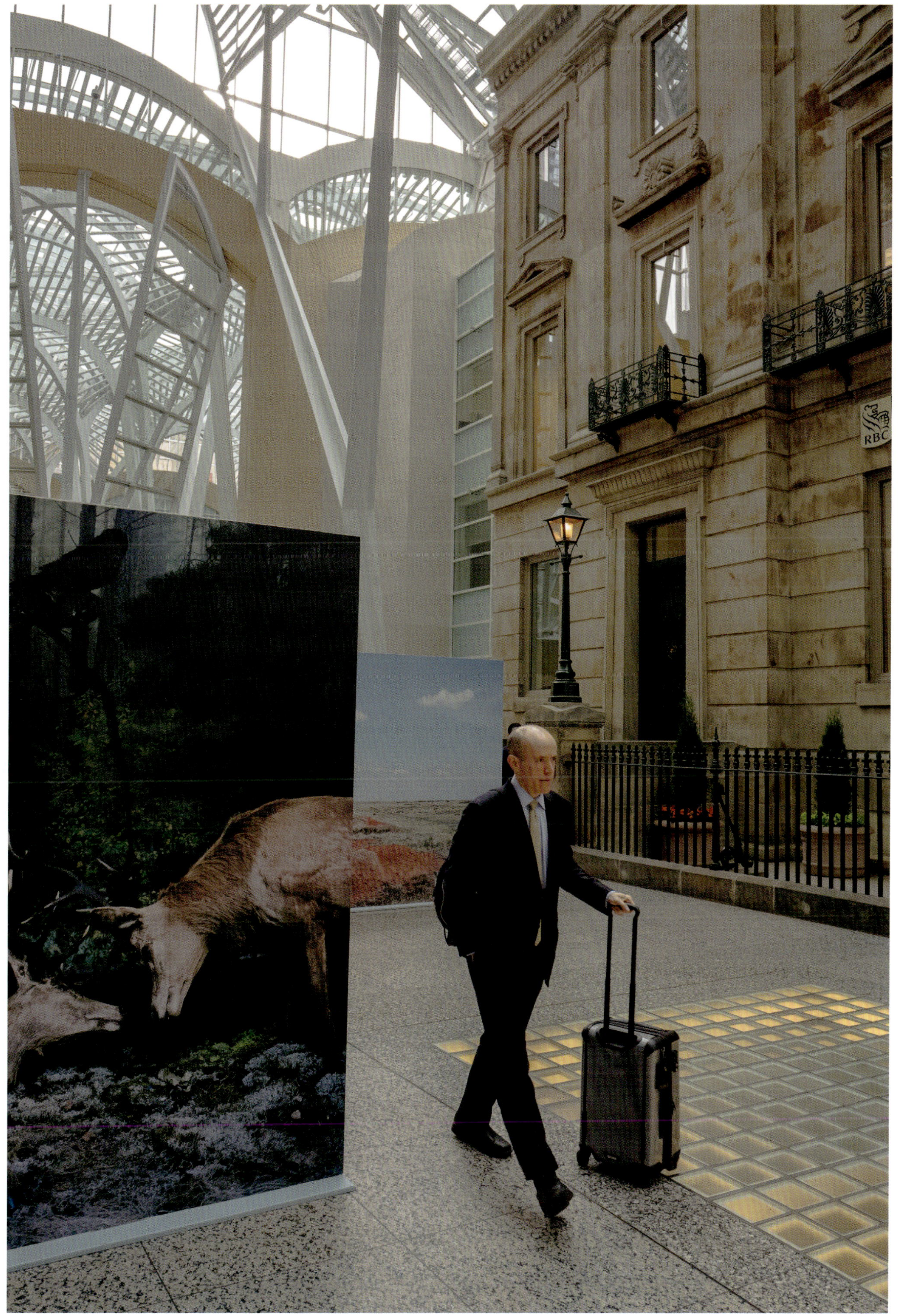
RBC

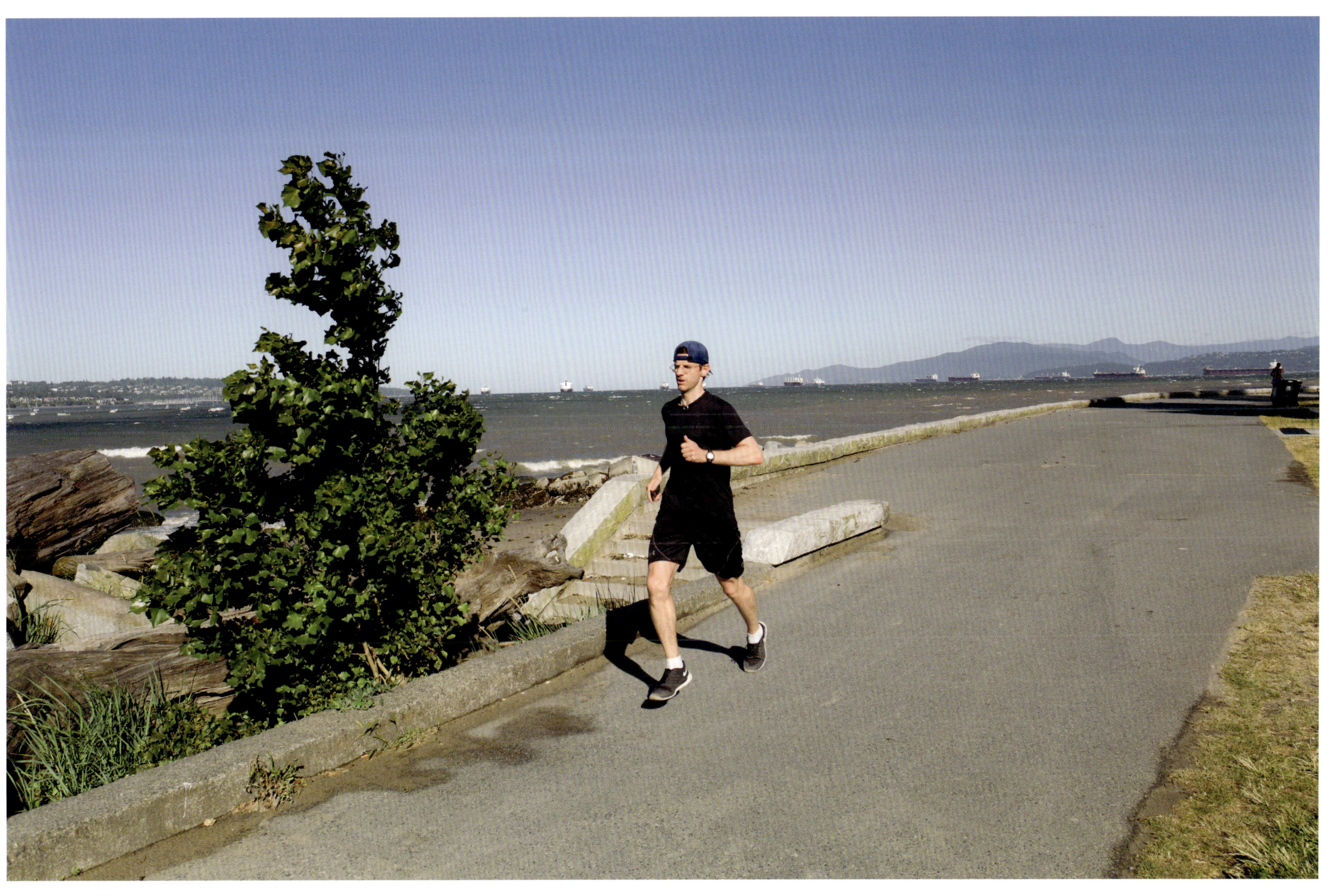

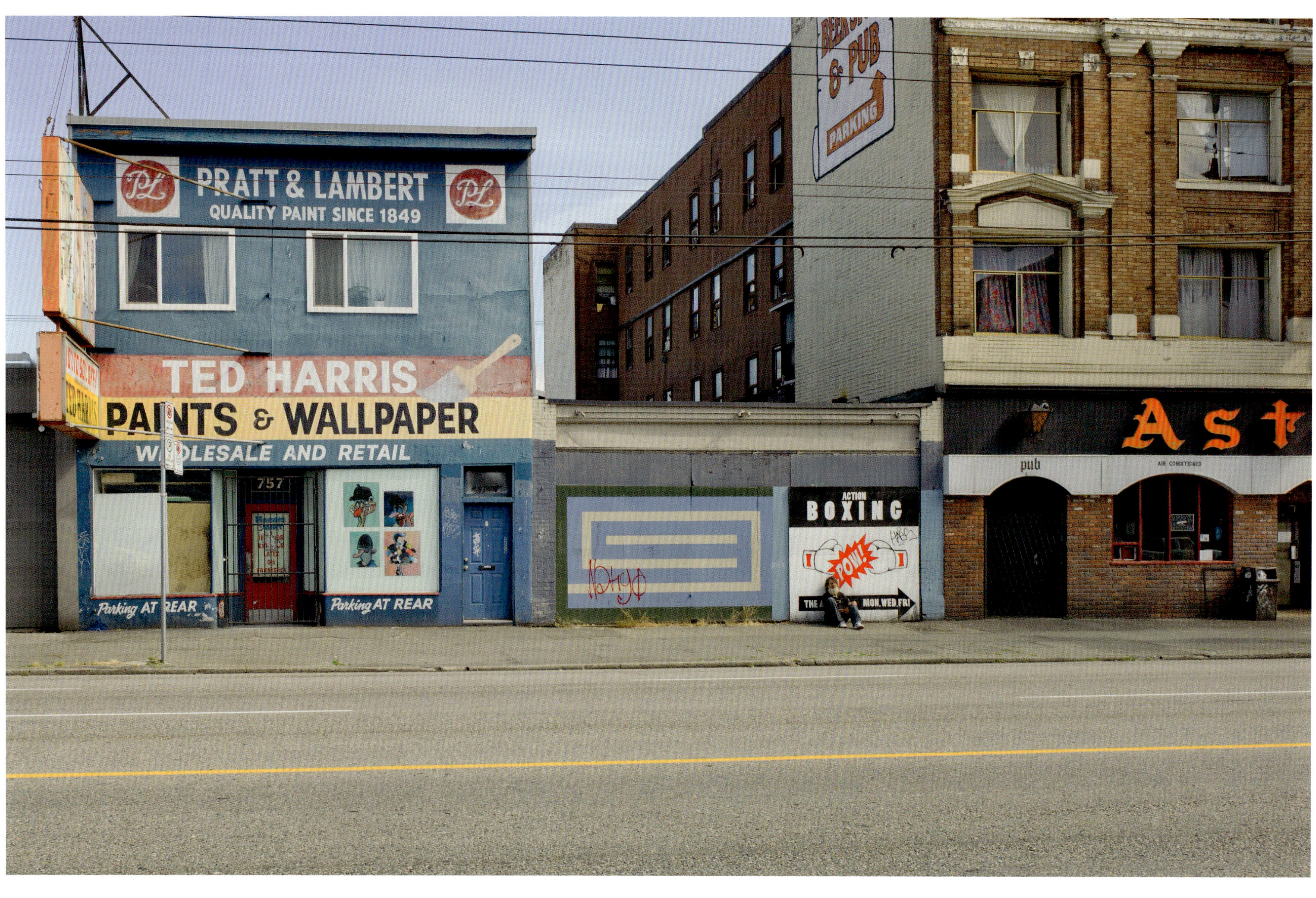
PRATT & LAMBERT
QUALITY PAINT SINCE 1849
PL
TED HARRIS
& WALLPAPER
Parking AT REAR
757
& PUB
PARKING
ACTION
BOXING
POW!
MON,WED,FRI
pub
AIR CONDITIONED

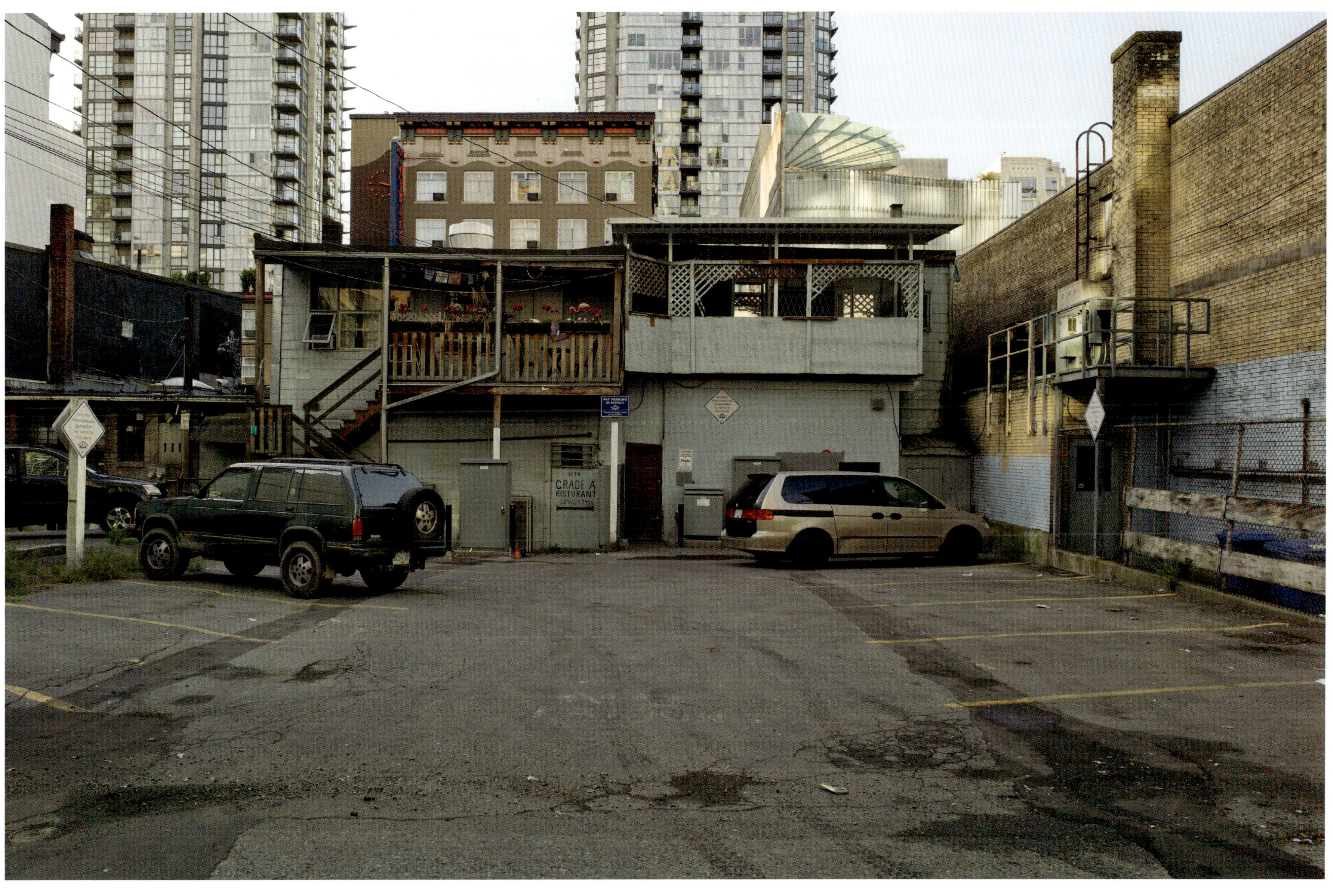
PAY PARKING
IN EFFECT
GRADE A
RESTURANT

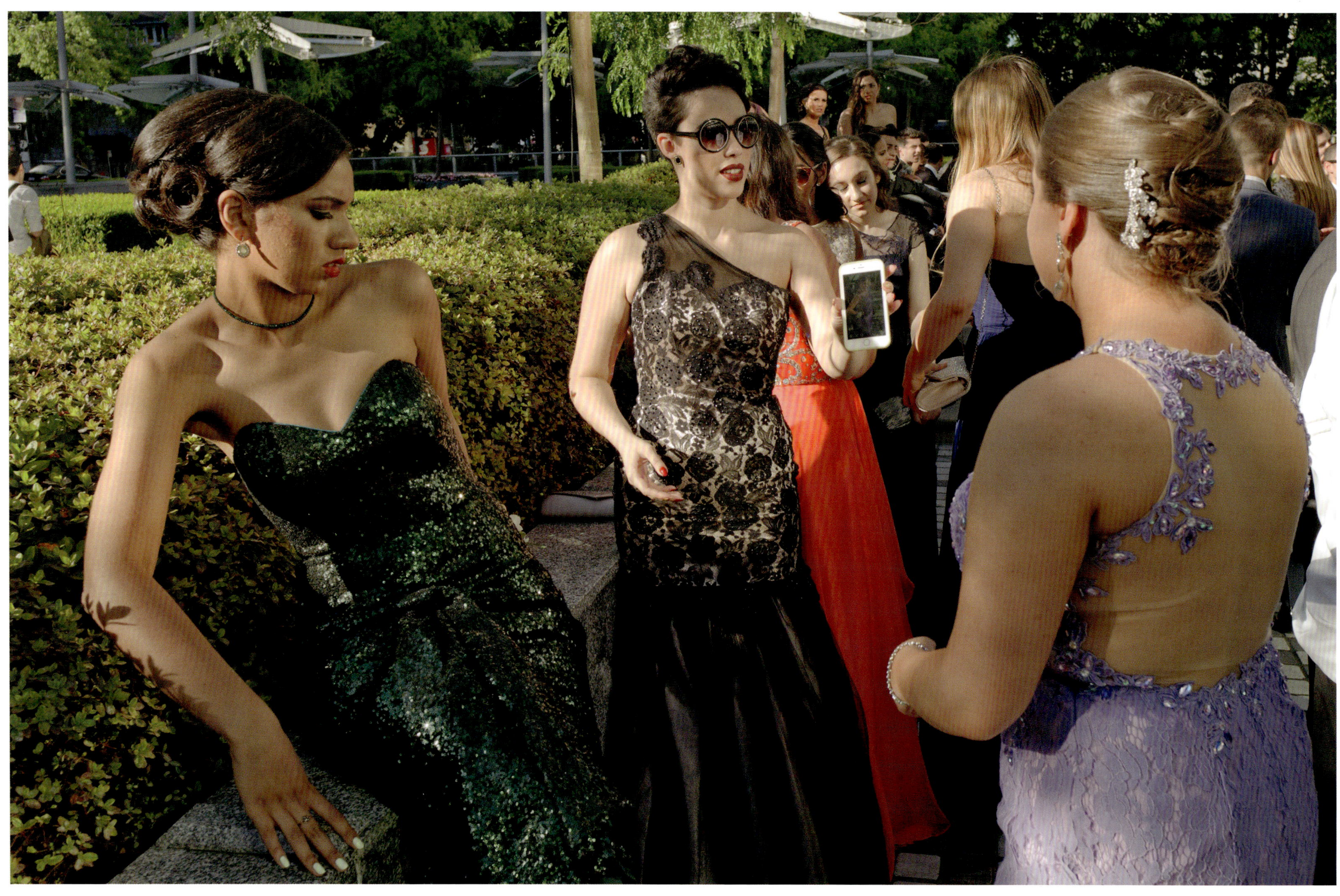

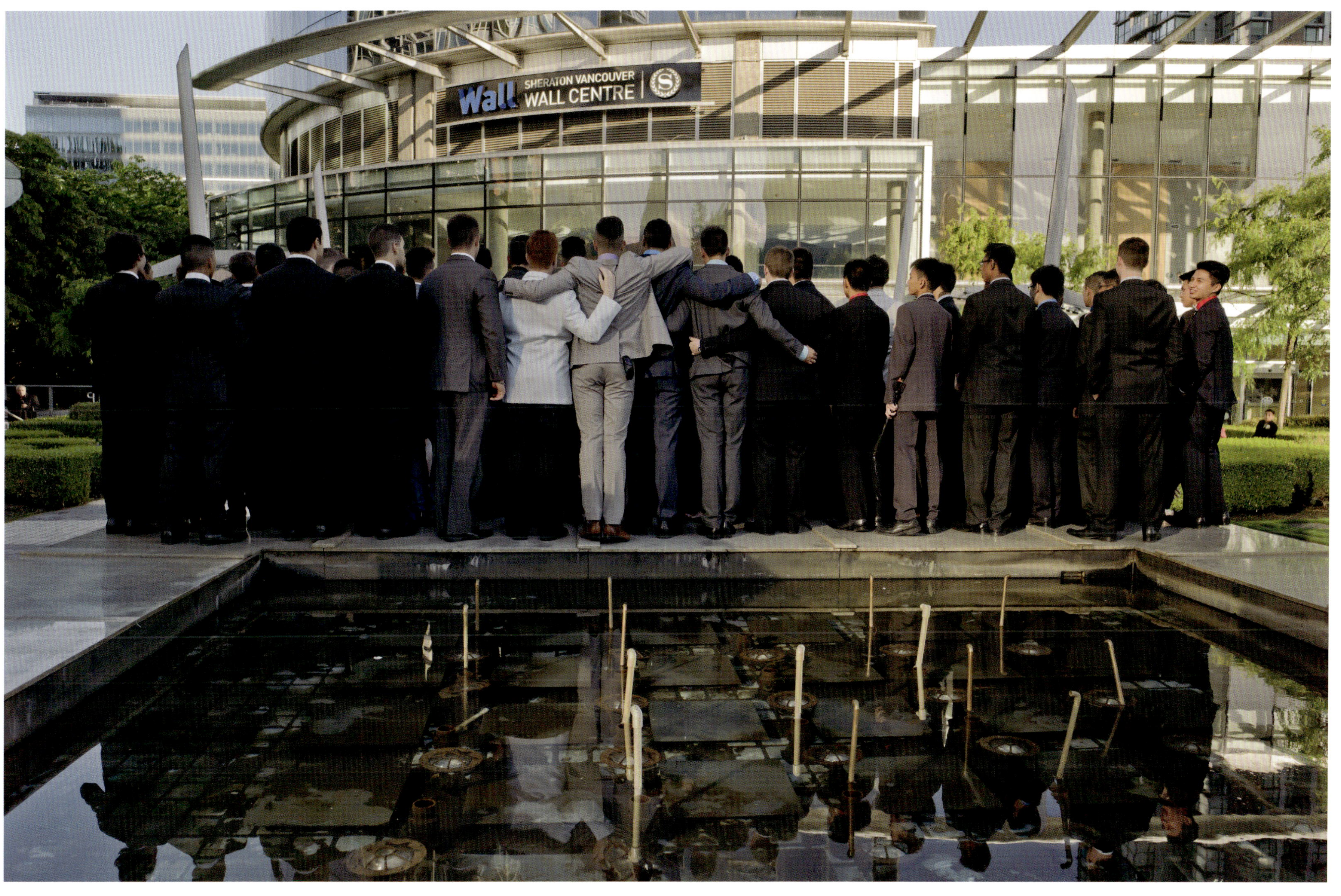
Wall
SHERATON VANCOUVER
WALL CENTRE

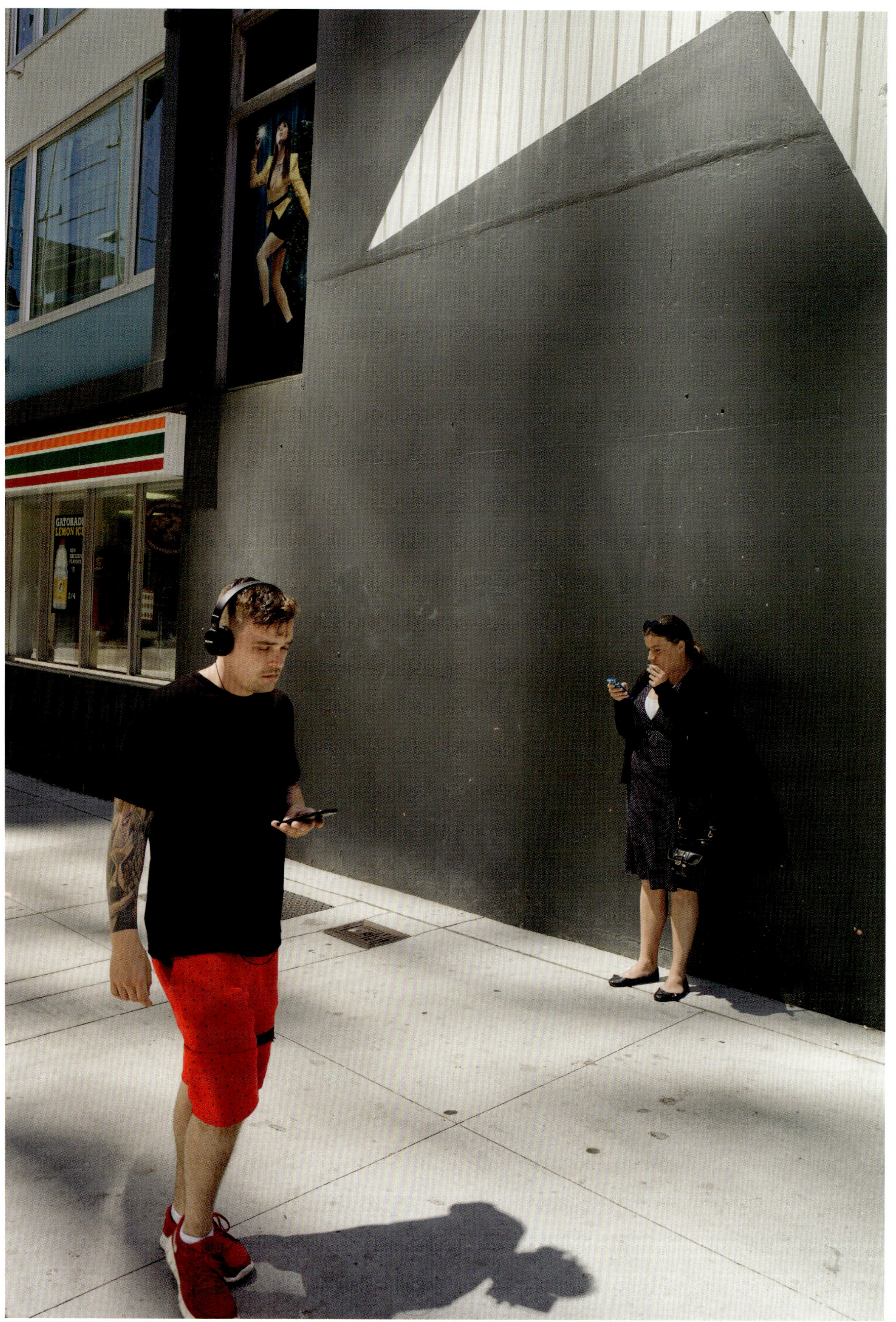

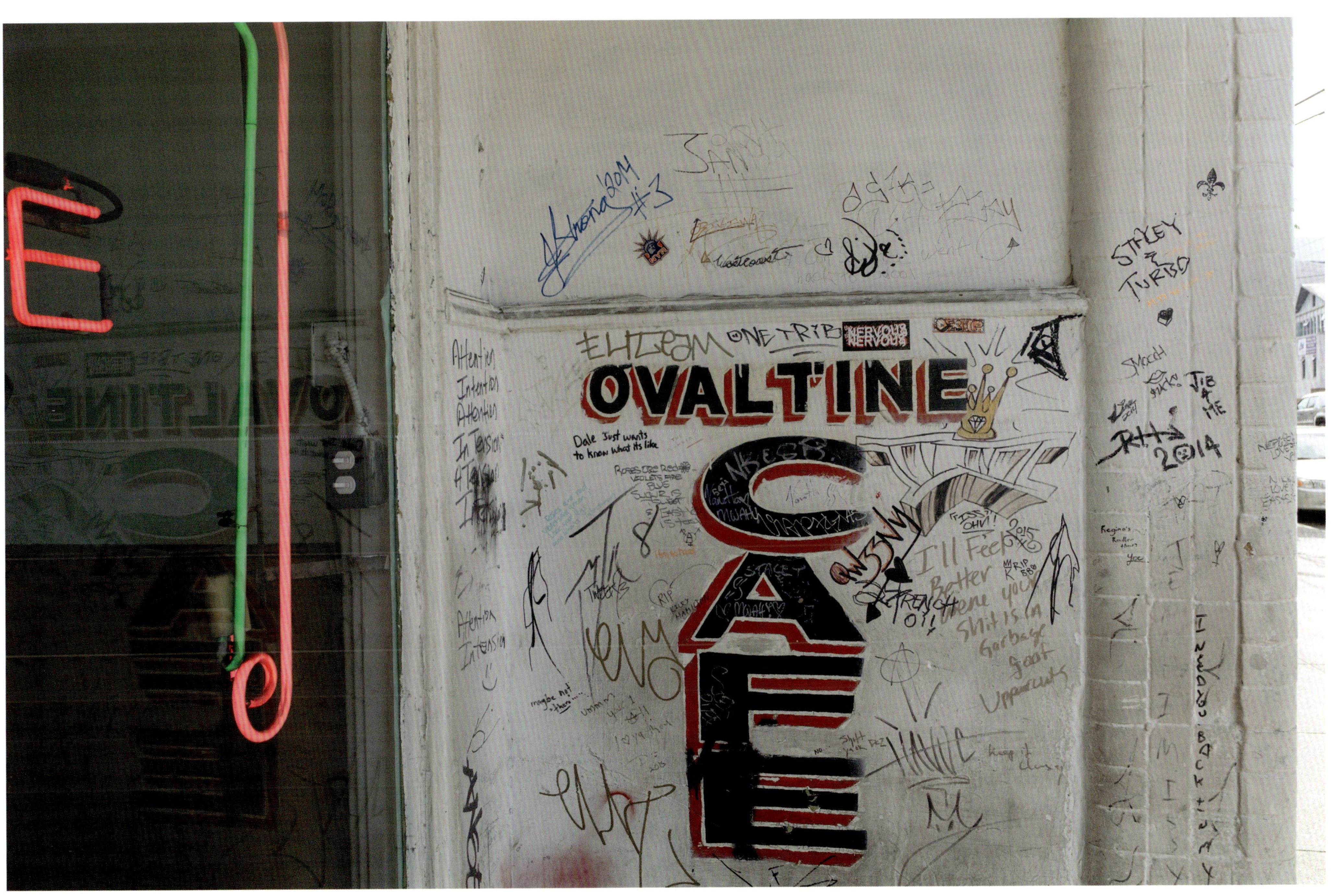
OVALTINE
CAFE

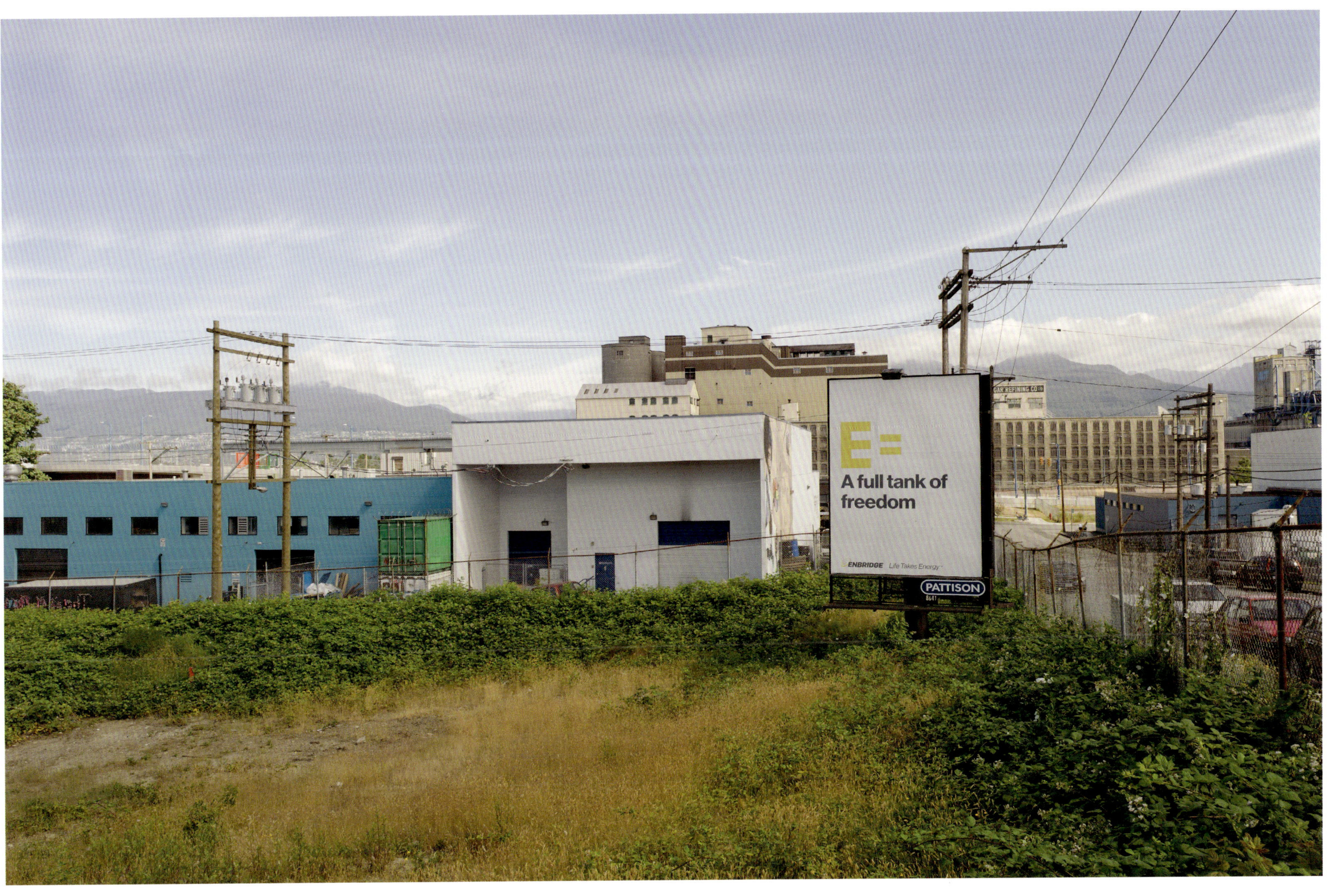
E=
A full tank of freedom
ENBRIDGE Life Takes Energy
PATTISON

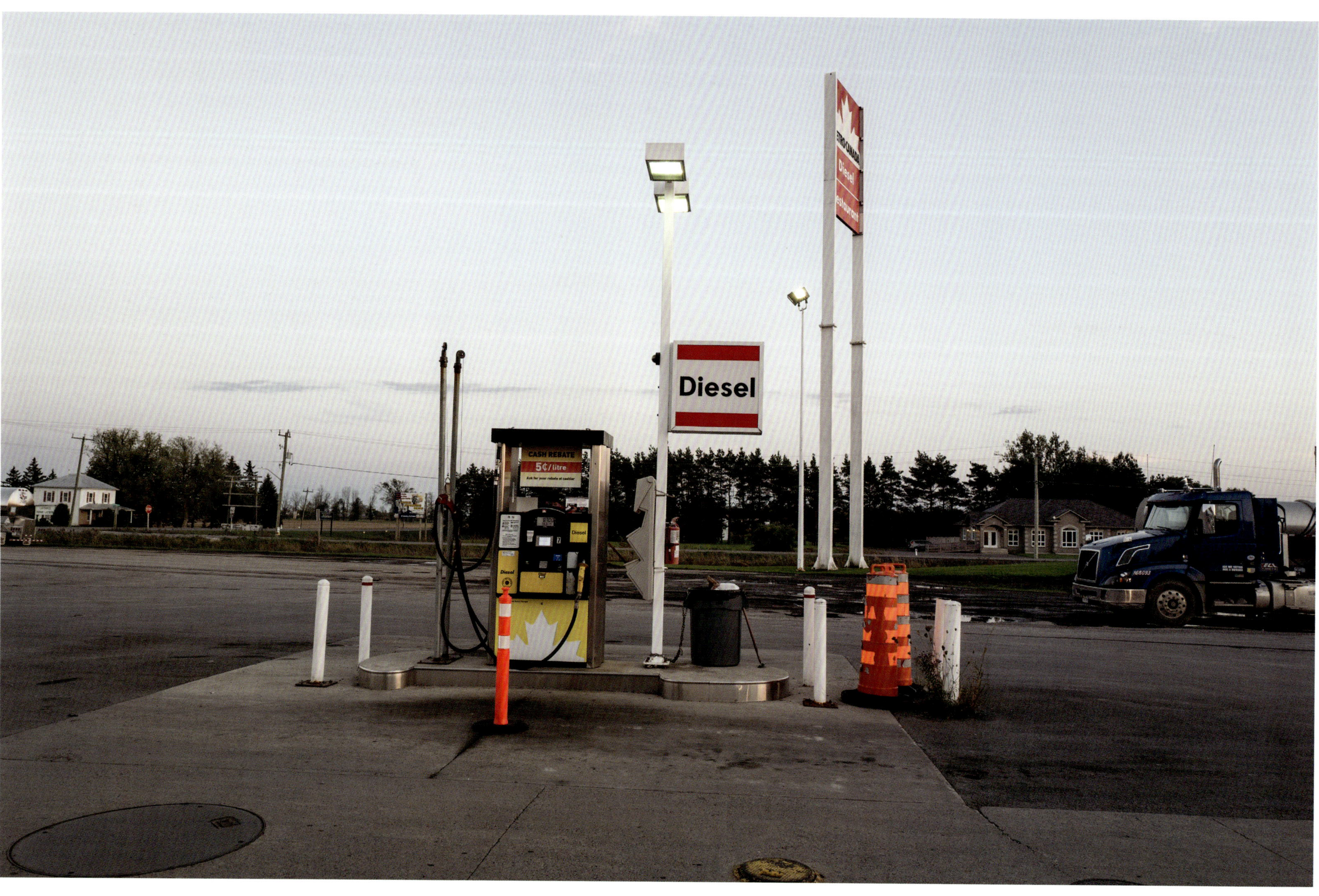
CASH REBATE
5¢/litre
Diesel

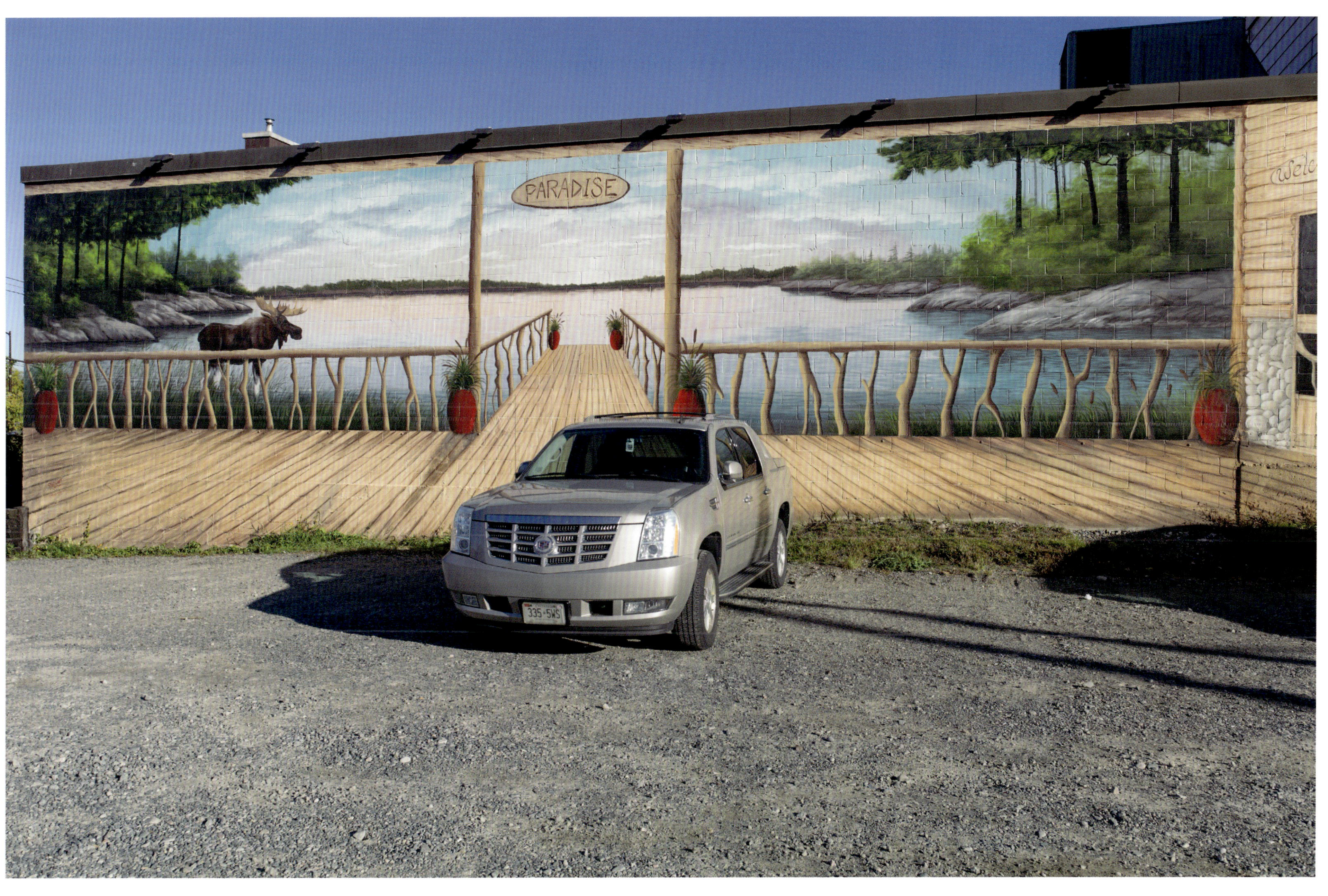
PARADISE
335-5WS

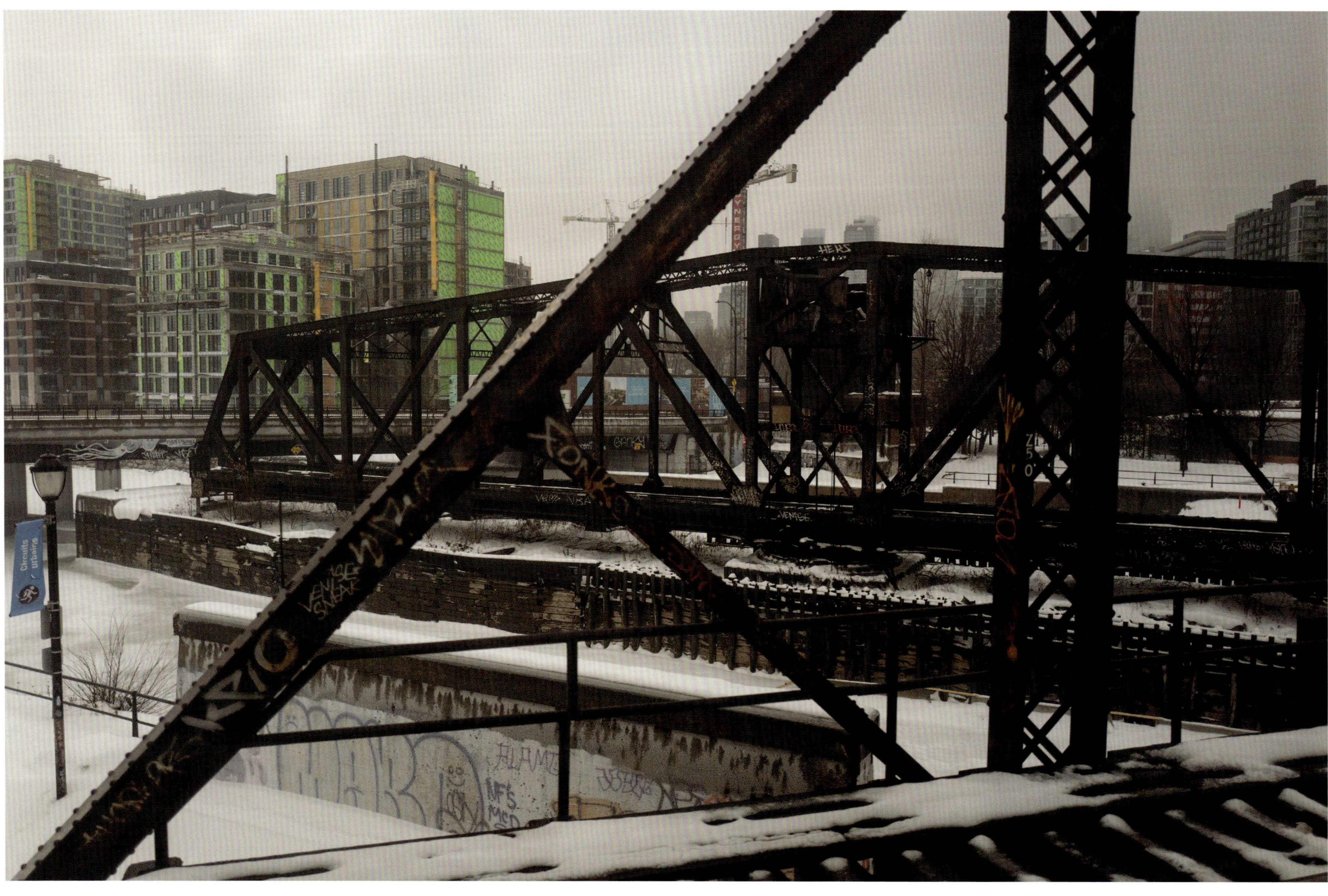
Circuits
urbains

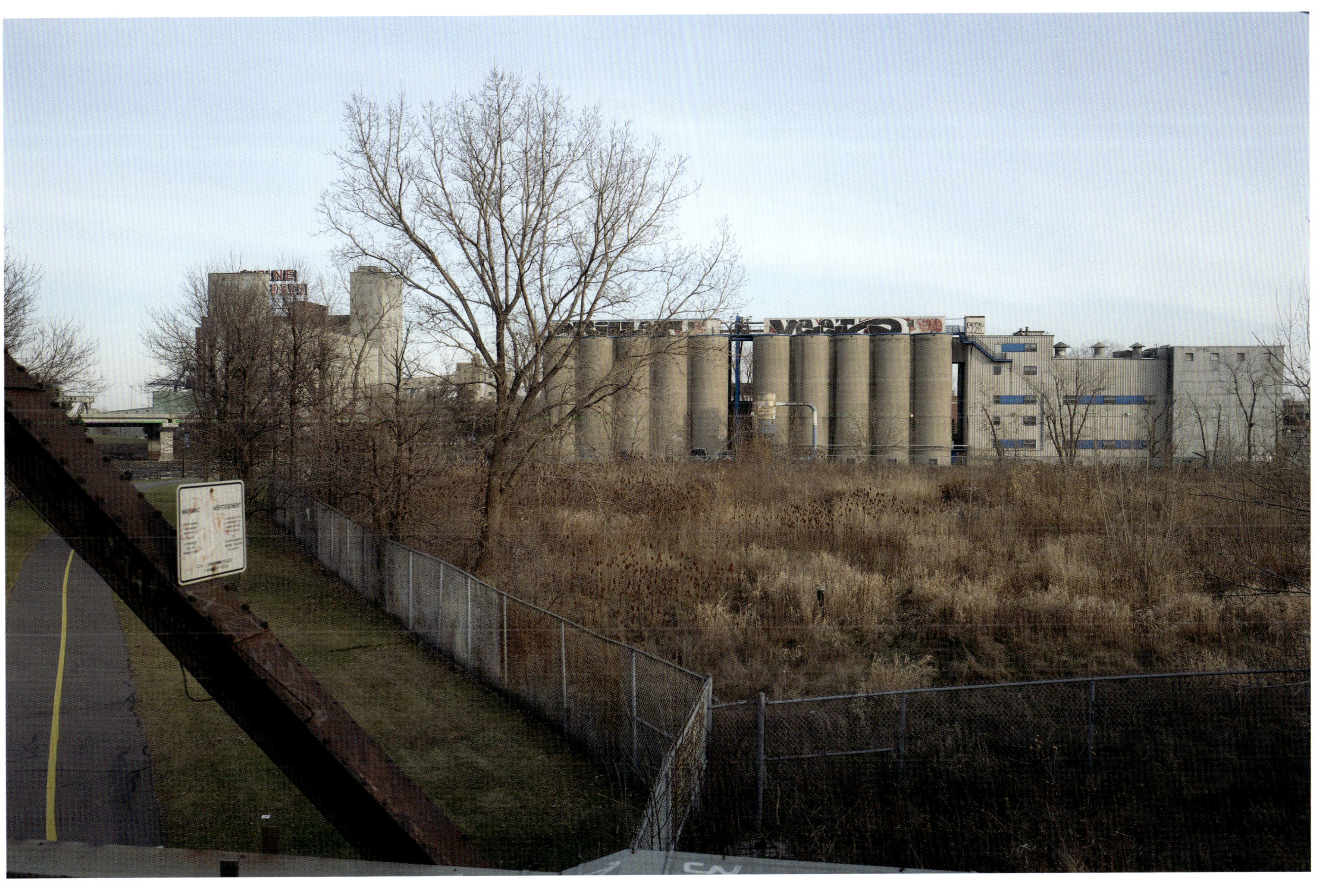

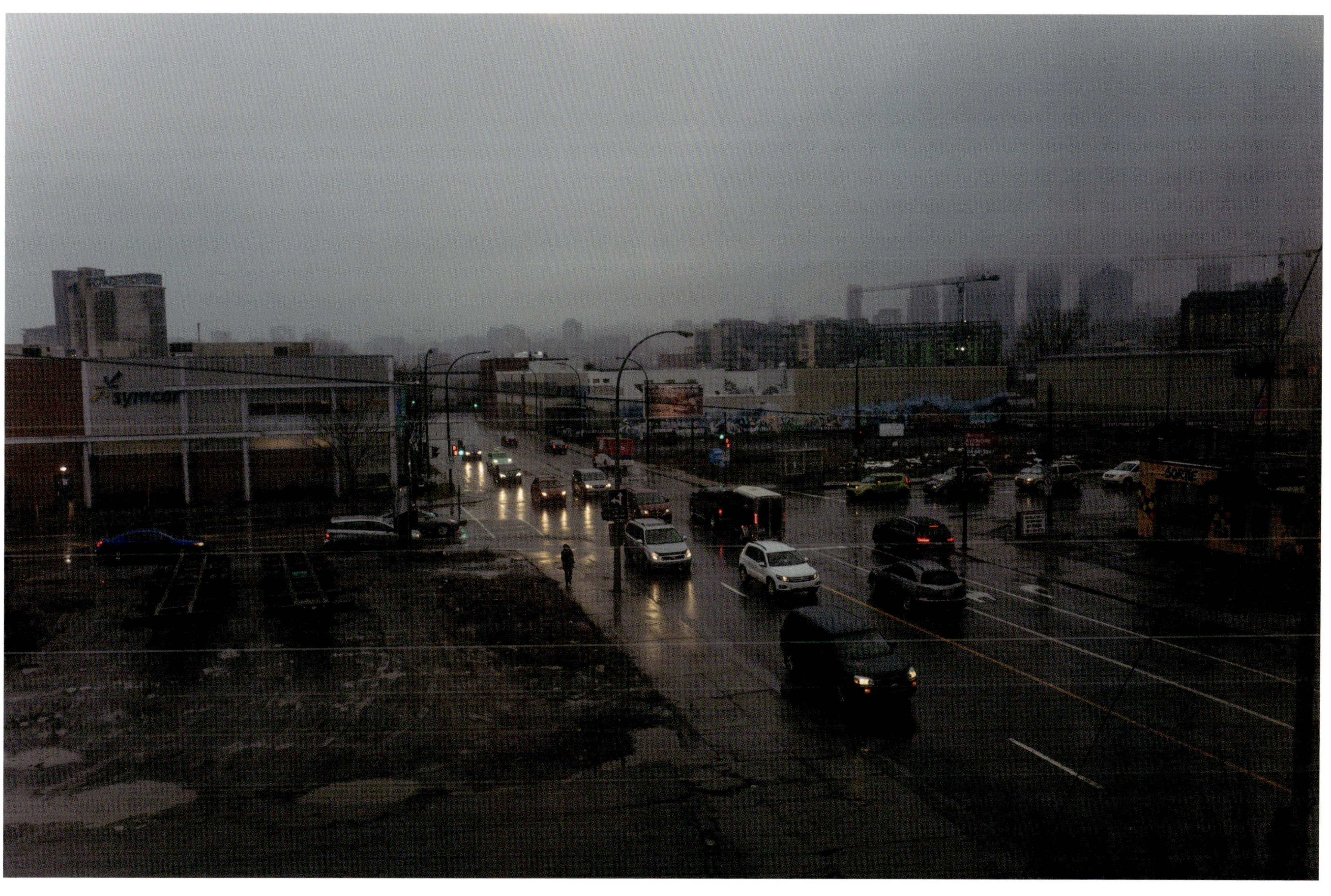
symcor

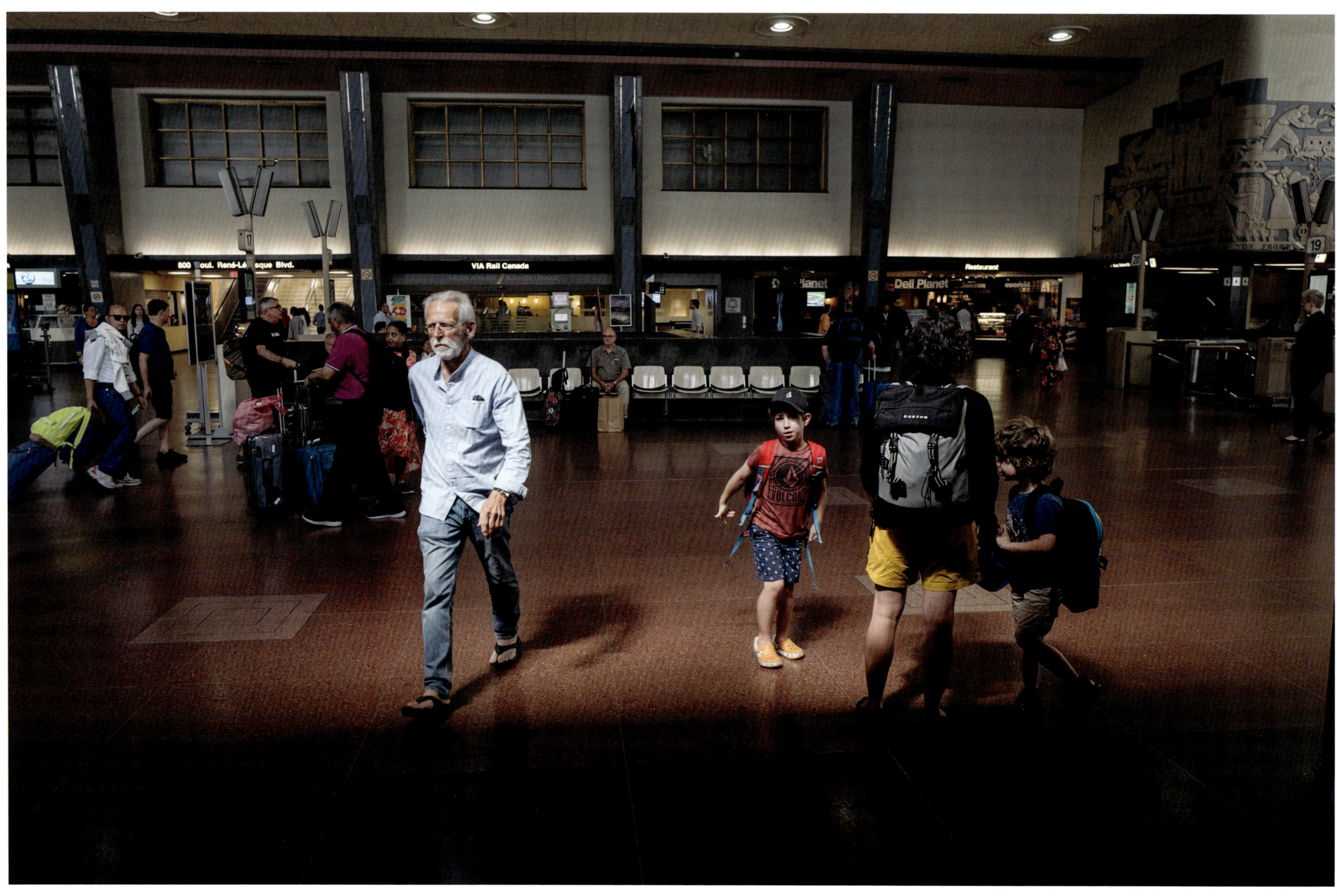
VIA Rail Canada
Restaurant
Deli Planet

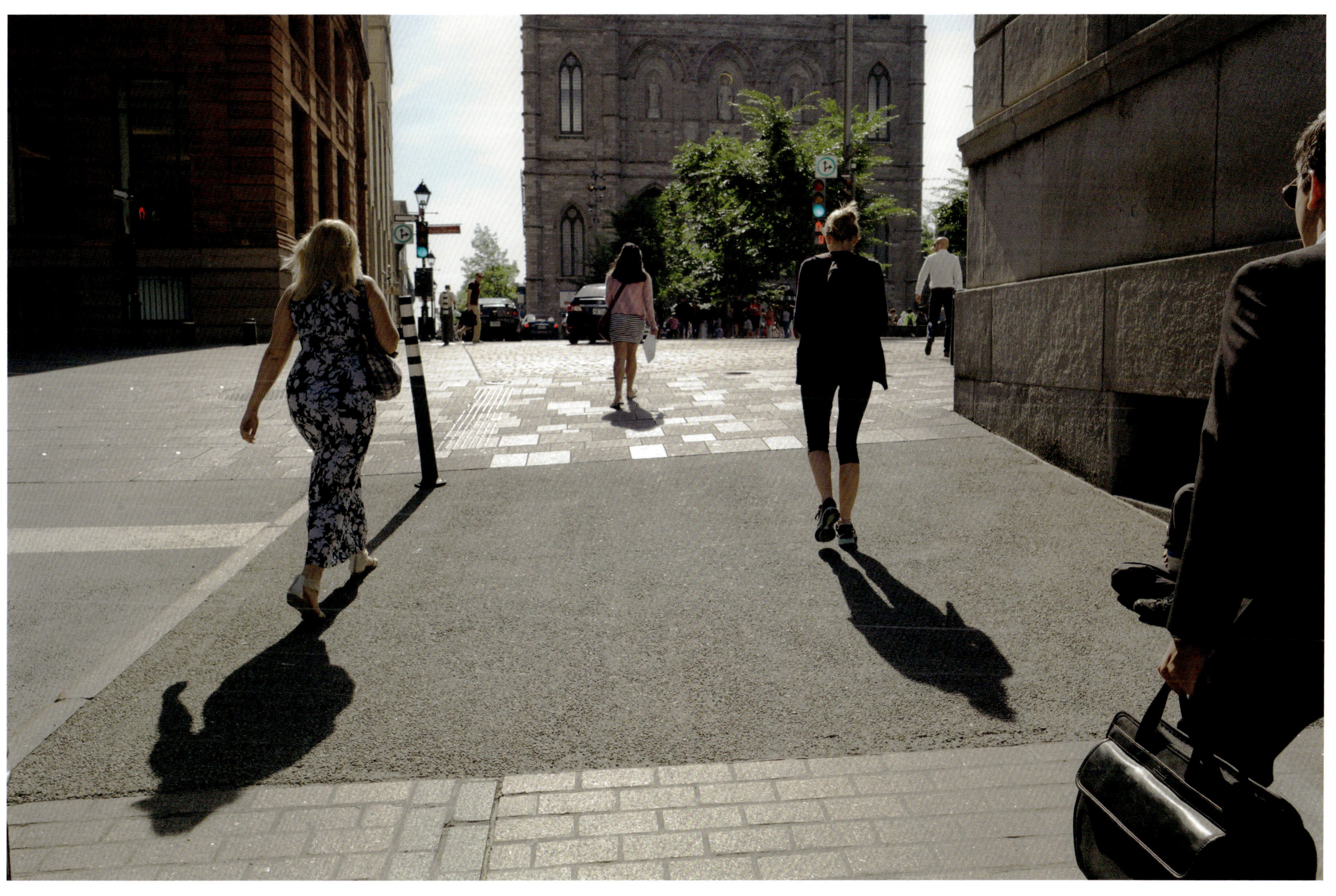

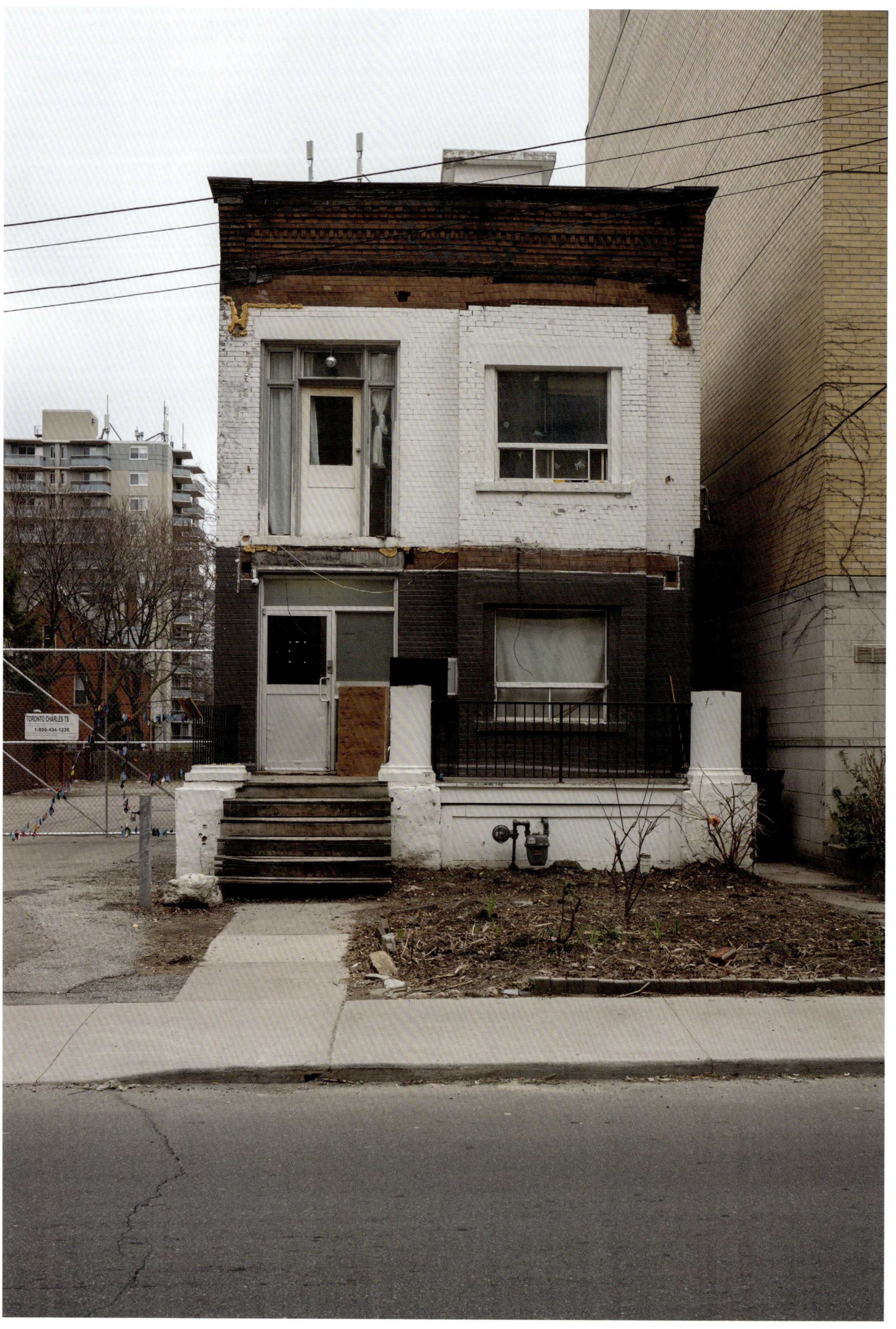
TORONTO CHARLES TS
1-800-434-1235

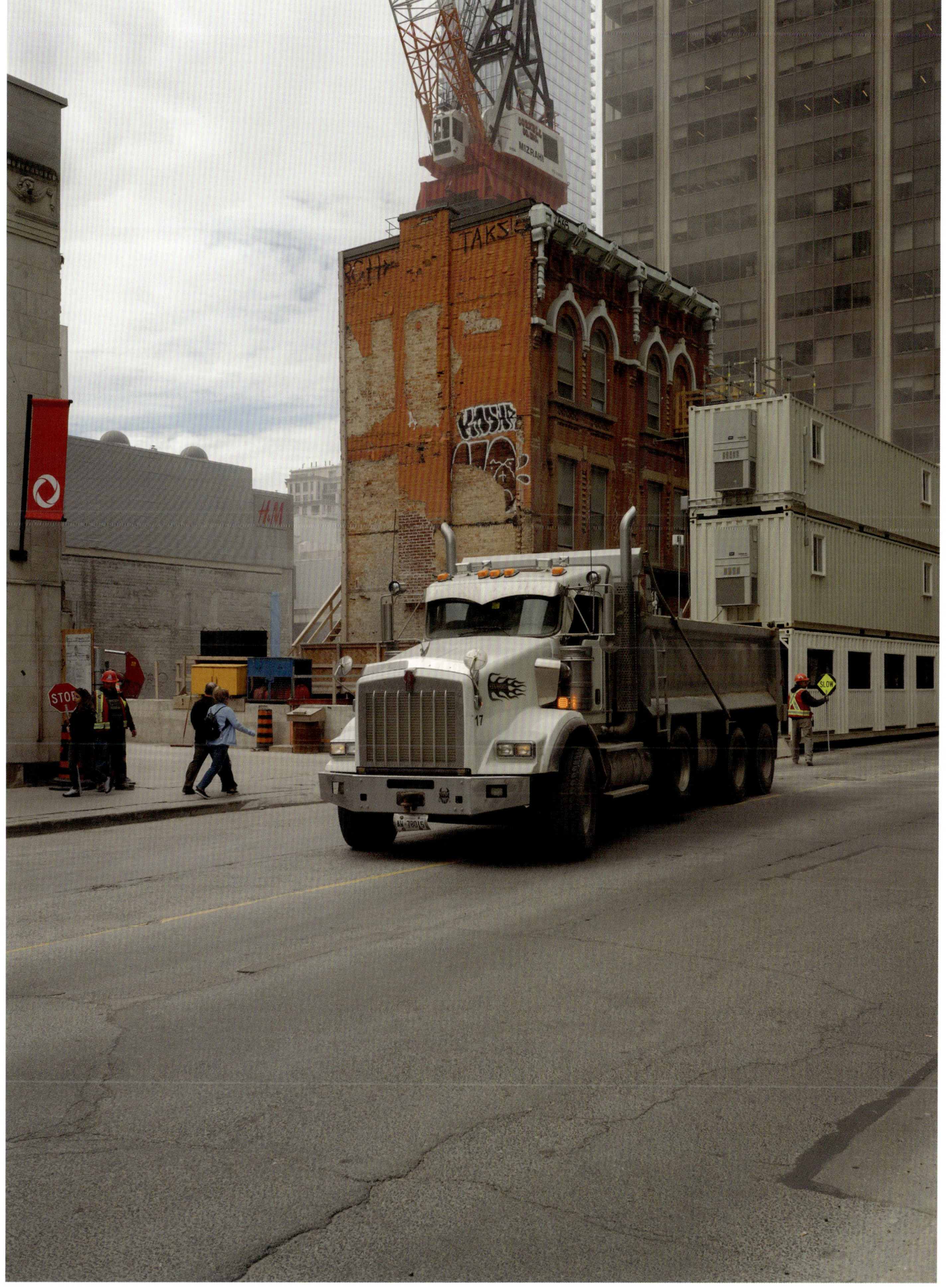
MIZRAHI
H&M
SLOW

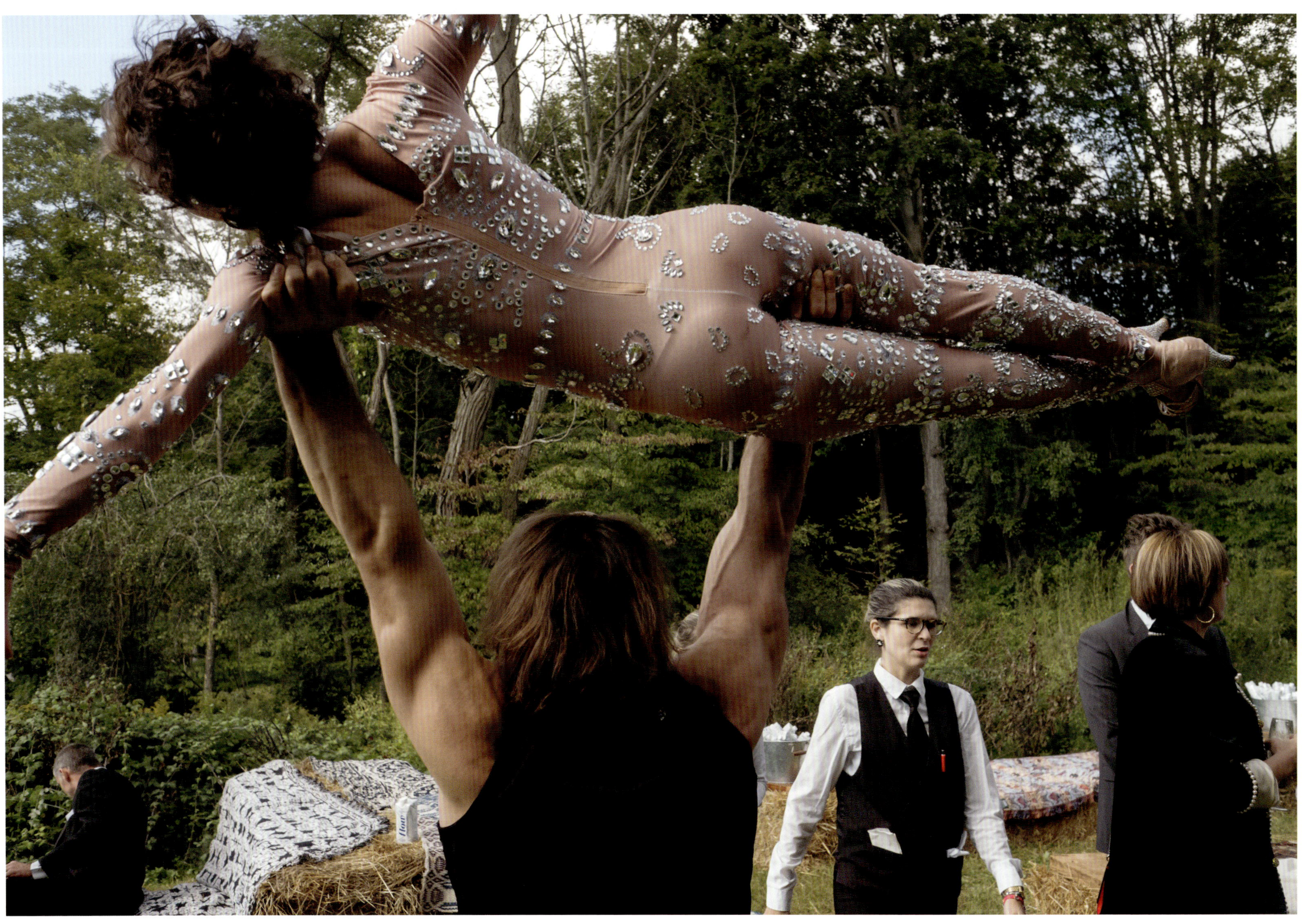

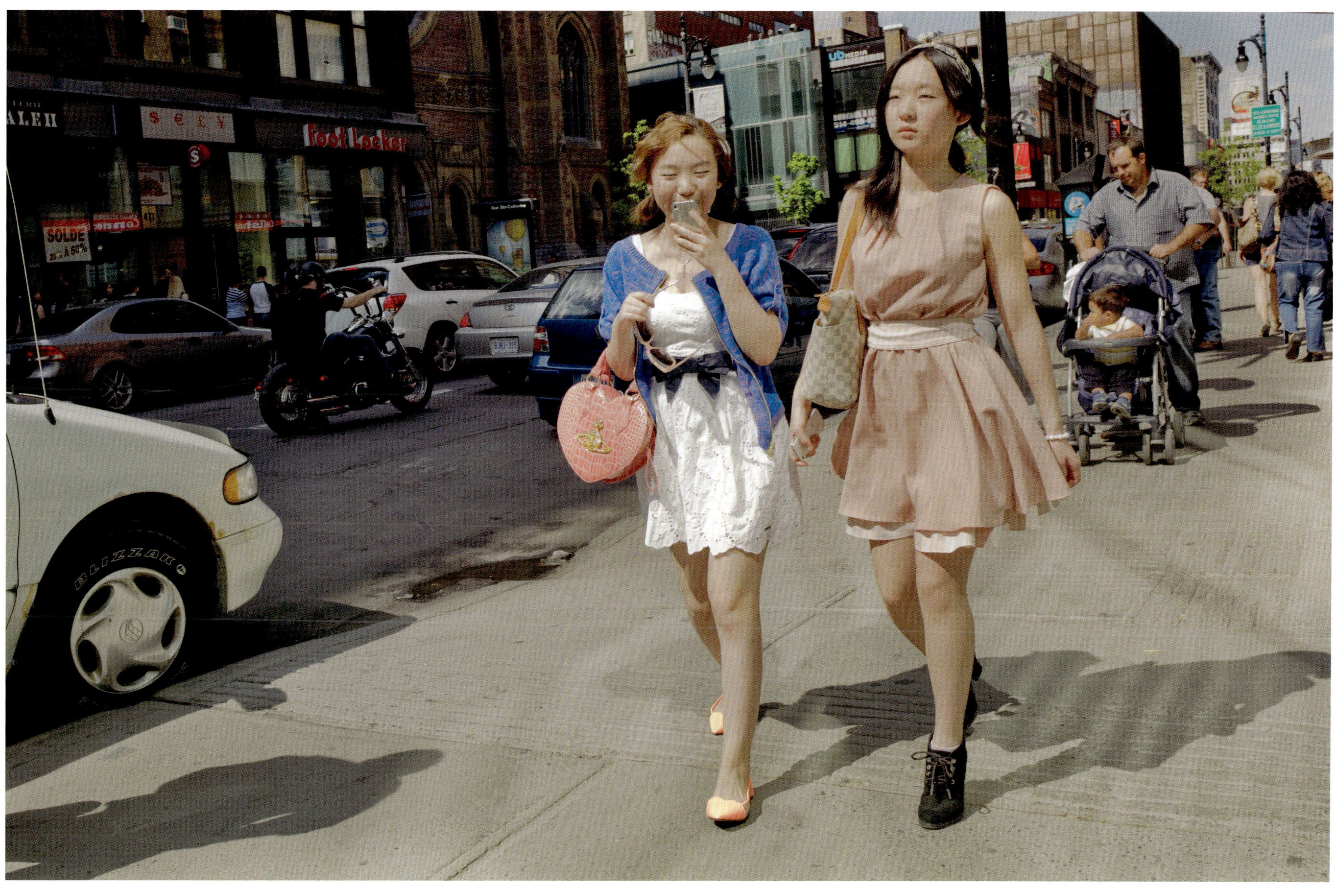
Foot Locker
SOLDE

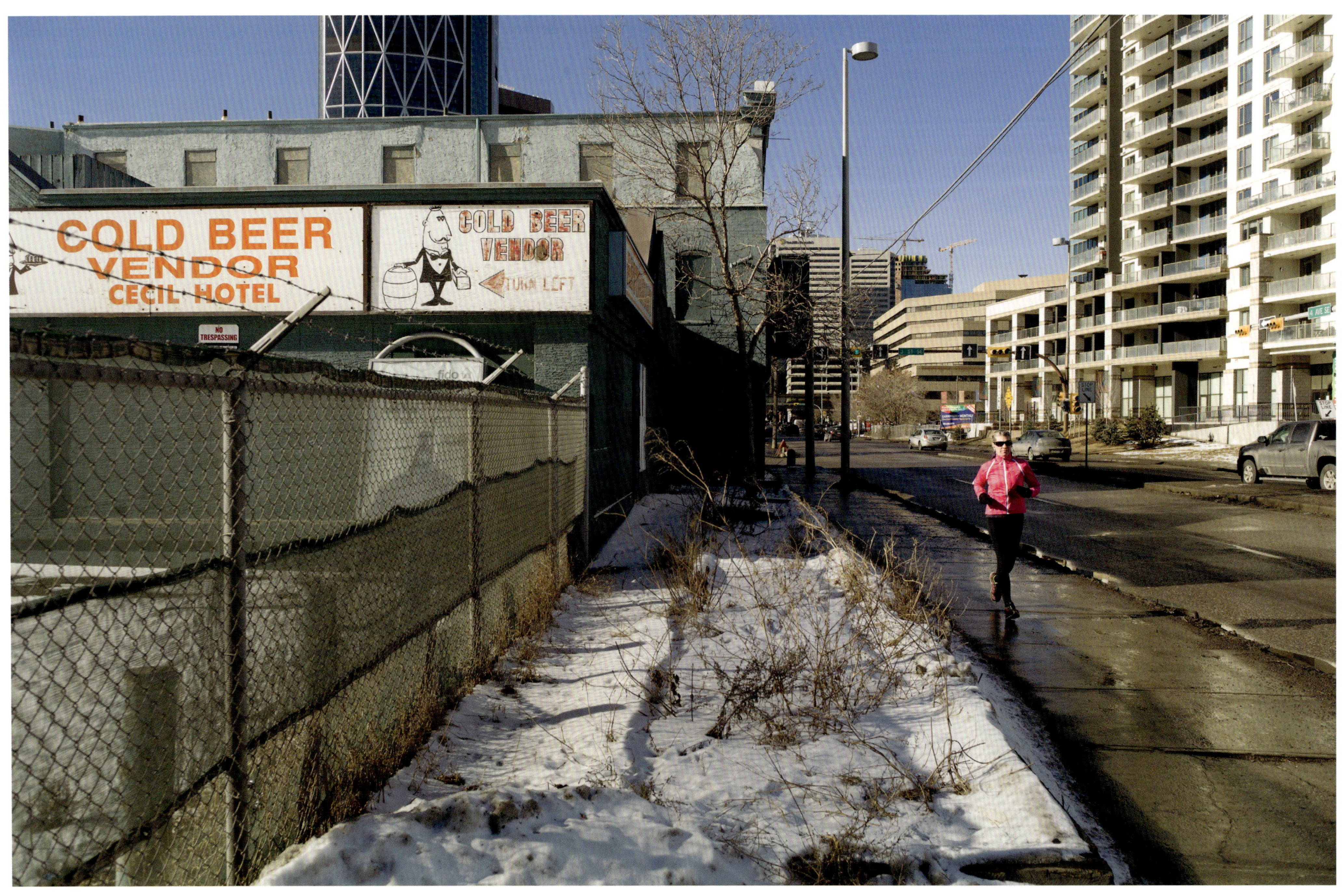
COLD BEER
VENDOR
CECIL HOTEL
COLD BEER
VENDOR
TURN LEFT
NO
TRESPASSING

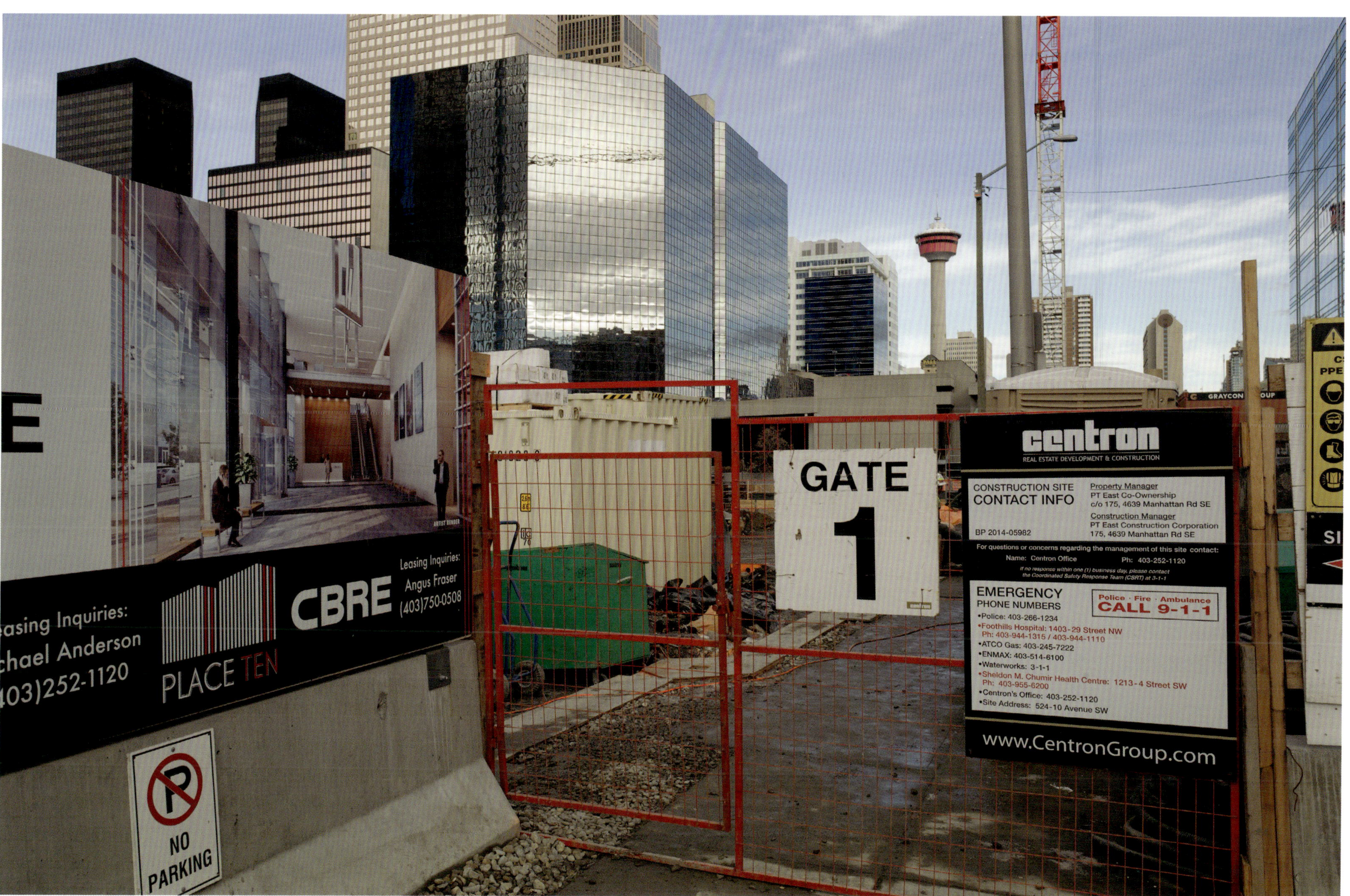

easing Inquiries:
chael Anderson
403)252-1120
PLACE TEN
CBRE
Leasing Inquiries:
Angus Fraser
(403)750-0508
NO PARKING
GATE 1
GRAYCON
centron
REAL ESTATE DEVELOPMENT & CONSTRUCTION
CONSTRUCTION SITE CONTACT INFO
BP 2014-05982
Property Manager
PT East Co-Ownership
c/o 175, 4639 Manhattan Rd SE
Construction Manager
PT East Construction Corporation
175, 4639 Manhattan Rd SE
For questions or concerns regarding the management of this site contact:
Name: Centron Office Ph: 403-252-1120
If no response within one (1) business day, please contact the Coordinated Safety Response Team (CSRT) at 3-1-1
EMERGENCY PHONE NUMBERS
Police · Fire · Ambulance CALL 9-1-1
•Police: 403-266-1234
•Foothills Hospital: 1403-29 Street NW Ph: 403-944-1315 / 403-944-1110
•ATCO Gas: 403-245-7222
•ENMAX: 403-514-6100
•Waterworks: 3-1-1
•Sheldon M. Chumir Health Centre: 1213-4 Street SW Ph: 403-955-6200
•Centron's Office: 403-252-1120
•Site Address: 524-10 Avenue SW
www.CentronGroup.com

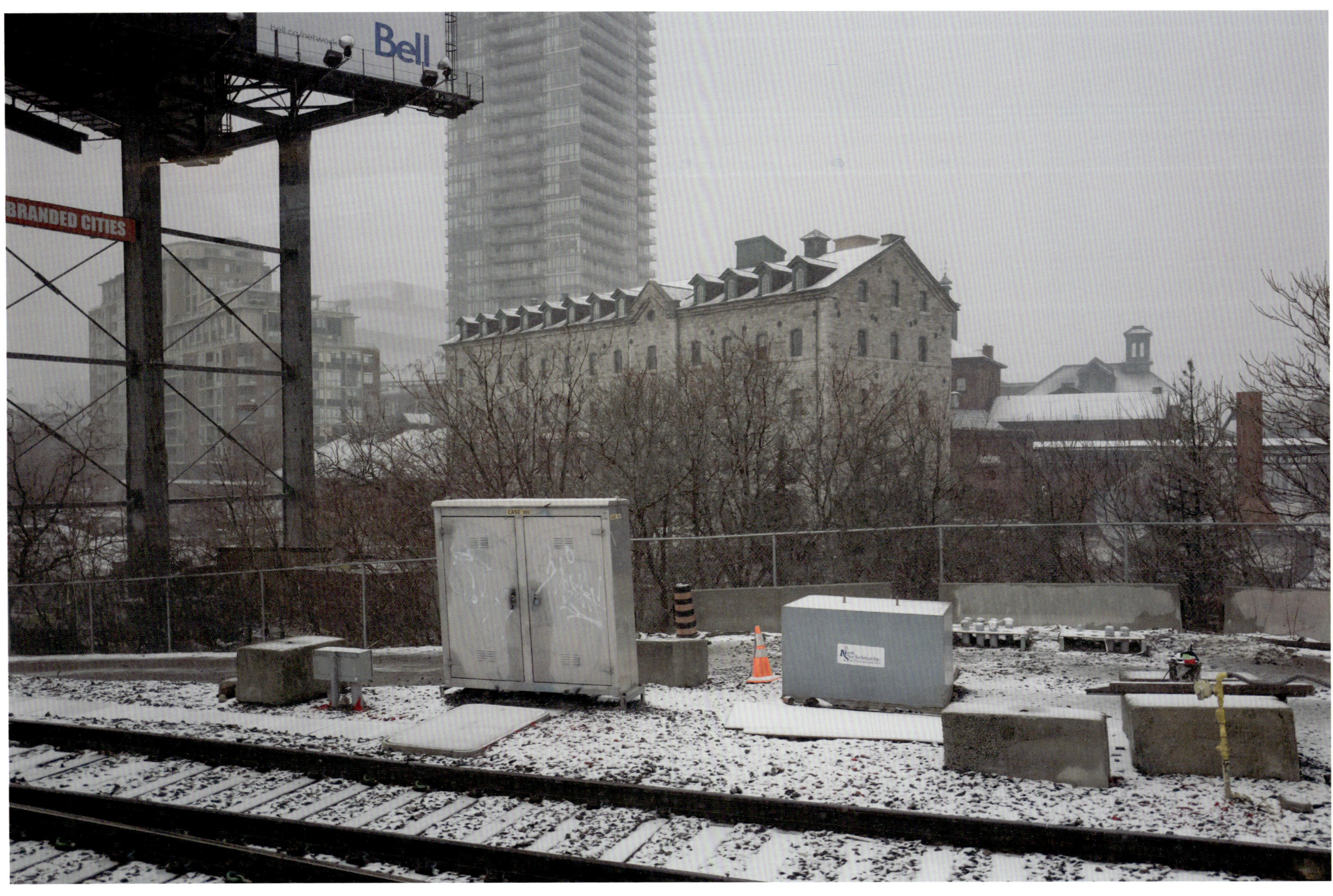
Bell
BRANDED CITIES

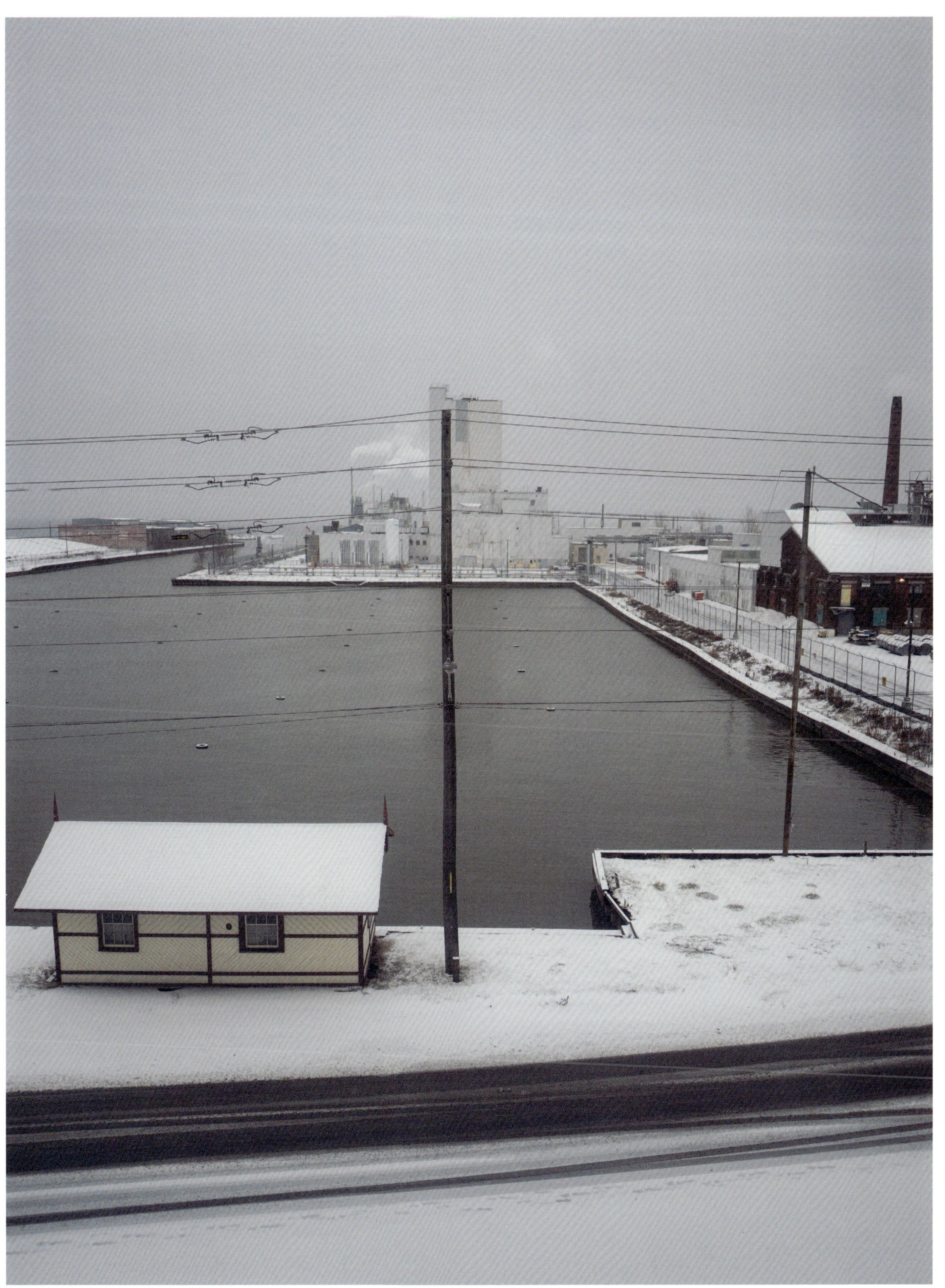

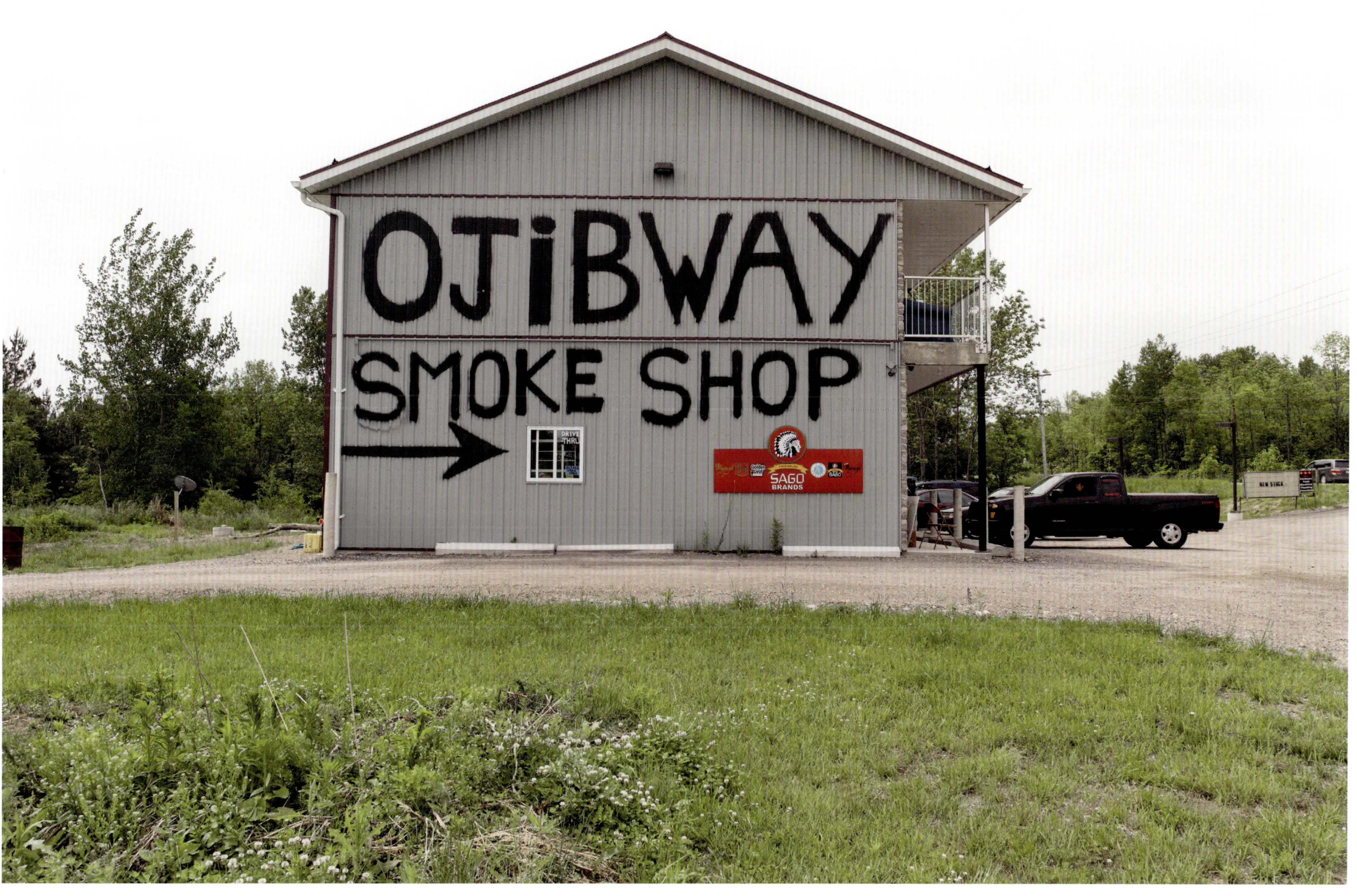
OJIBWAY
SMOKE SHOP
DRIVE THRU
SAGO BRANDS

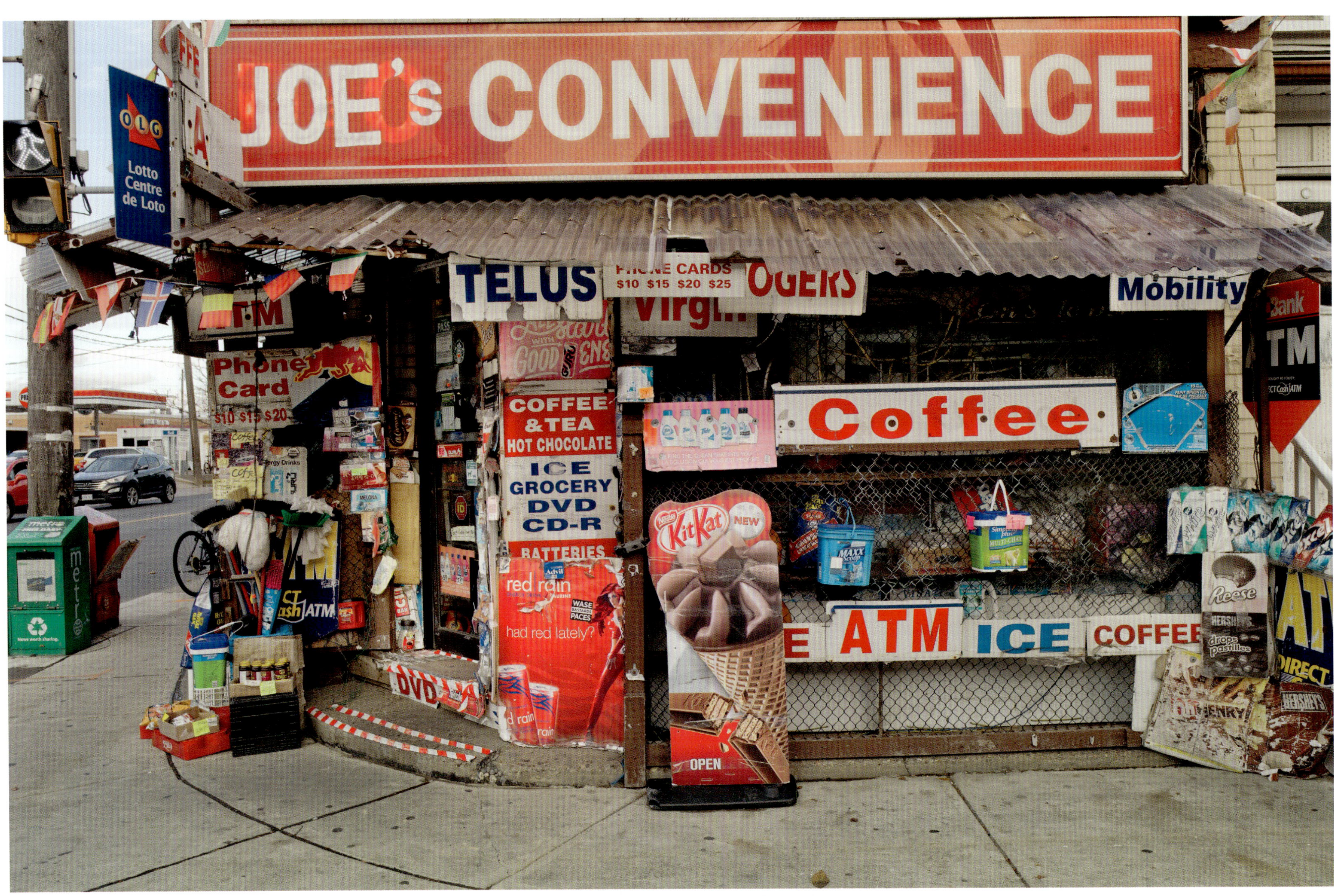
JOE's CONVENIENCE
OLG
Lotto
Centre
de Loto
TELUS
PHONE CARDS
$10 $15 $20 $25
Mobility
Phone
Card
$10 $15 $20
COFFEE
&TEA
HOT CHOCOLATE
ICE
GROCERY
DVD
CD-R
BATTERIES
Coffee
red rain
had red lately?
KitKat
NEW
OPEN
ATM
ICE
COFFEE
DVD
Reese
metro

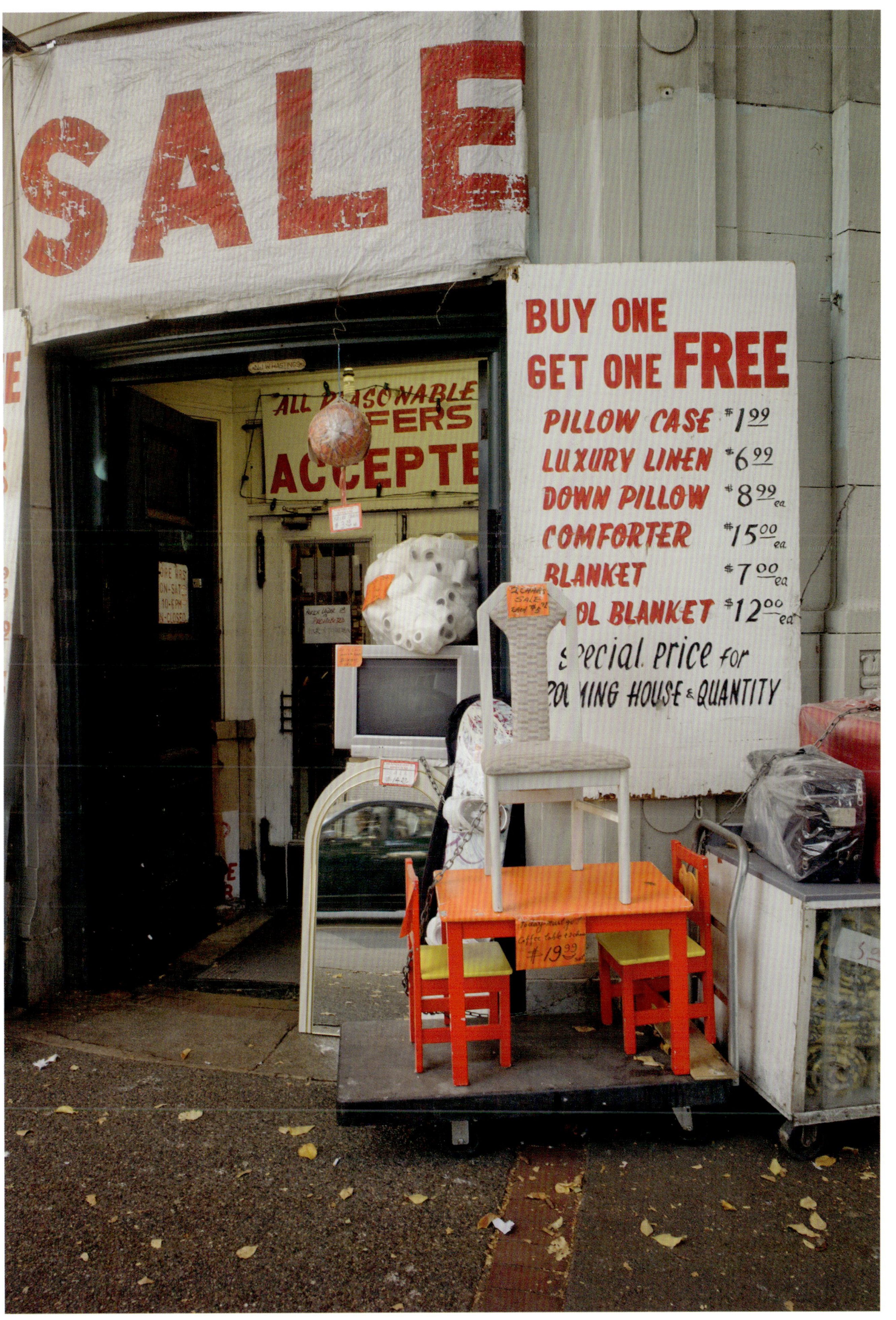
SALE
ALL
ASONABLE
FERS
ACCEPTE
BUY ONE
GET ONE FREE
PILLOW CASE $1.99
LUXURY LINEN $6.99
DOWN PILLOW $8.99 ea
COMFORTER $15.00 ea
BLANKET $7.00 ea
OL BLANKET $12.00 ea
ecial Price for
MING HOUSE & QUANTITY
$19.99

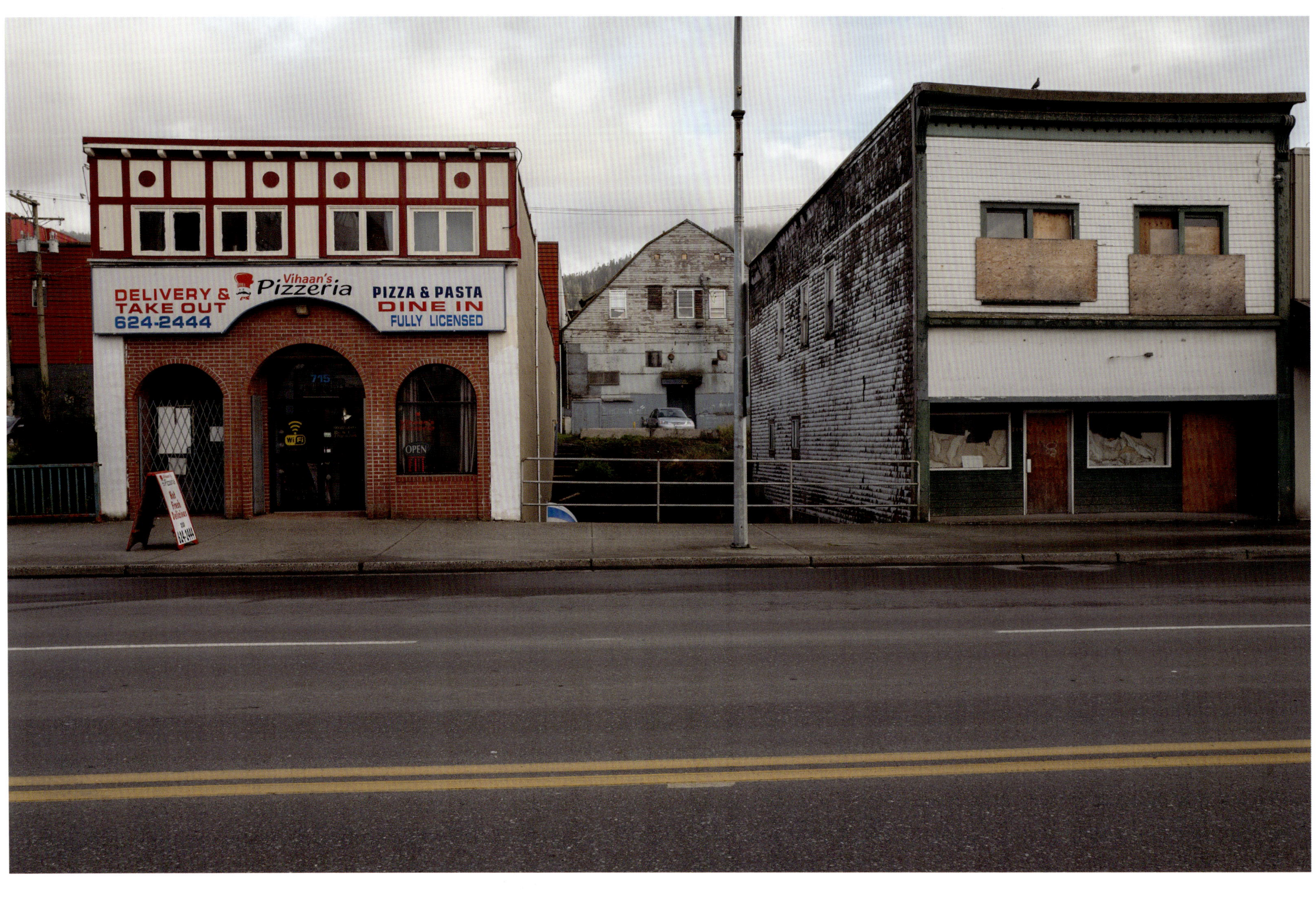
Vihaan's
Pizzeria
DELIVERY &
TAKE OUT
624-2444
PIZZA & PASTA
DINE IN
FULLY LICENSED
OPEN

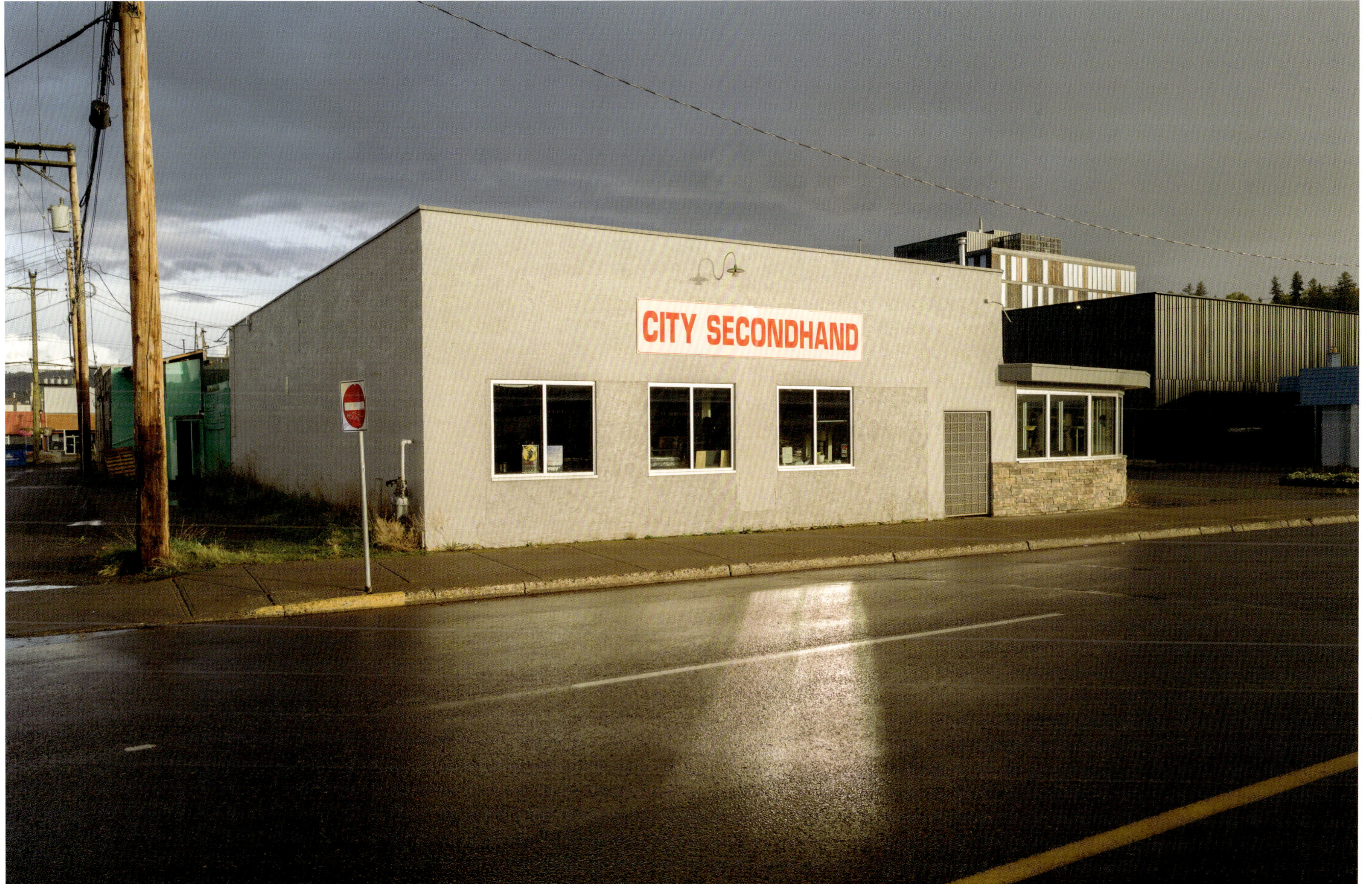
CITY SECONDHAND

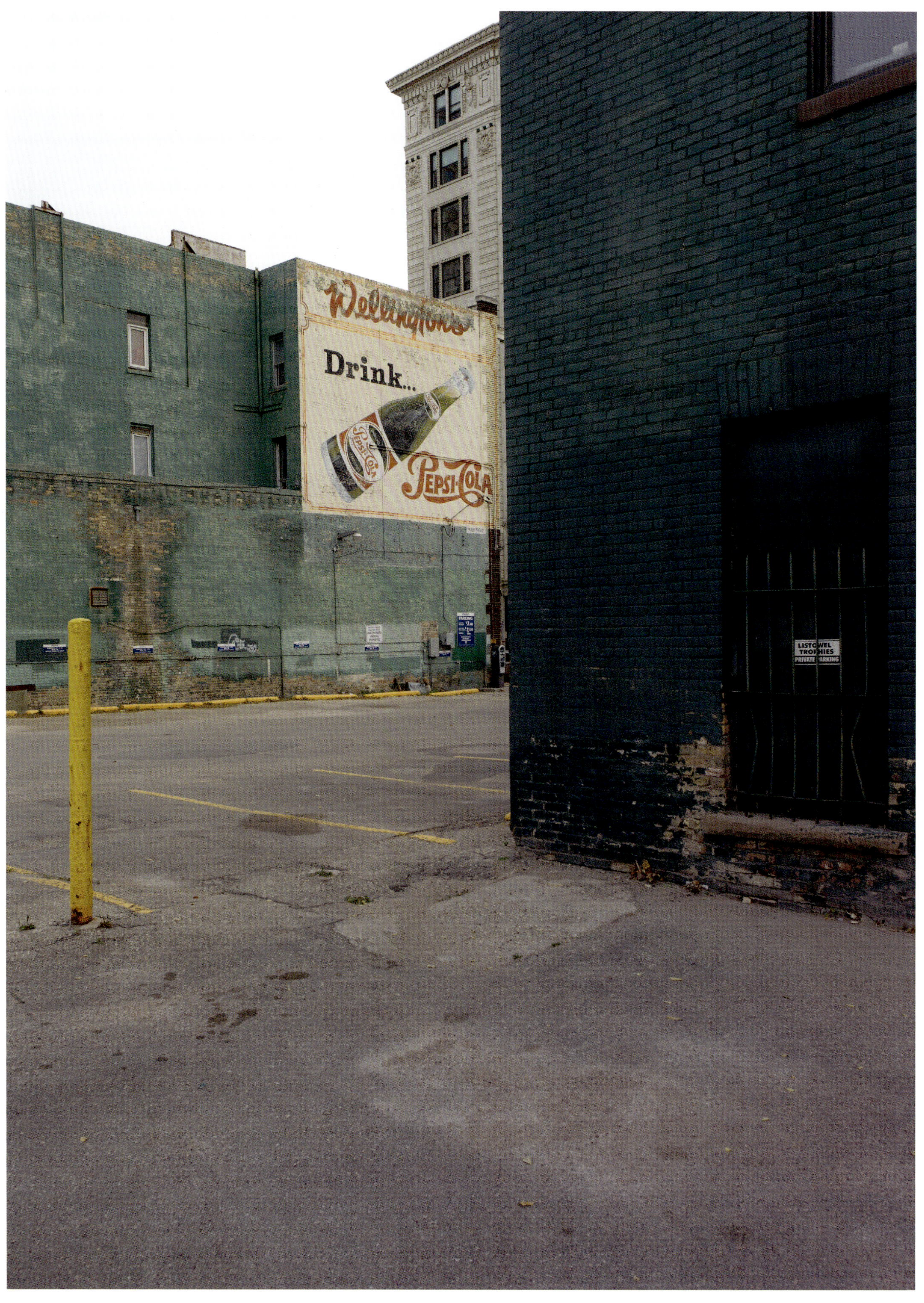
Wellington's
Drink...
Pepsi-Cola
LISTOWEL

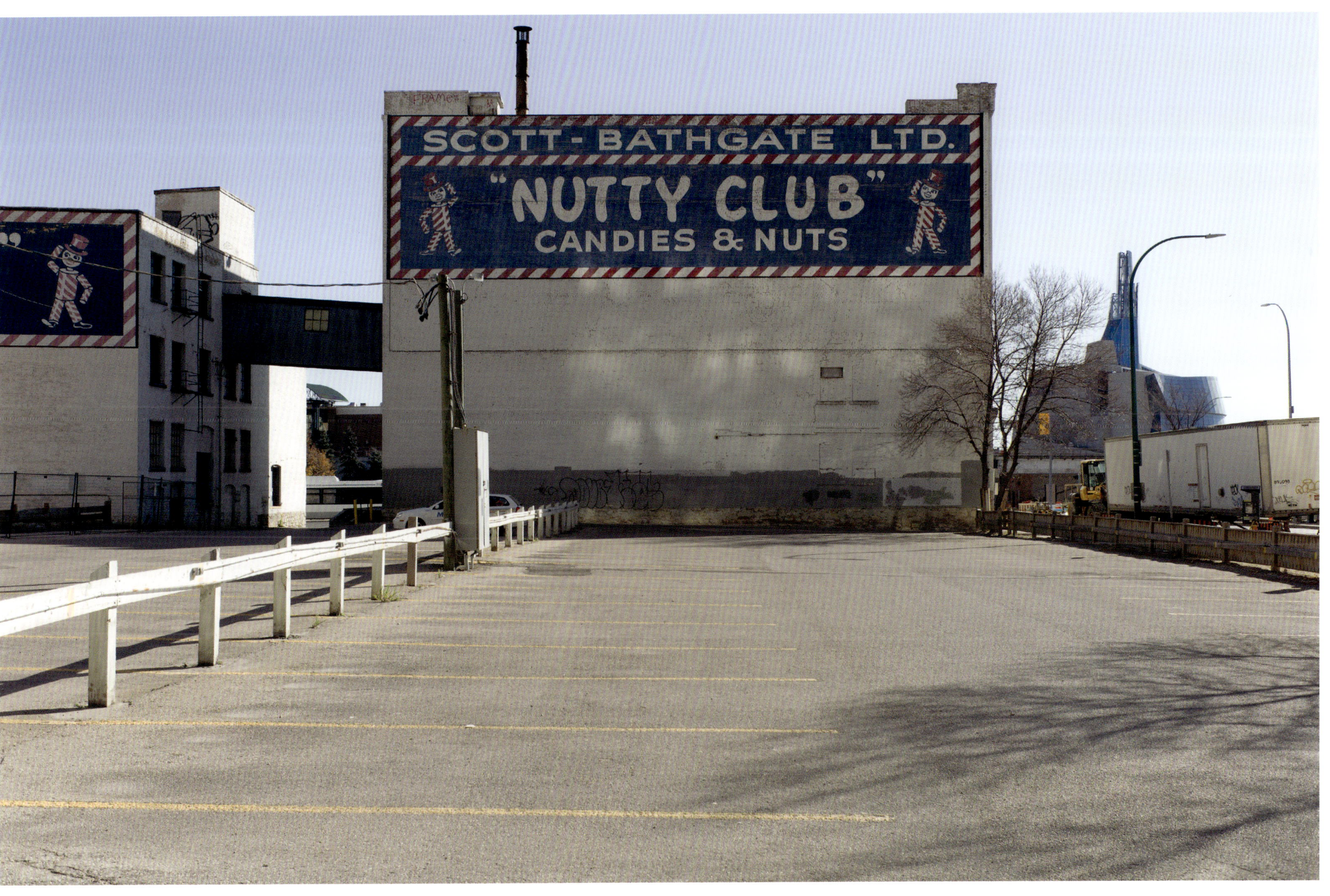
SCOTT - BATHGATE LTD.
"NUTTY CLUB"
CANDIES & NUTS

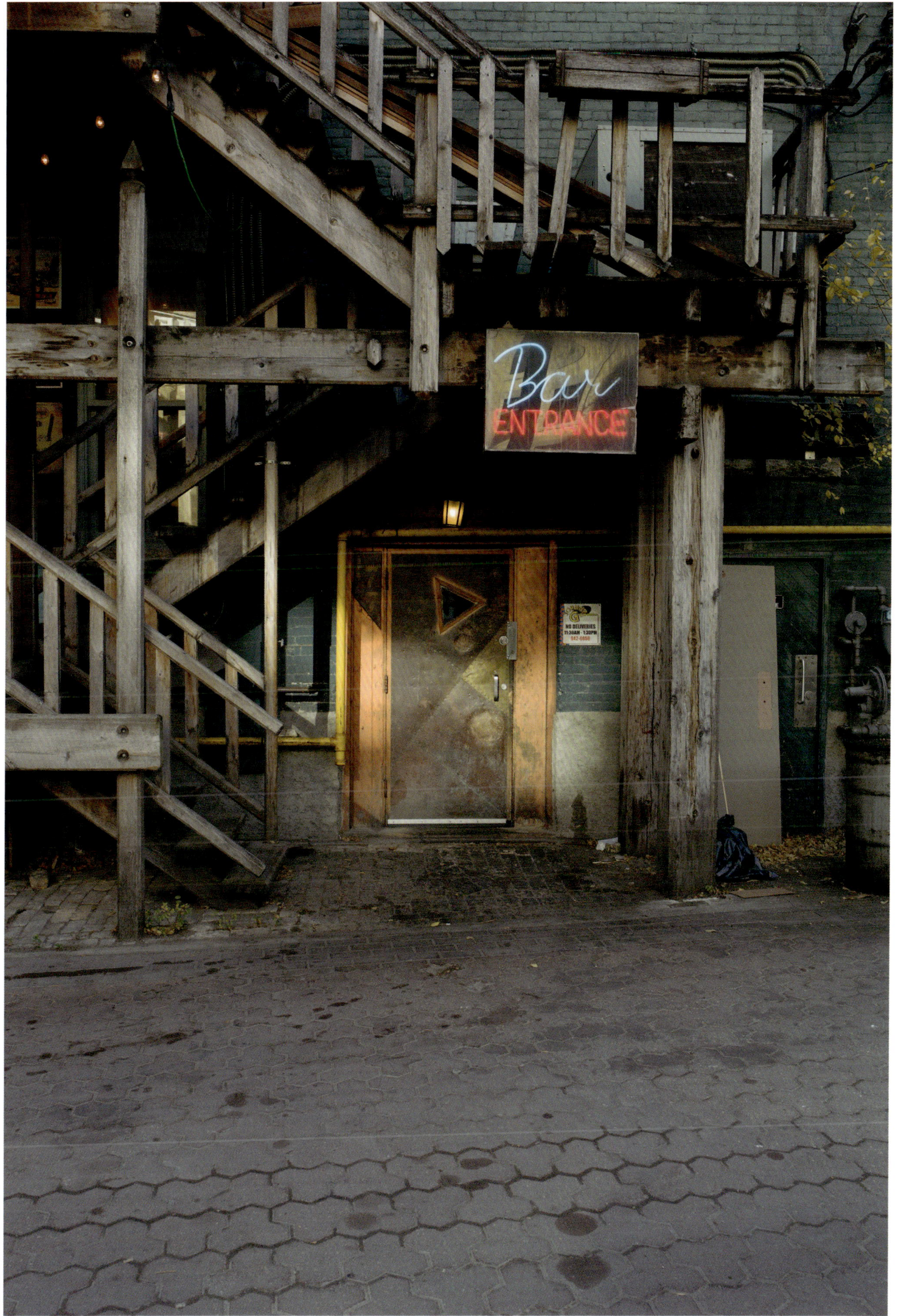
Bar
ENTRANCE
NO DELIVERIES
11:30AM - 1:30PM

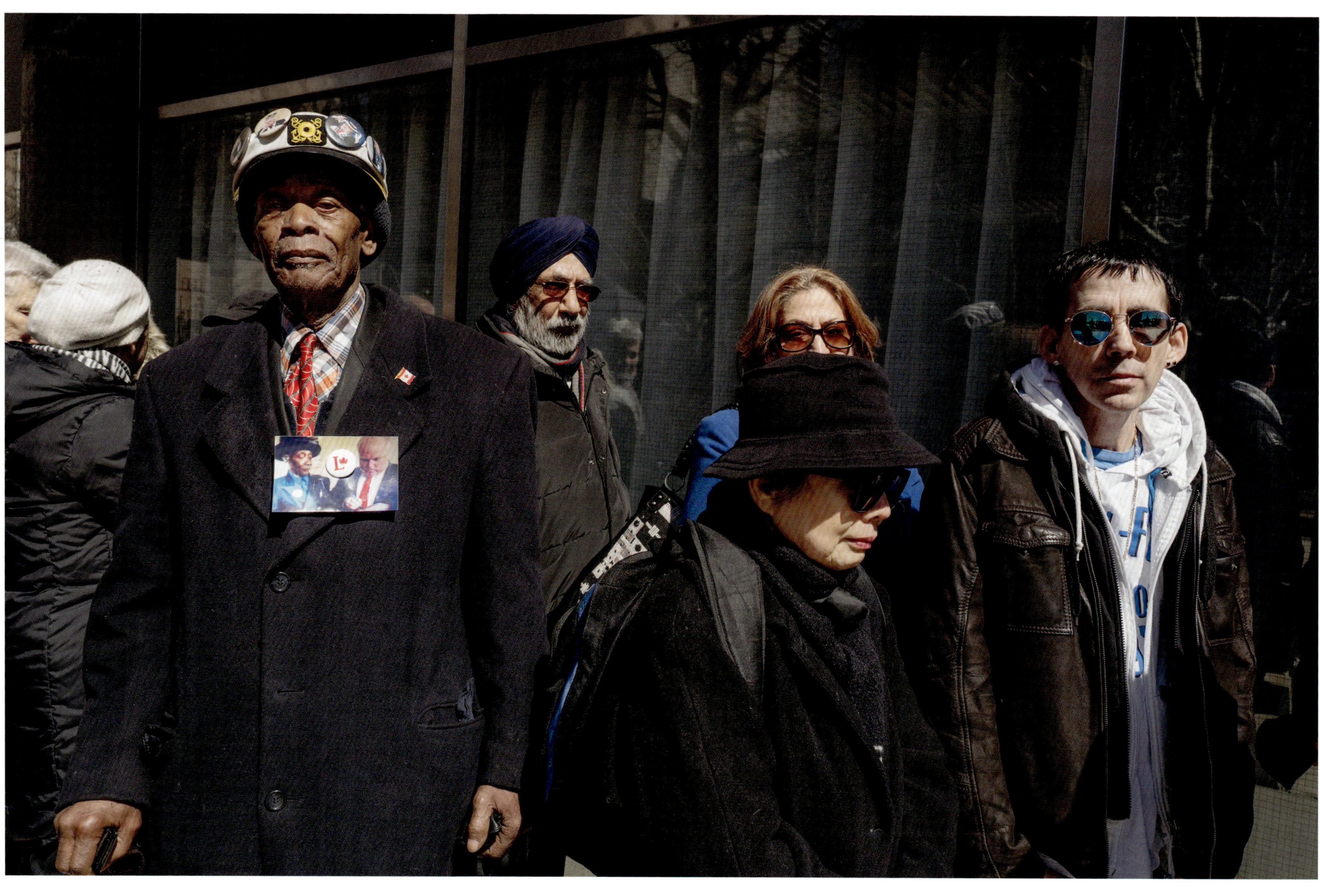

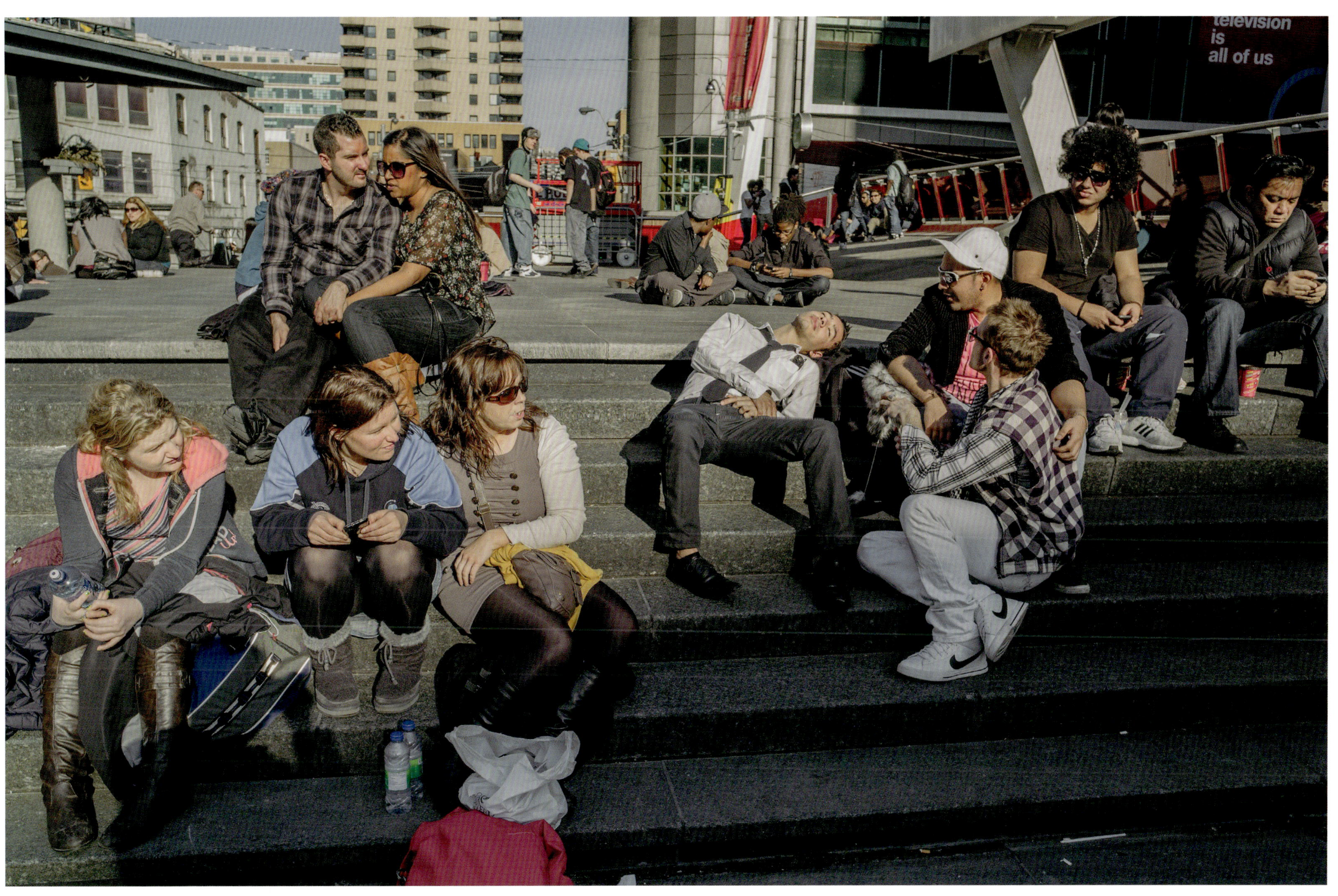
television
is
all of us

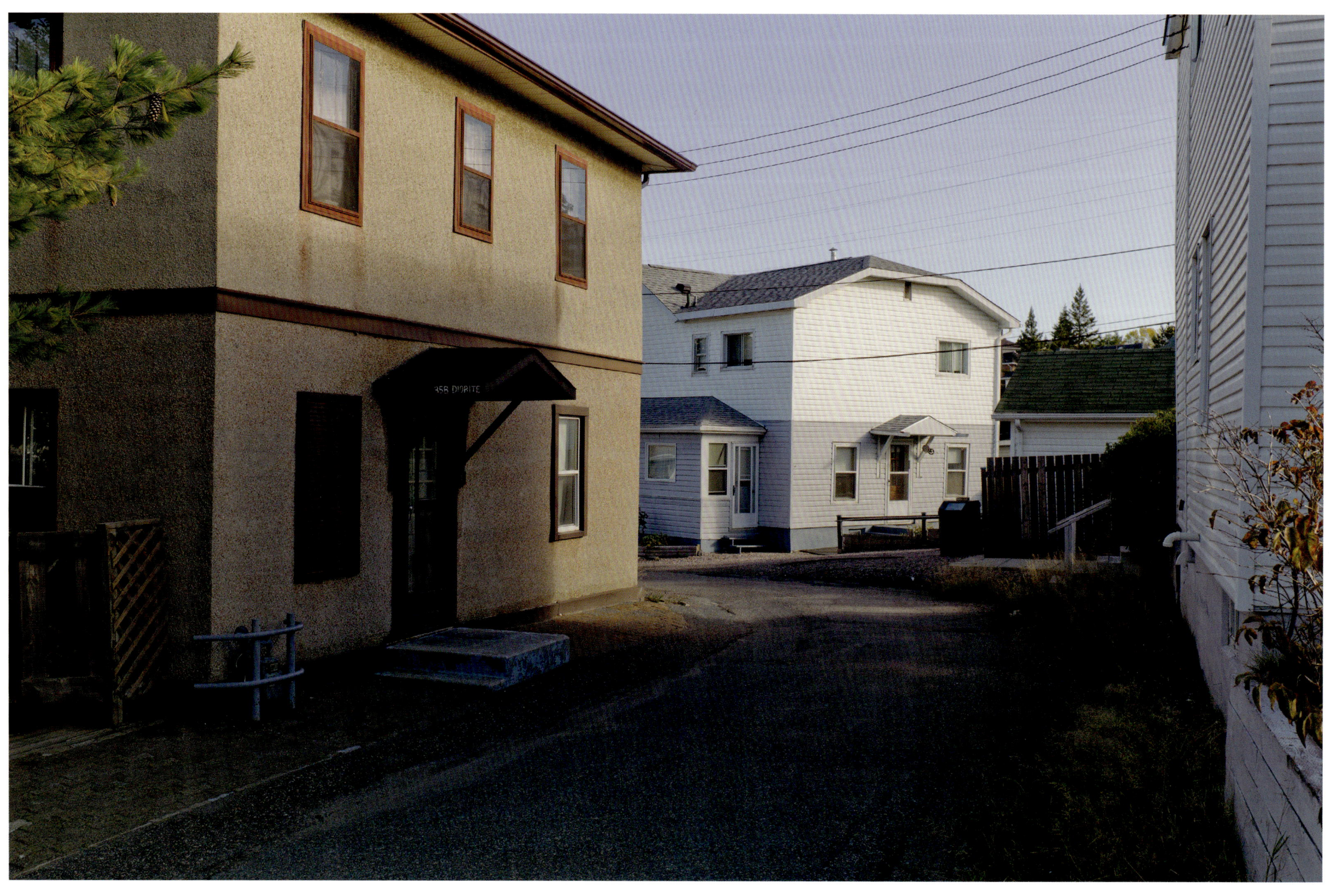
35B DIORITE

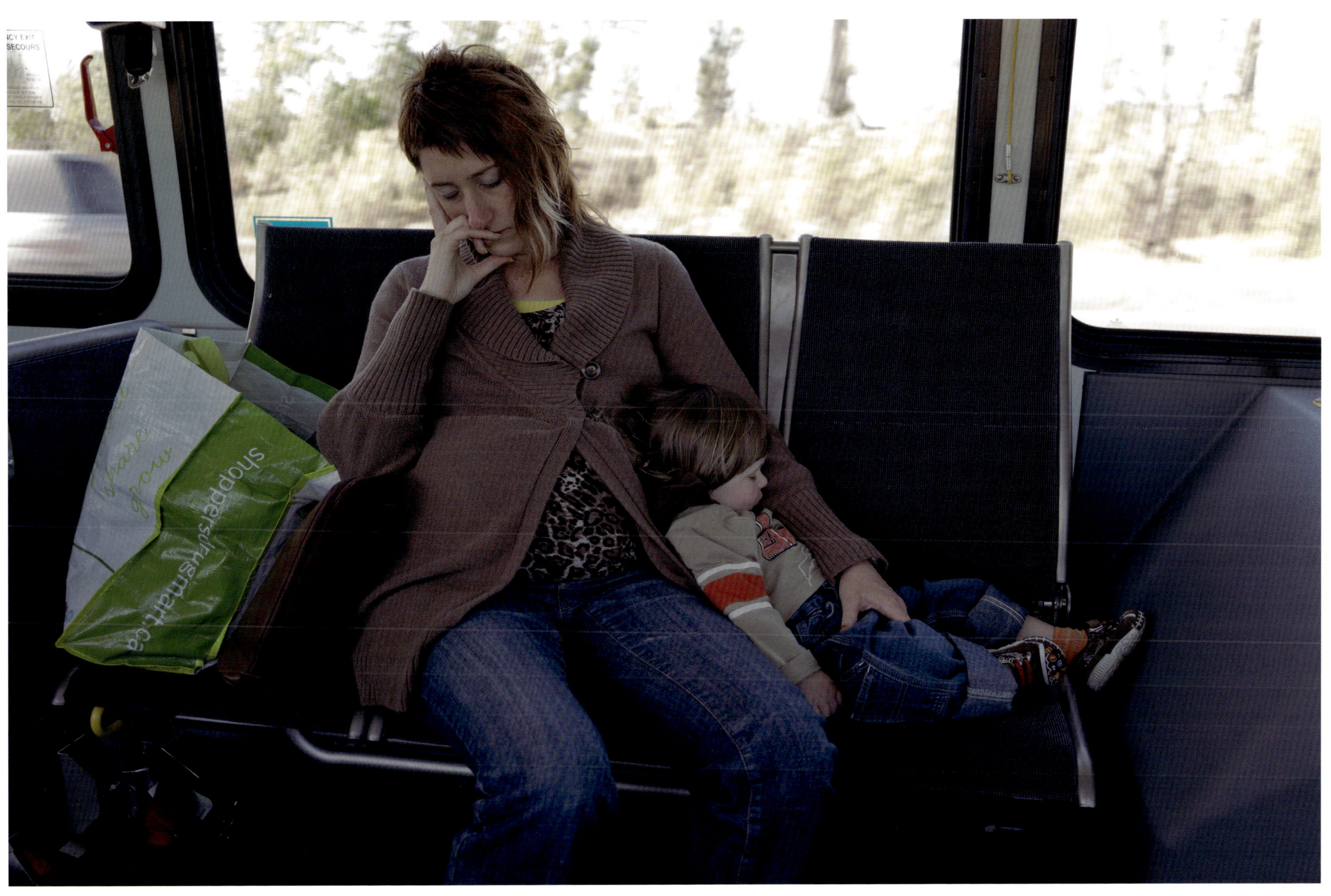
shoppersdrugmart.ca

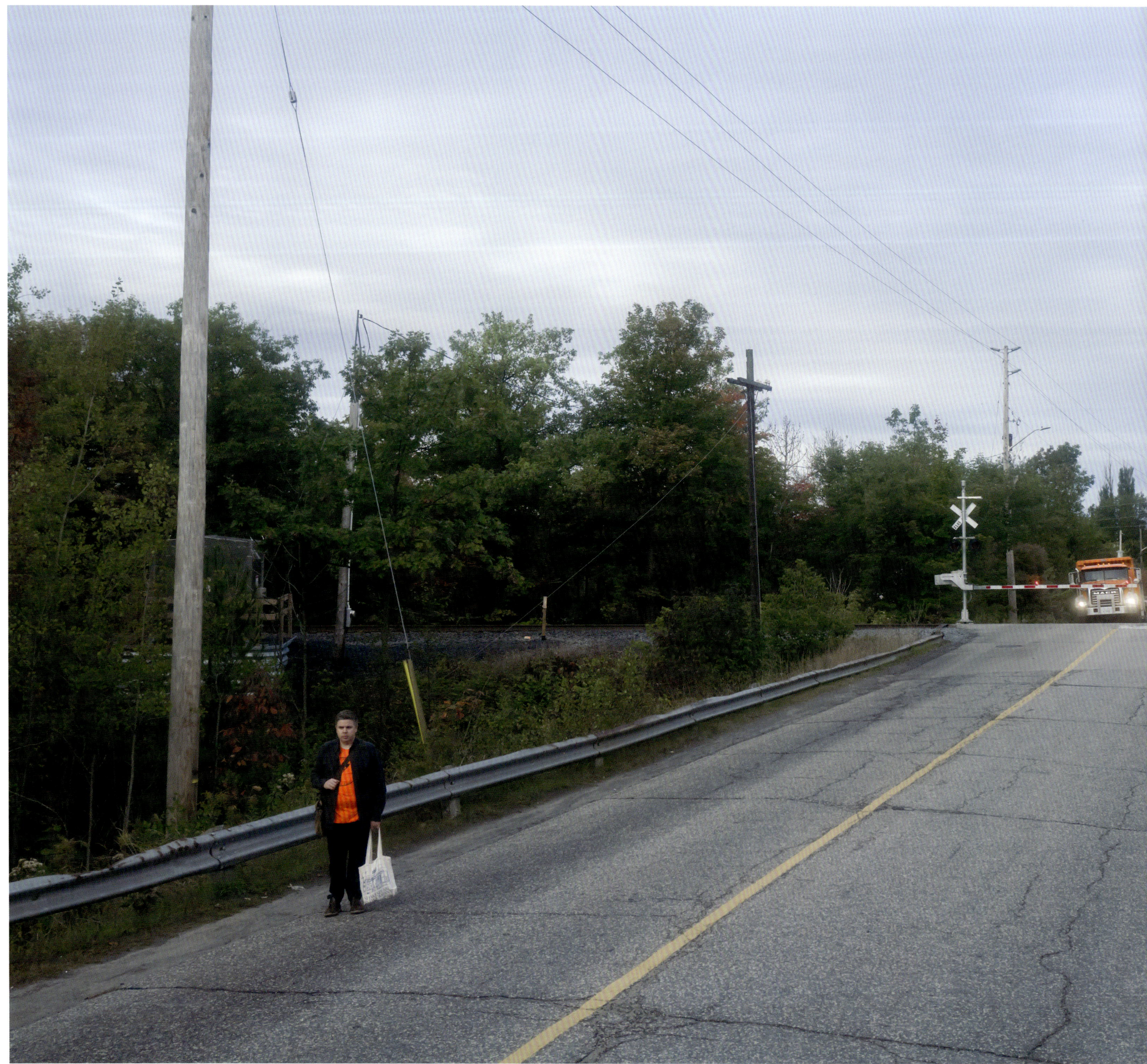

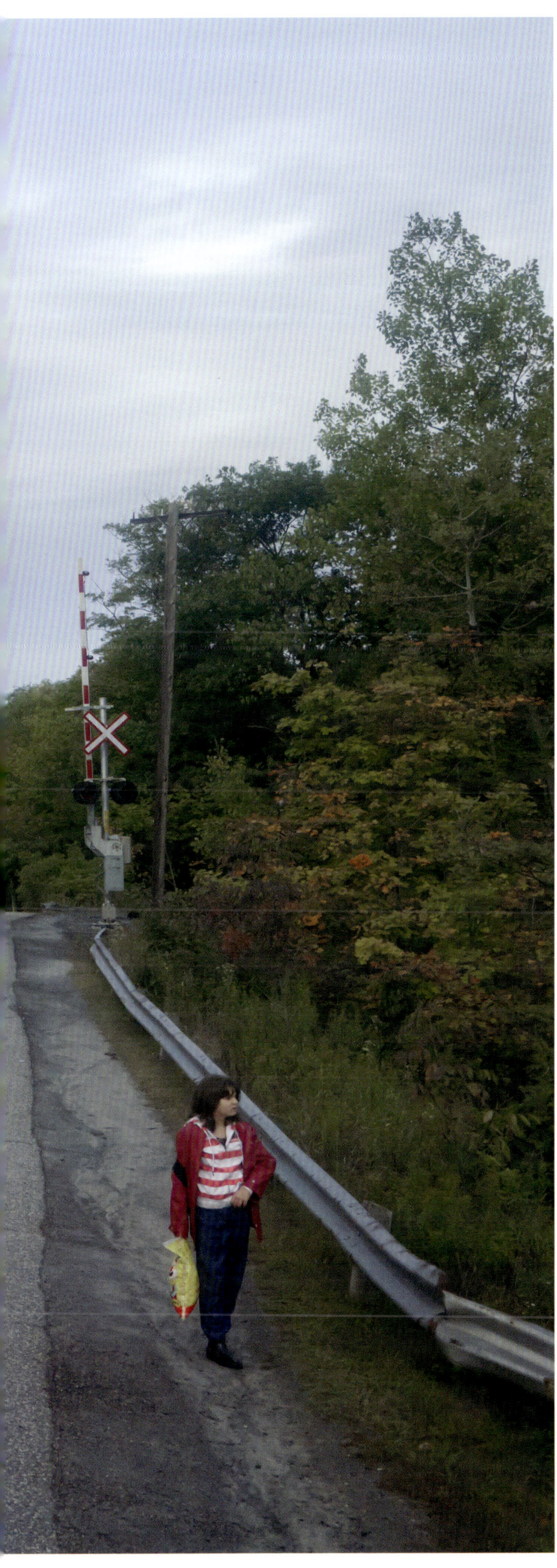

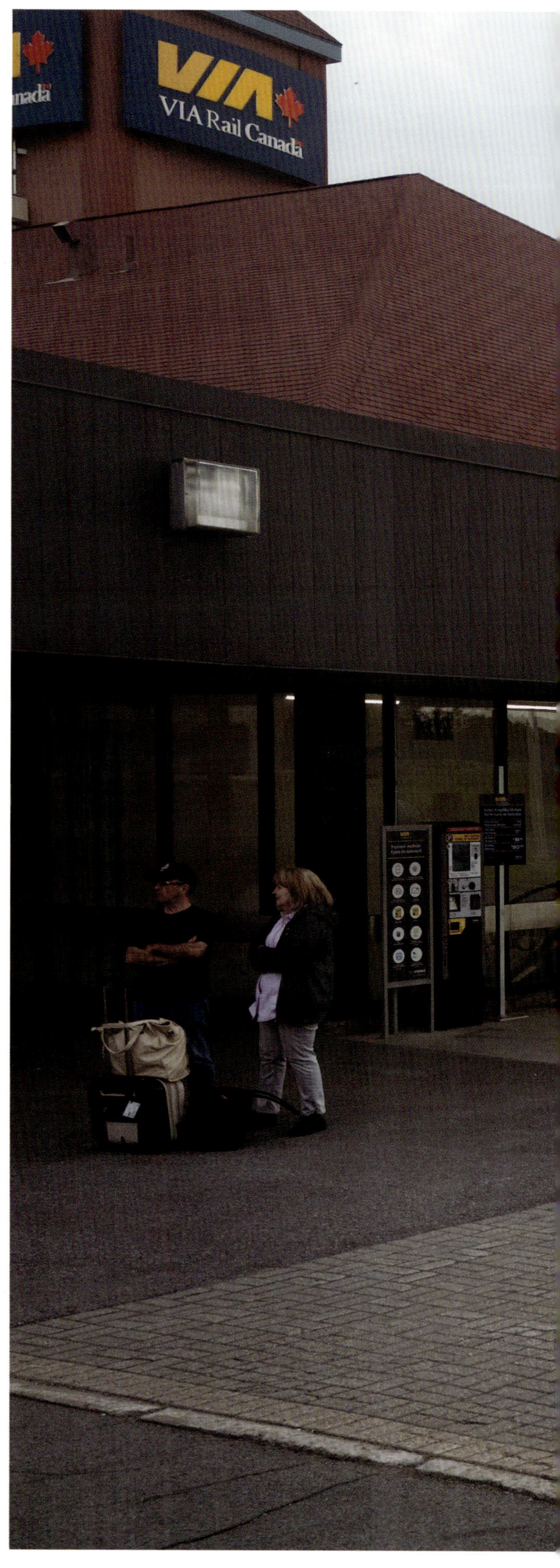
VIA
VIA Rail Canada

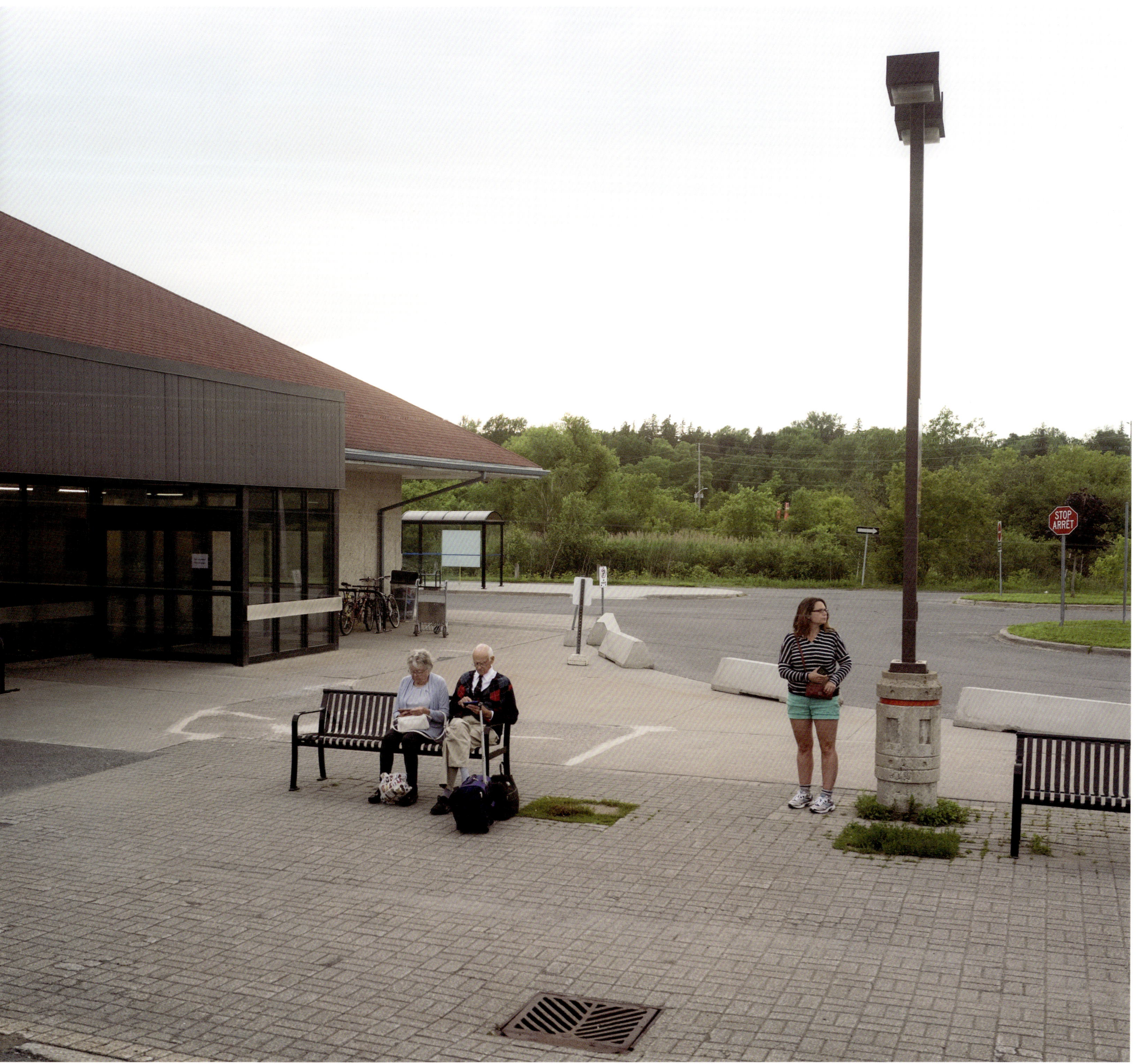
STOP
ARRÊT

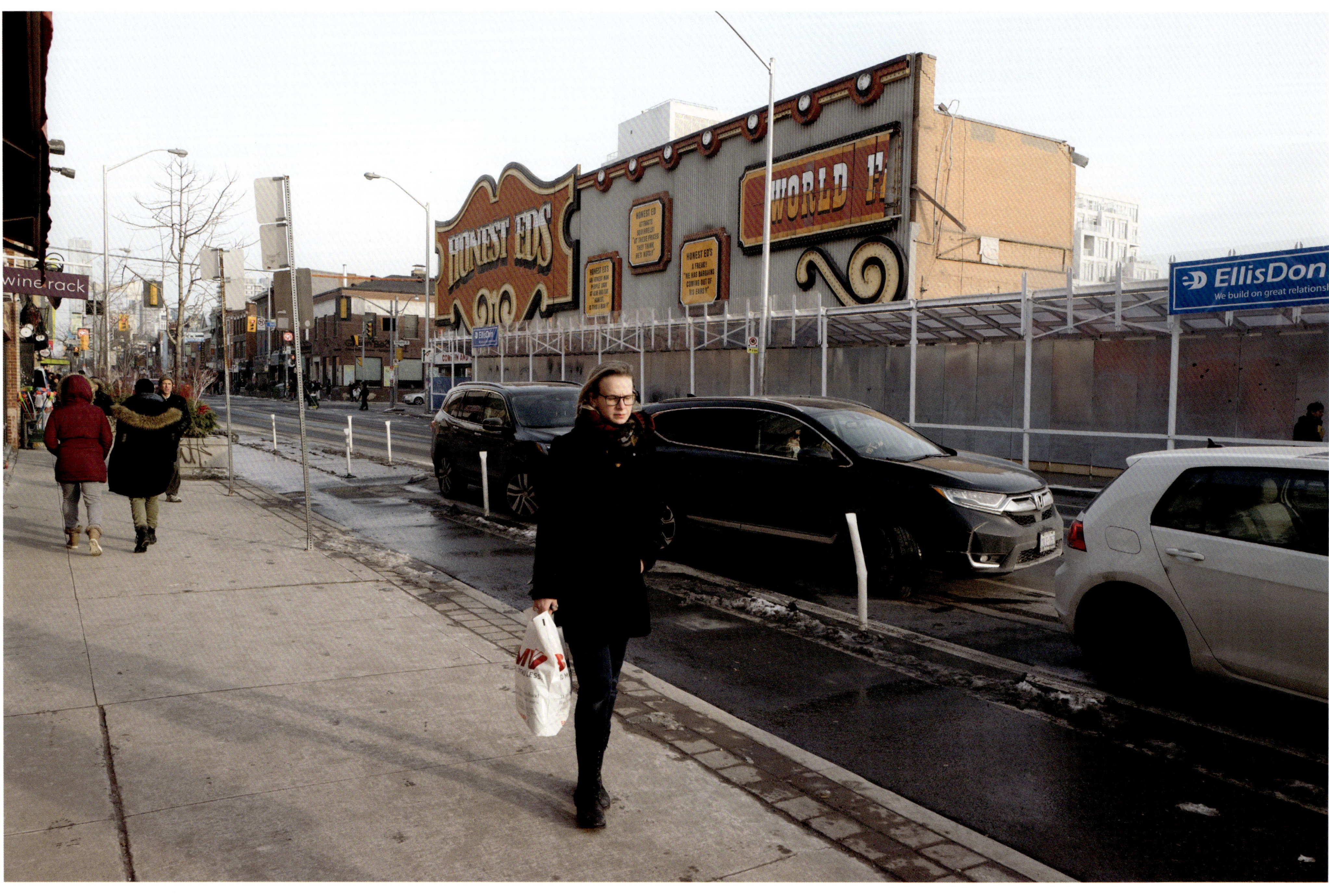
wine rack
HONEST EDS
WORLD
EllisDon

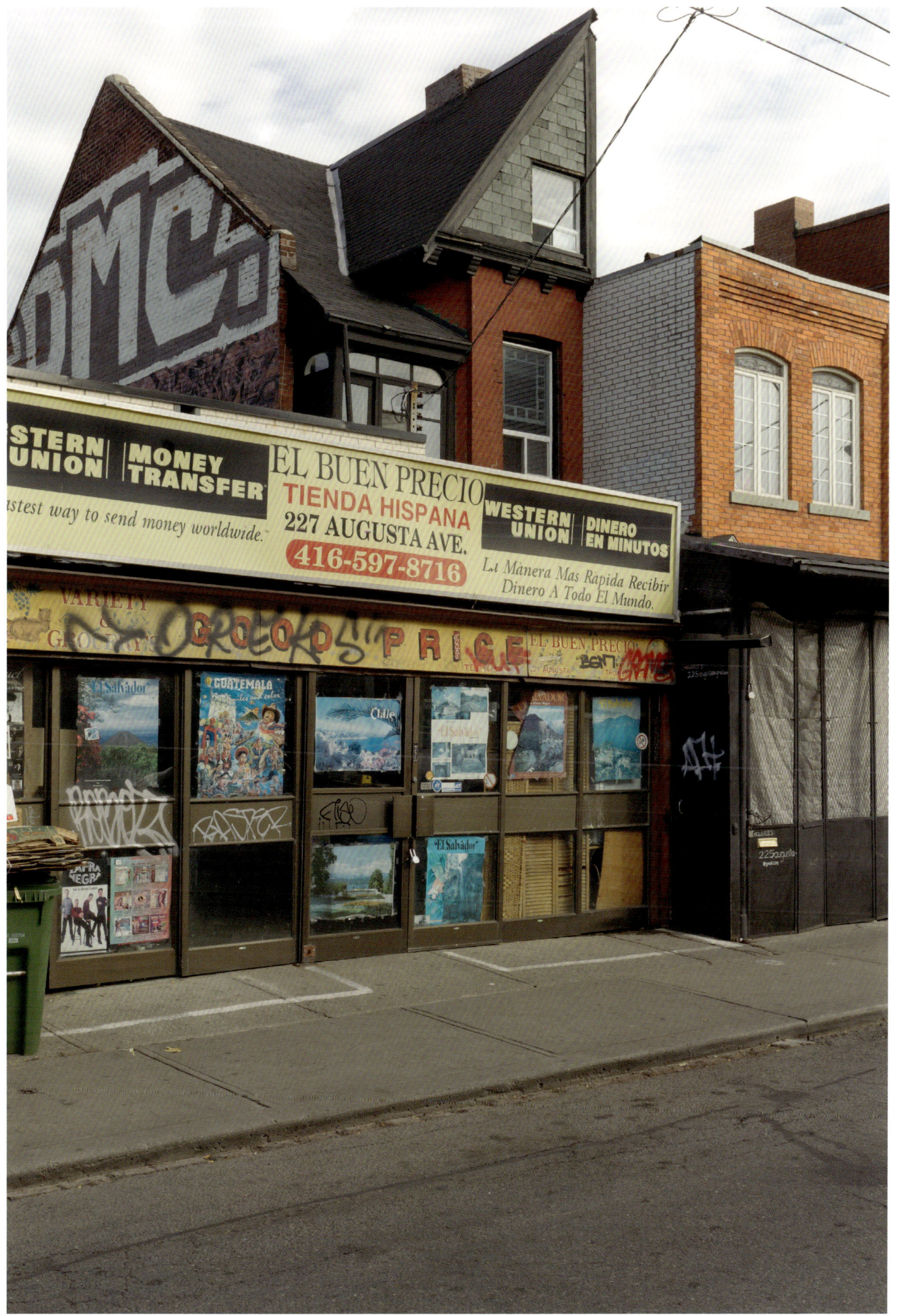

WESTERN UNION
MONEY TRANSFER
EL BUEN PRECIO
TIENDA HISPANA
227 AUGUSTA AVE.
416-597-8716
WESTERN UNION
DINERO EN MINUTOS
La Manera Mas Rapida Recibir Dinero A Todo El Mundo.
VARIETY
PRICE
EL BUEN PRECIO
El Salvador
GUATEMALA
Chile
El Salvador

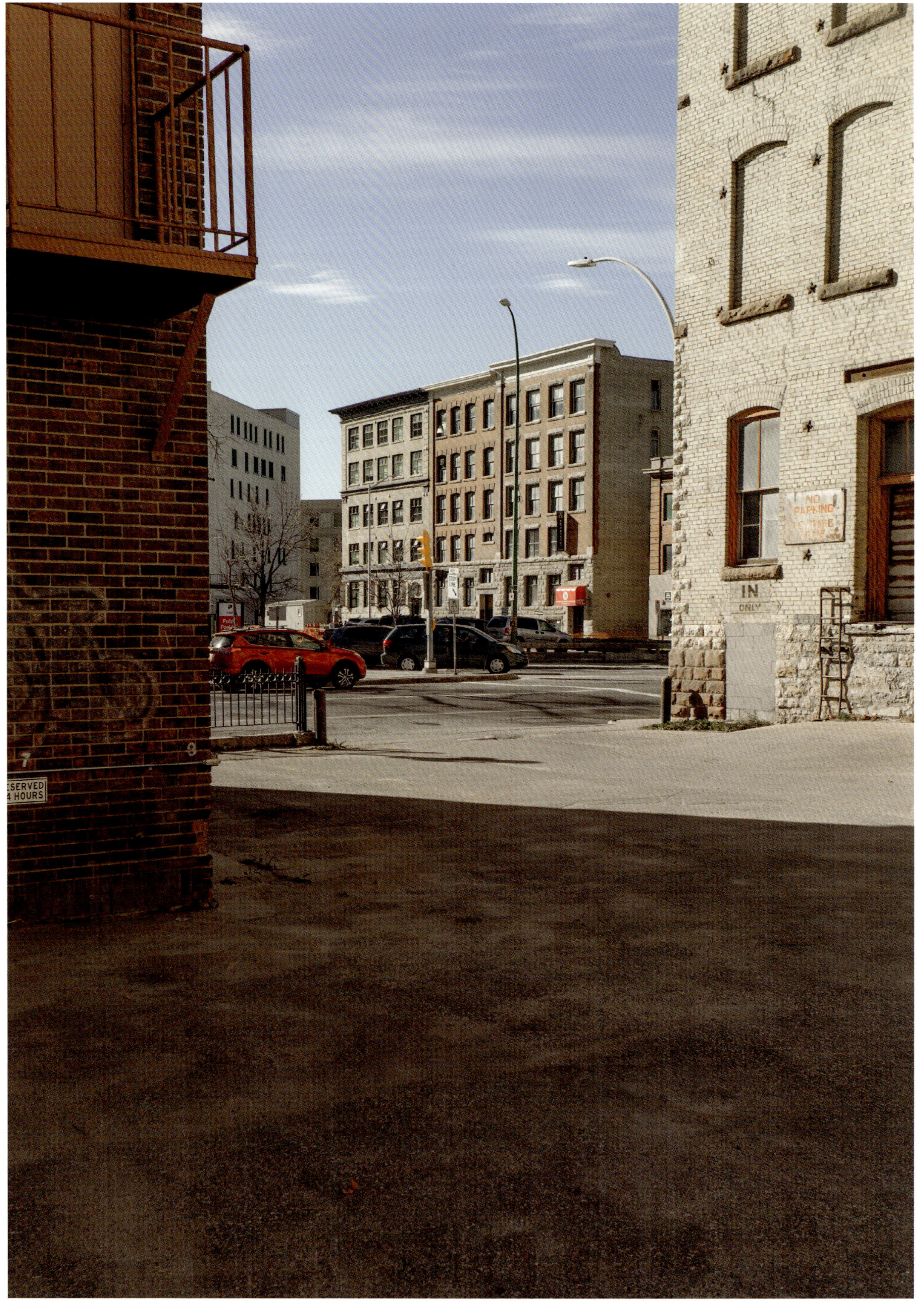
IN
ONLY

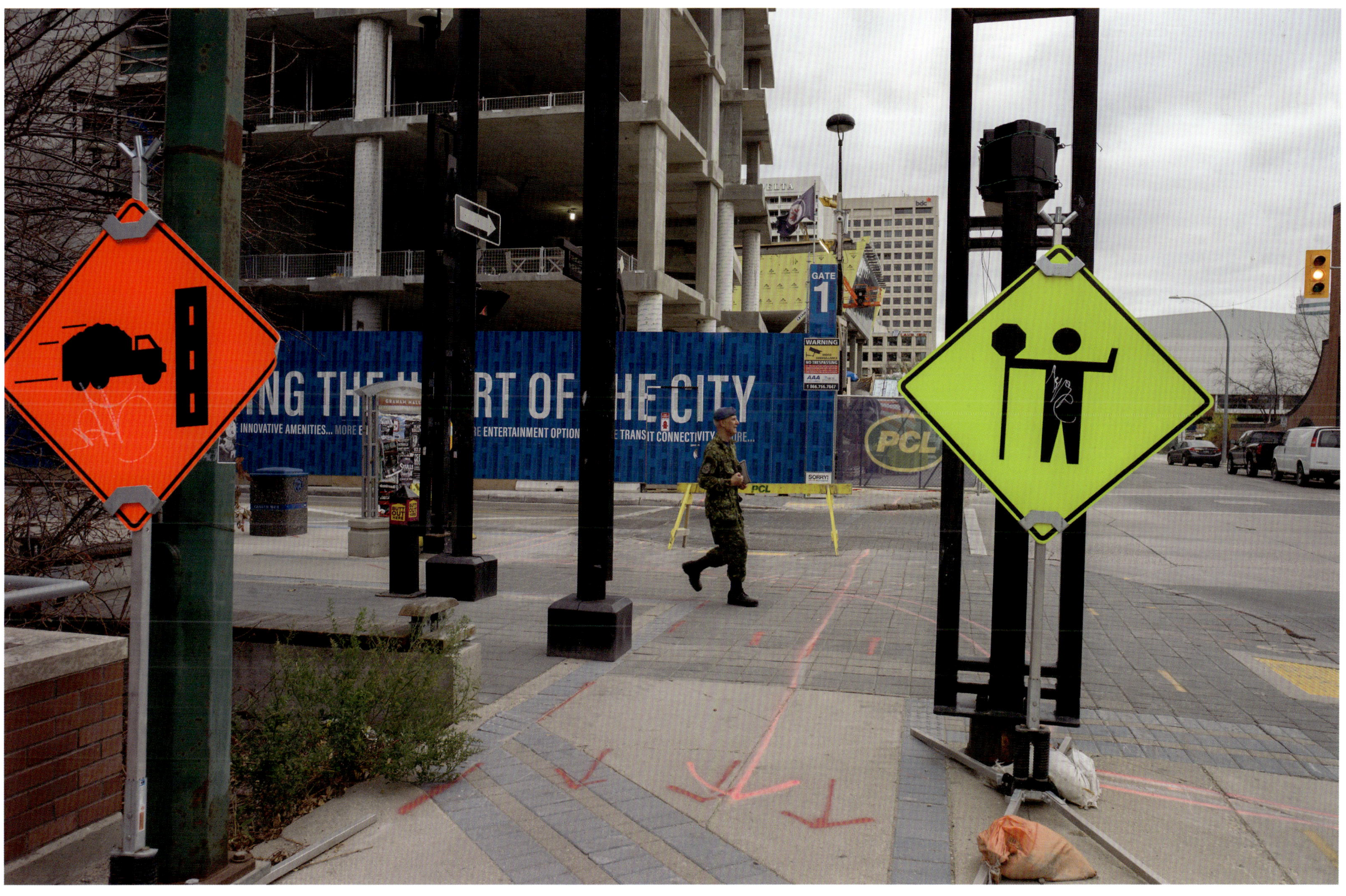
GATE
1
WARNING
NO TRESPASSING
PCL
SORRY!

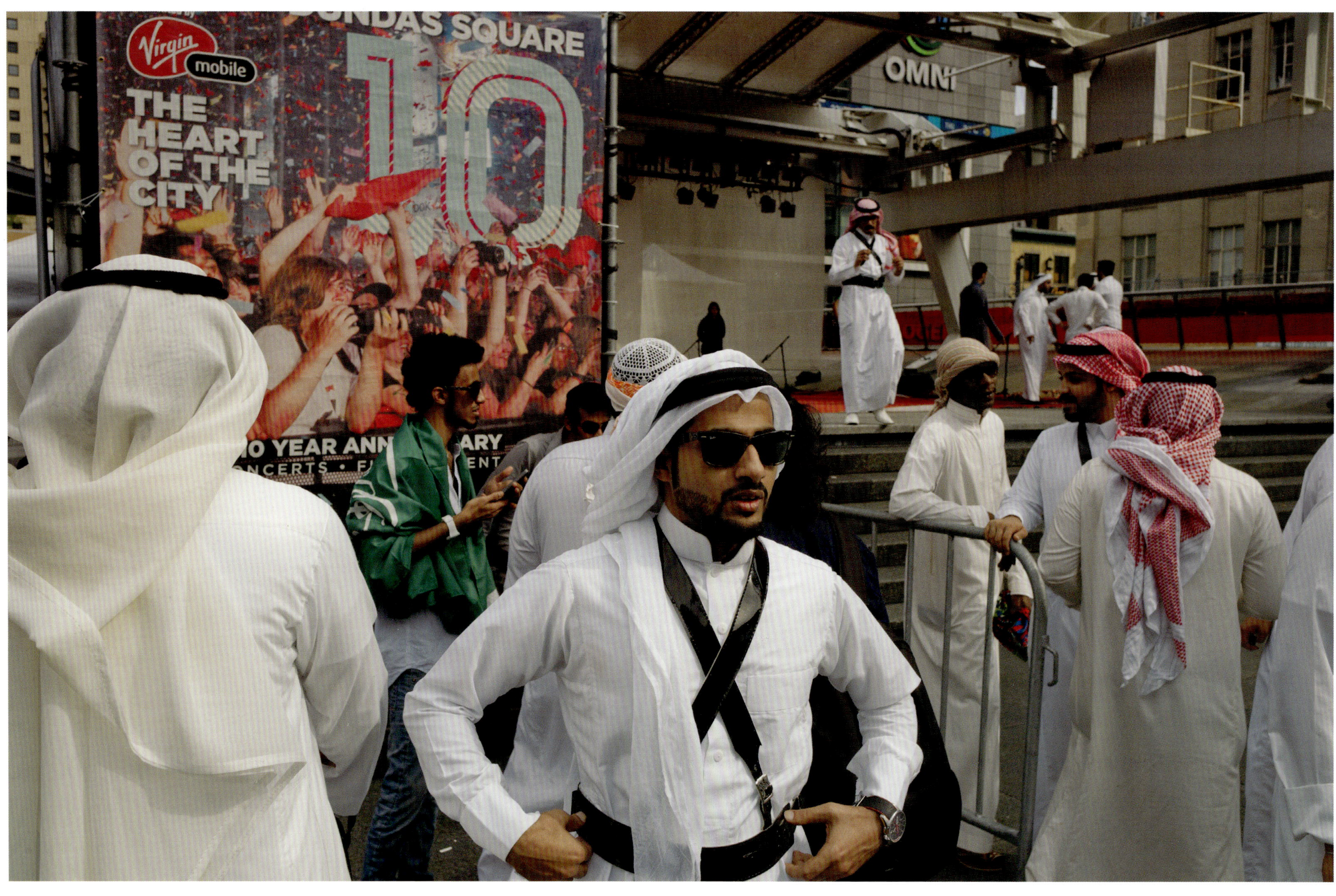
Virgin
mobile
UNDAS SQUARE
10
THE HEART OF THE CITY
0 YEAR ANN ARY
OMNI

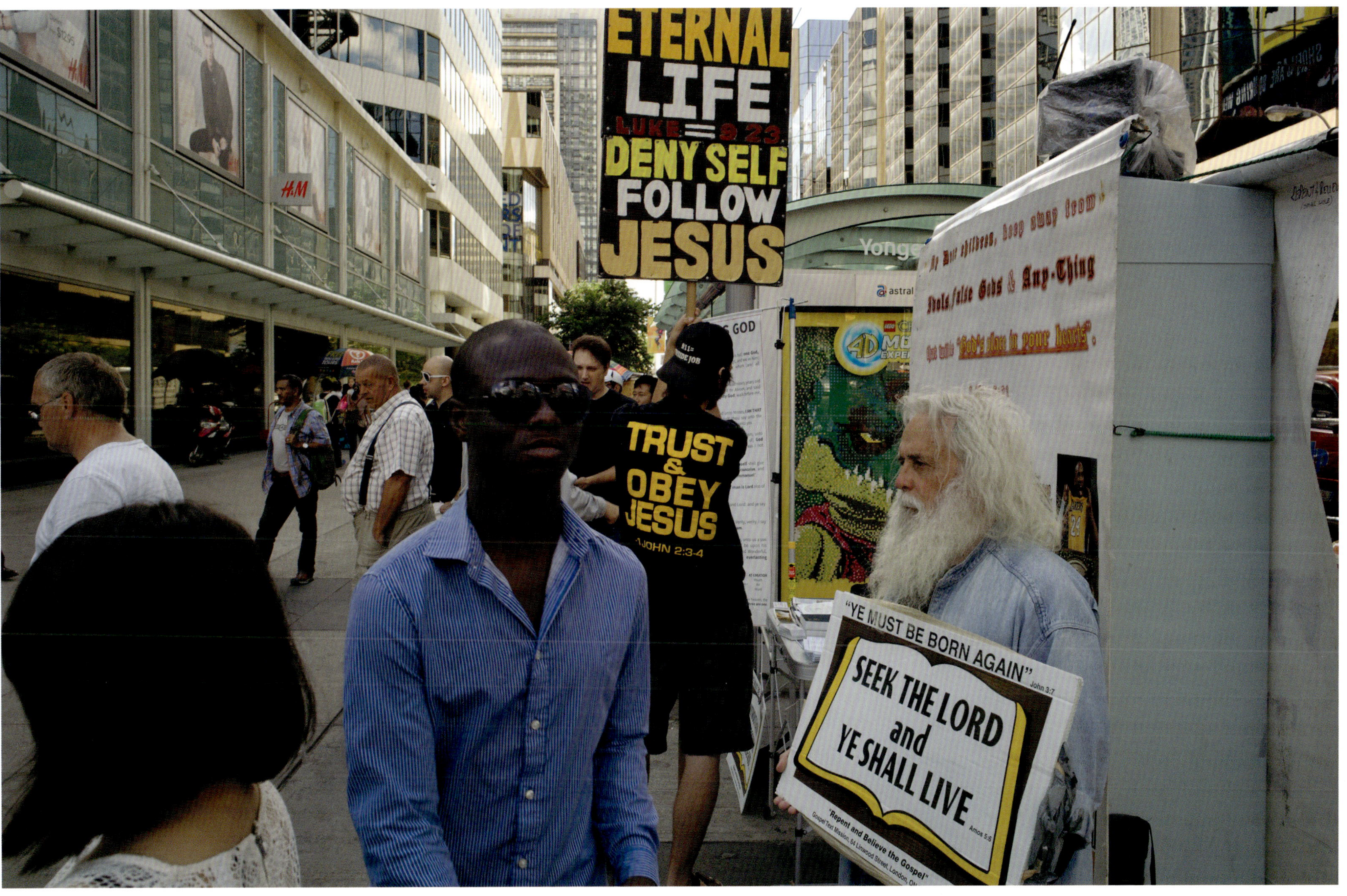
ETERNAL
LIFE
LUKE 9 23
DENY SELF
FOLLOW
JESUS
H&M
Yonge
astral
TRUST
&
OBEY
JESUS
JOHN 2:3-4
Idols/false Gods & Any-Thing
"God's place in your hearts".
"YE MUST BE BORN AGAIN" John 3:7
SEEK THE LORD
and
YE SHALL LIVE
Amos 5:6
"Repent and Believe the Gospel"

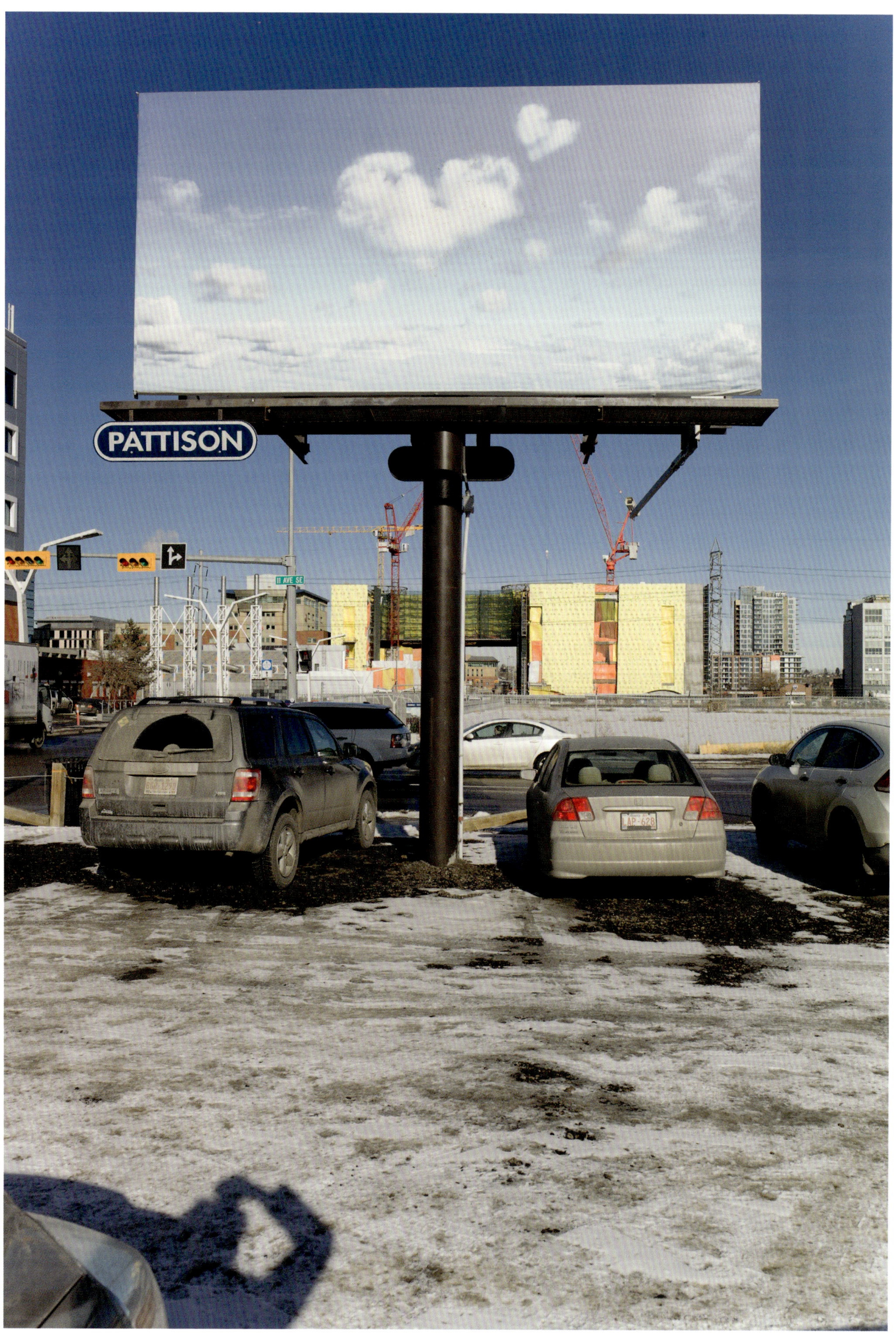
PATTISON
11 AVE SE

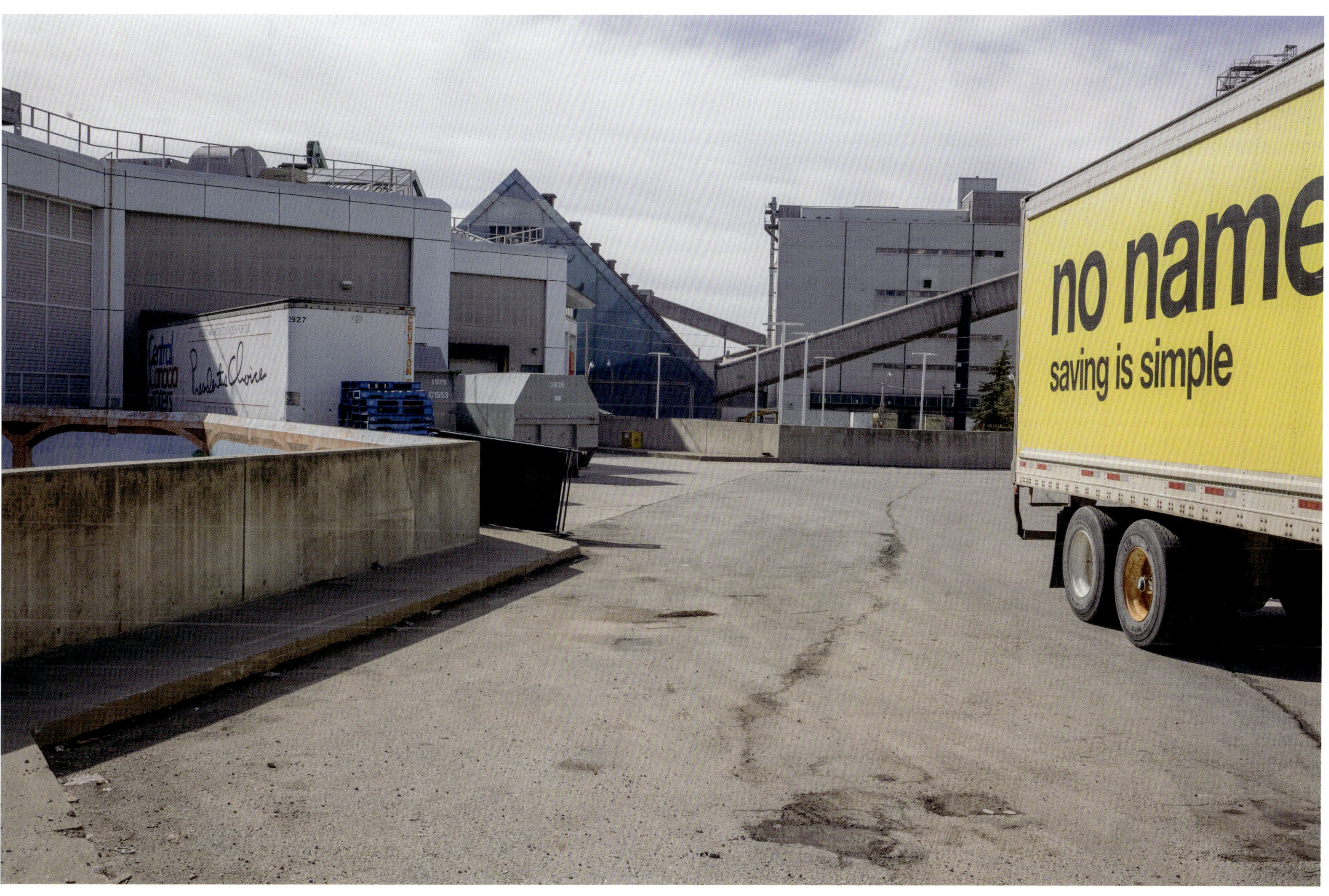
no name
saving is simple

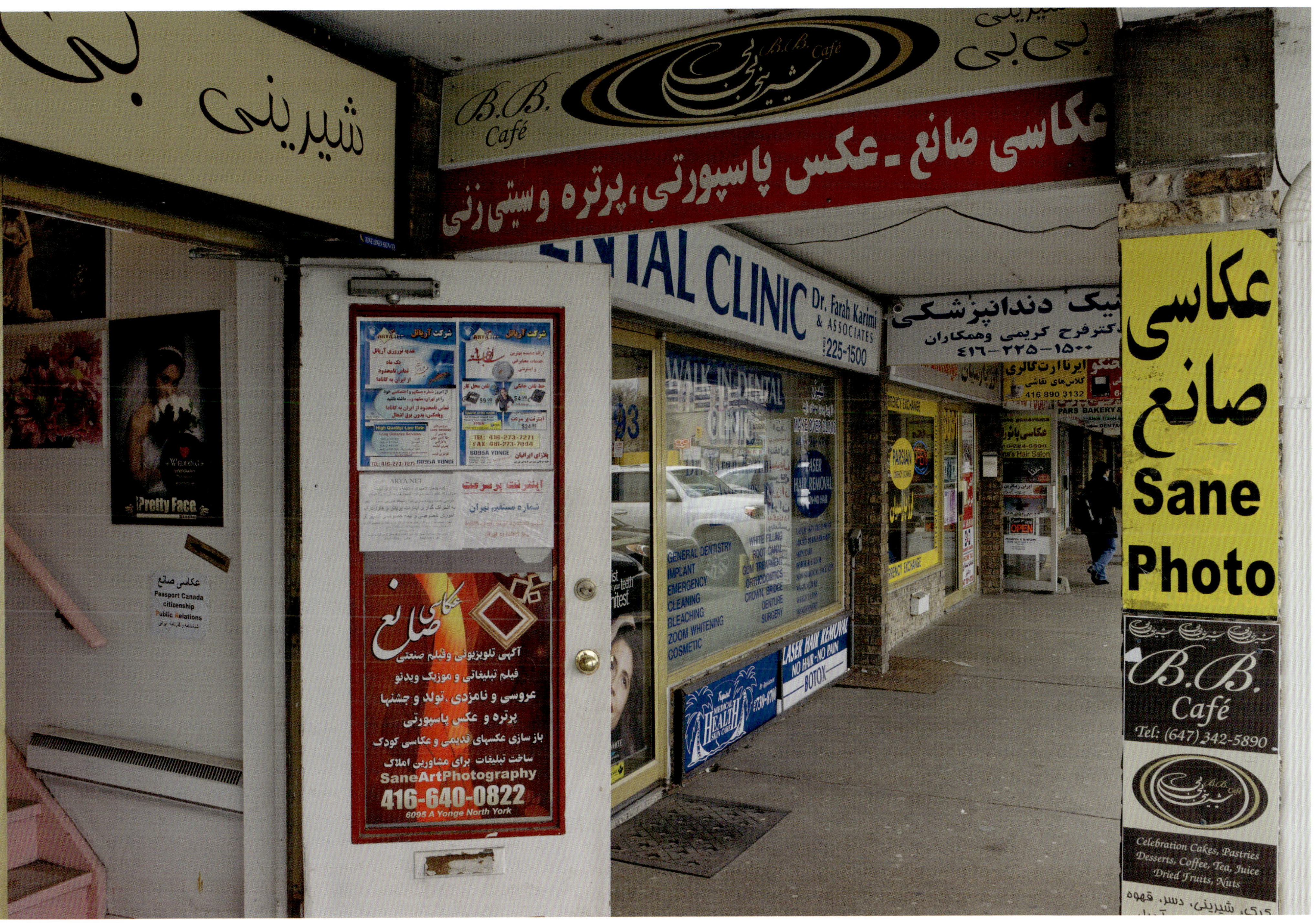
شیرینی
B.B. Café
عکاسی صانع ـ عکس پاسپورتی، پرتره و سیتی زنی
NTAL CLINIC
Dr. Farah Karimi & ASSOCIATES
225-1500
WALK IN DENTAL
GENERAL DENTISTRY
IMPLANT
EMERGENCY
CLEANING
BLEACHING
ZOOM WHITENING
COSMETIC
LASER HAIR REMOVAL
NO HAIR-NO PAIN
BOTOX
عکاسی صانع
Passport Canada
citizenship
Public Relations
Pretty Face
آگهی تلویزیونی وفیلم صنعتی
فیلم تبلیغاتی و موزیک ویدئو
عروسی و نامزدی، تولد و جشنها
پرتره و عکس پاسپورتی
باز سازی عکسهای قدیمی و عکاسی کودک
ساخت تبلیغات برای مشاورین املاک
SaneArtPhotography
416-640-0822
6095 A Yonge North York
عکاسی صانع
Sane Photo
B.B. Café
Tel: (647) 342-5890
Celebration Cakes, Pastries
Desserts, Coffee, Tea, Juice
Dried Fruits, Nuts

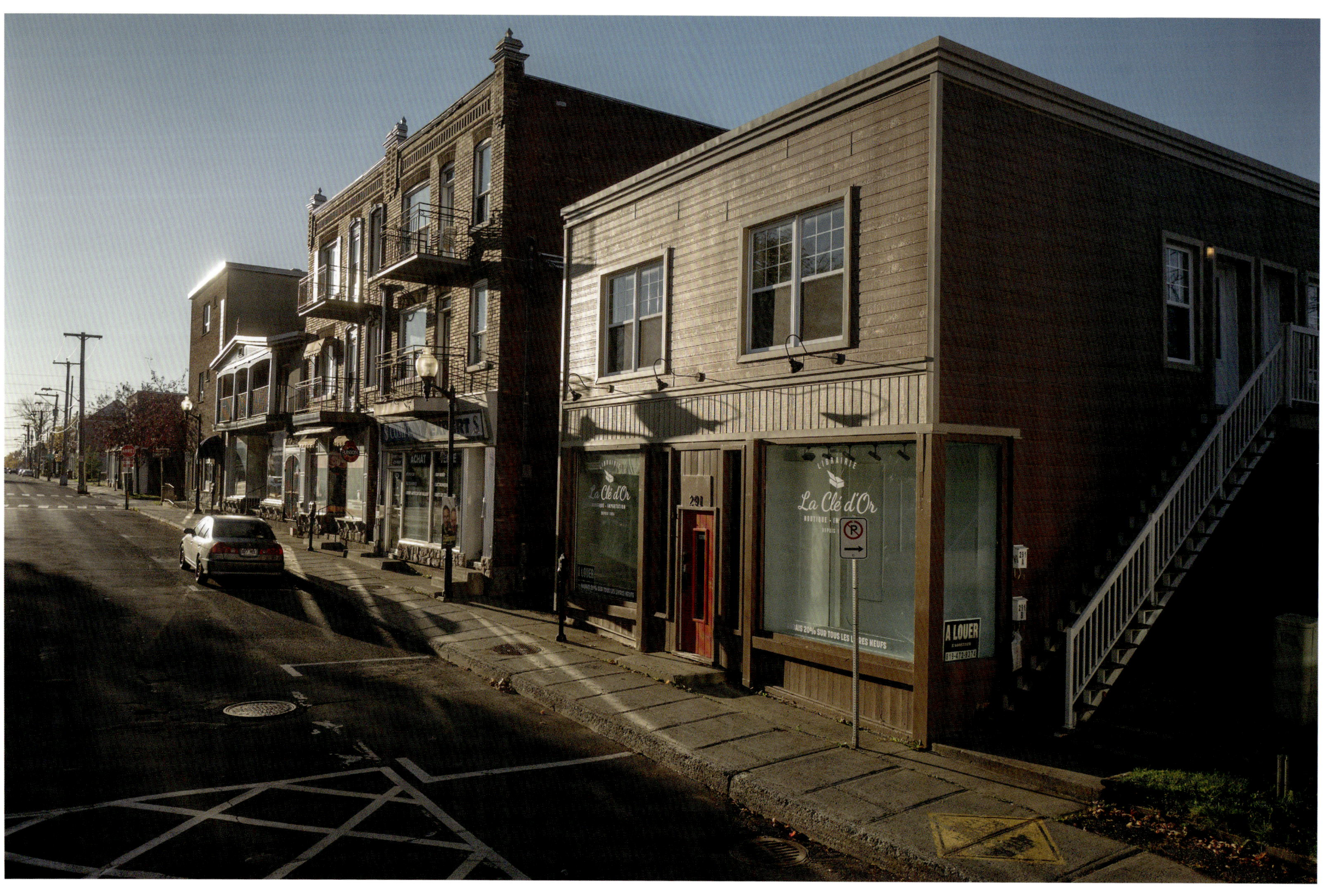
LIBRAIRIE
La Clé d'Or
BOUTIQUE - IMPORTATION
291
A LOUER
AIS 20% SUR TOUS LES L RES NEUFS
A LOUER
819-472-9374
ACHAT

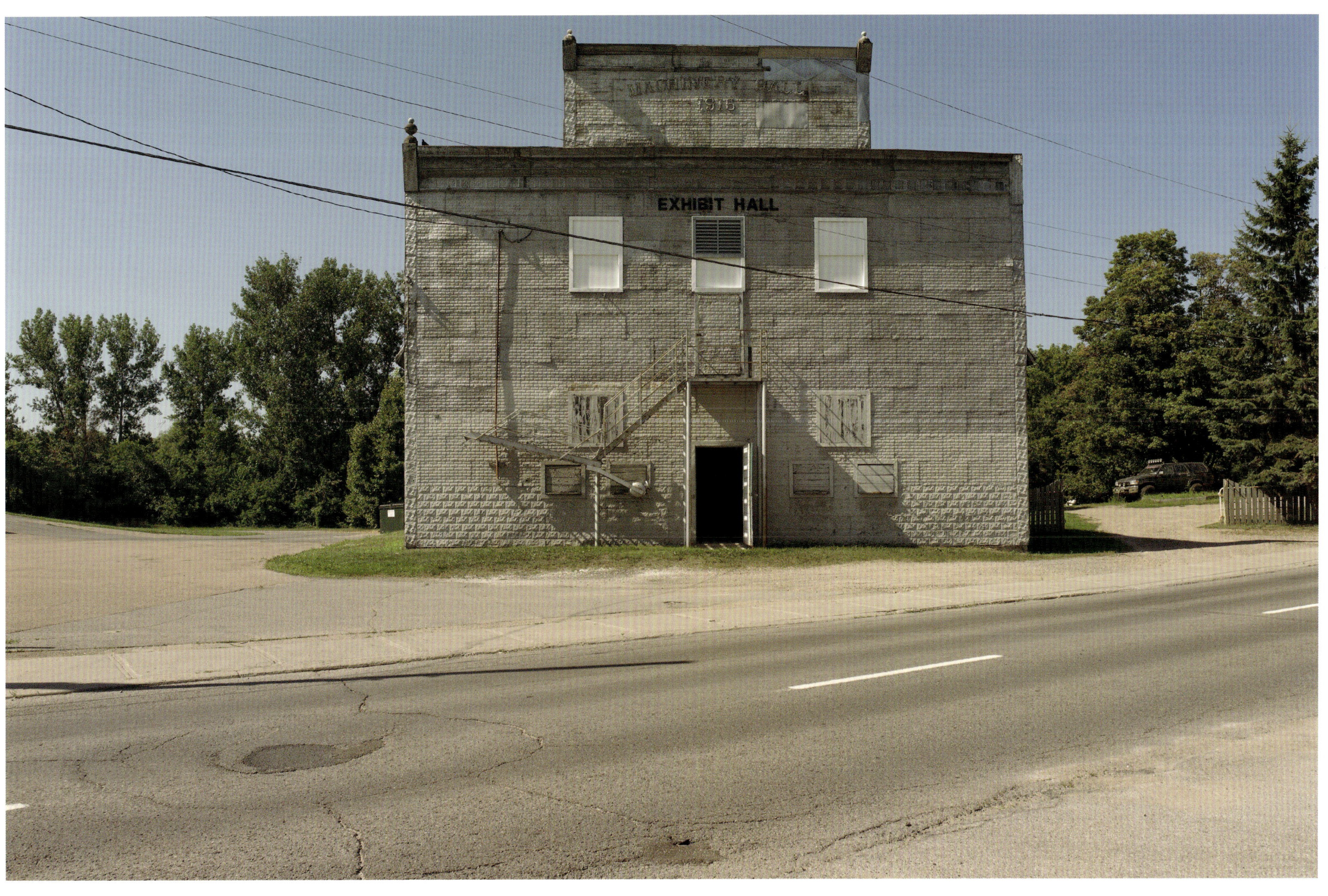
EXHIBIT HALL

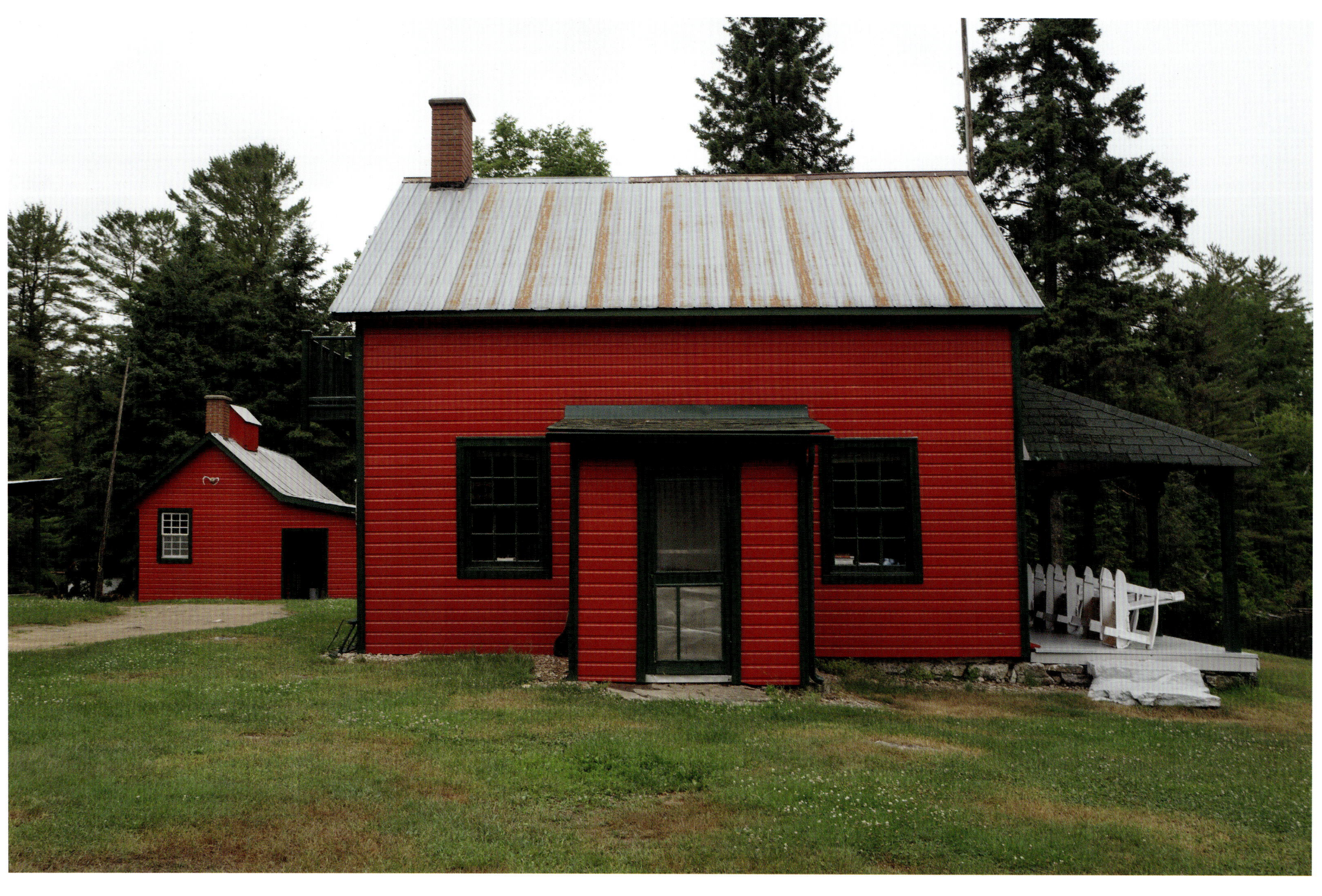

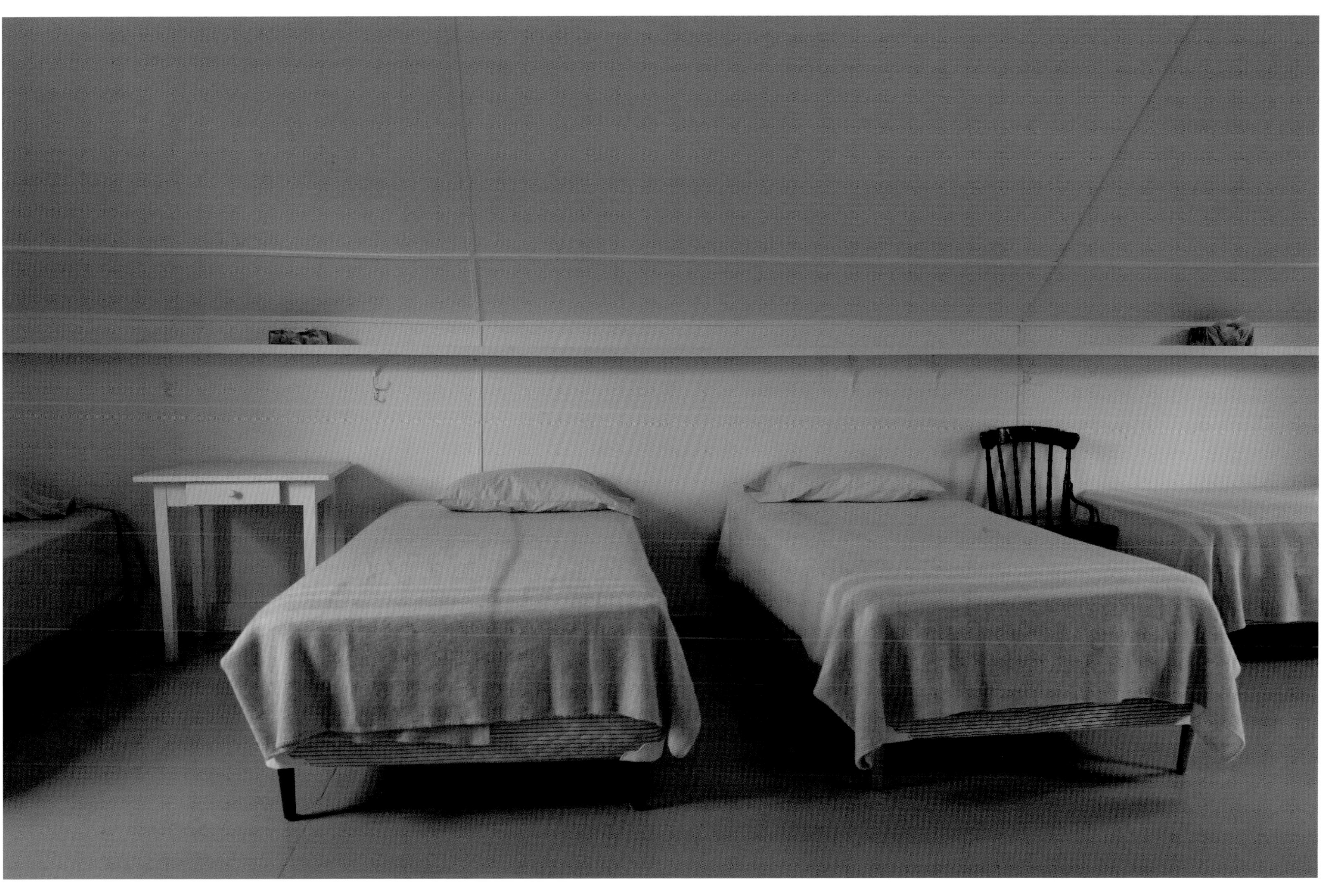

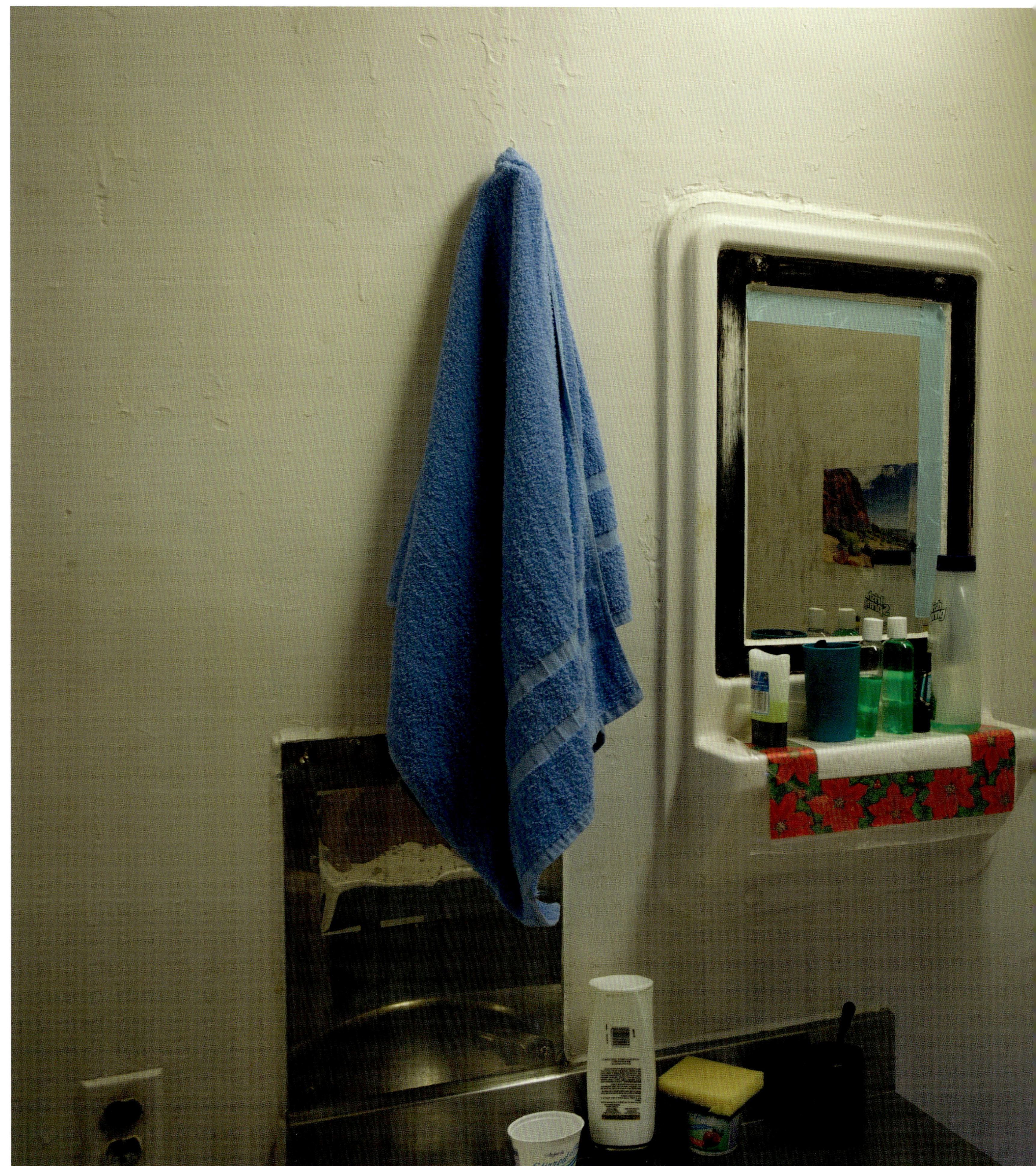

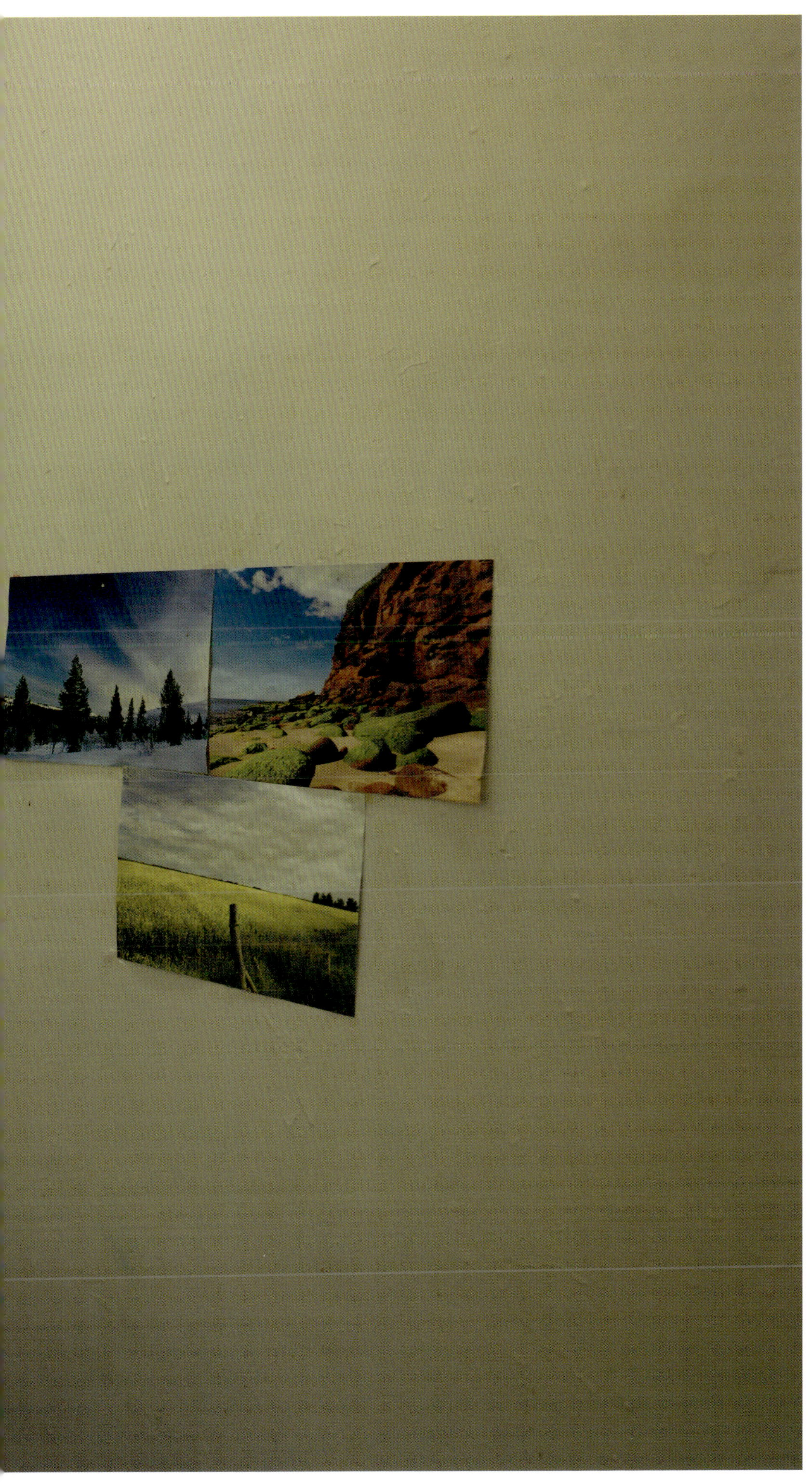

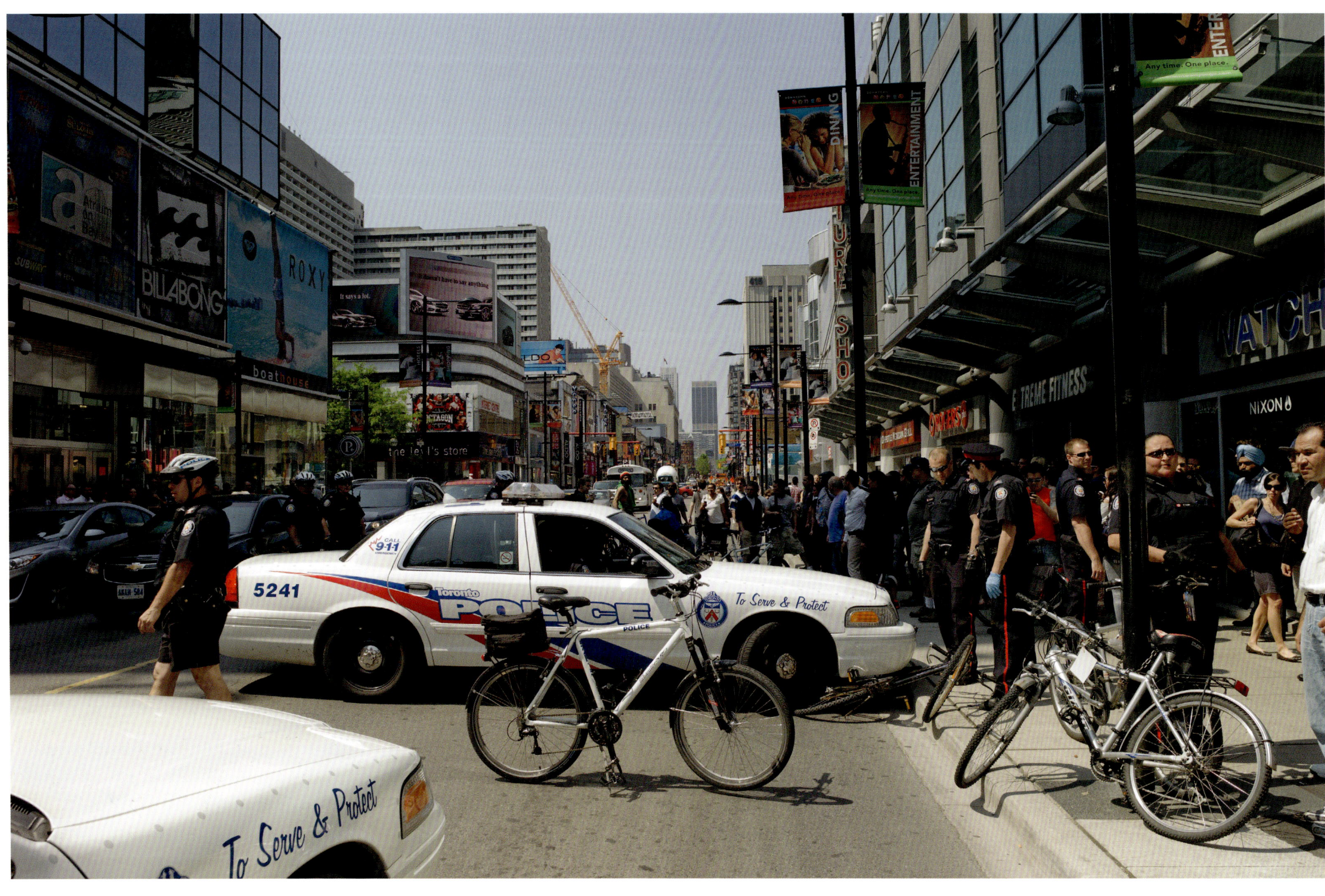
BILLABONG
ROXY
boathouse
DINING
ENTERTAINMENT
Any time. One place.
NIXON
5241
Toronto
POLICE
To Serve & Protect
To Serve & Protect

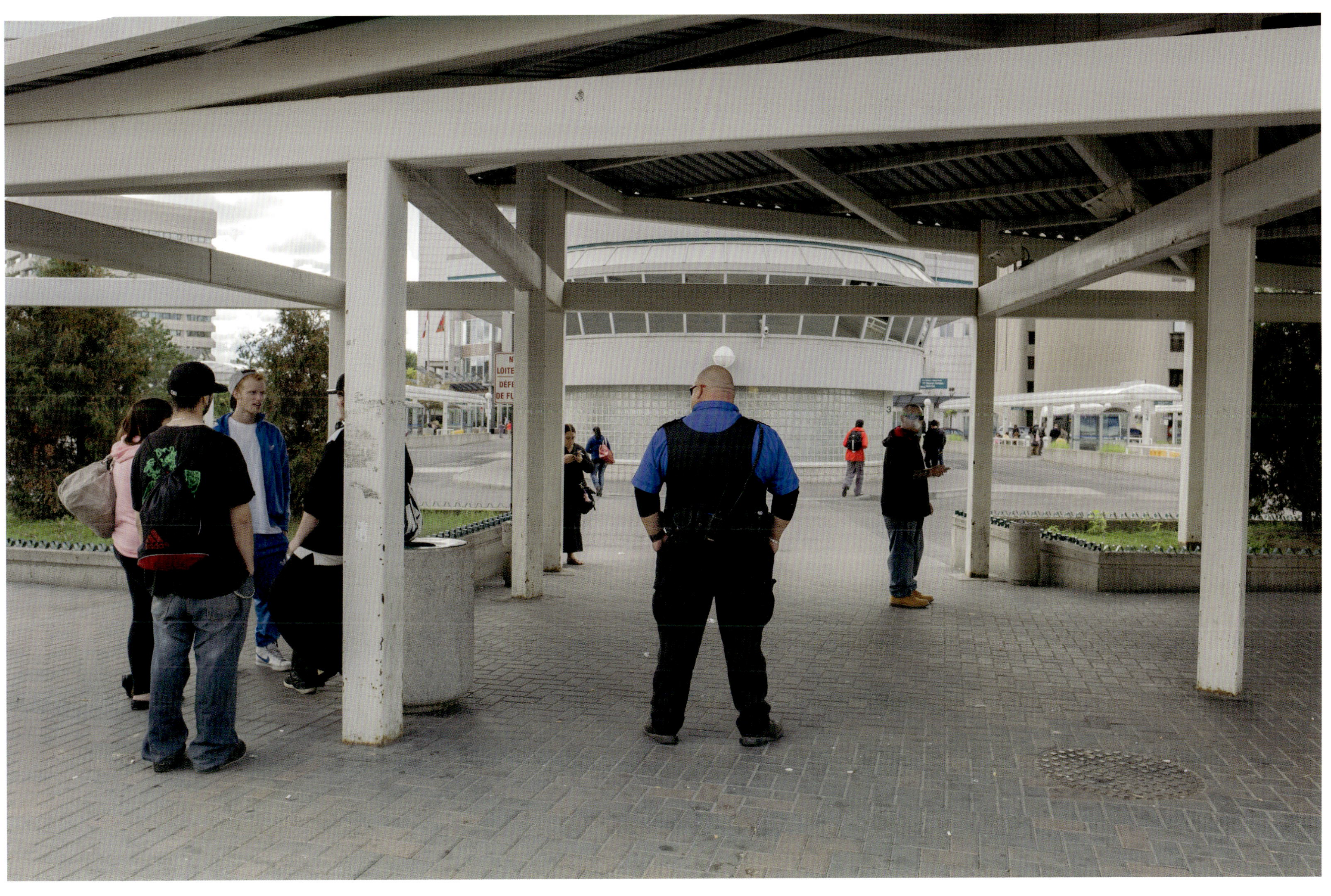

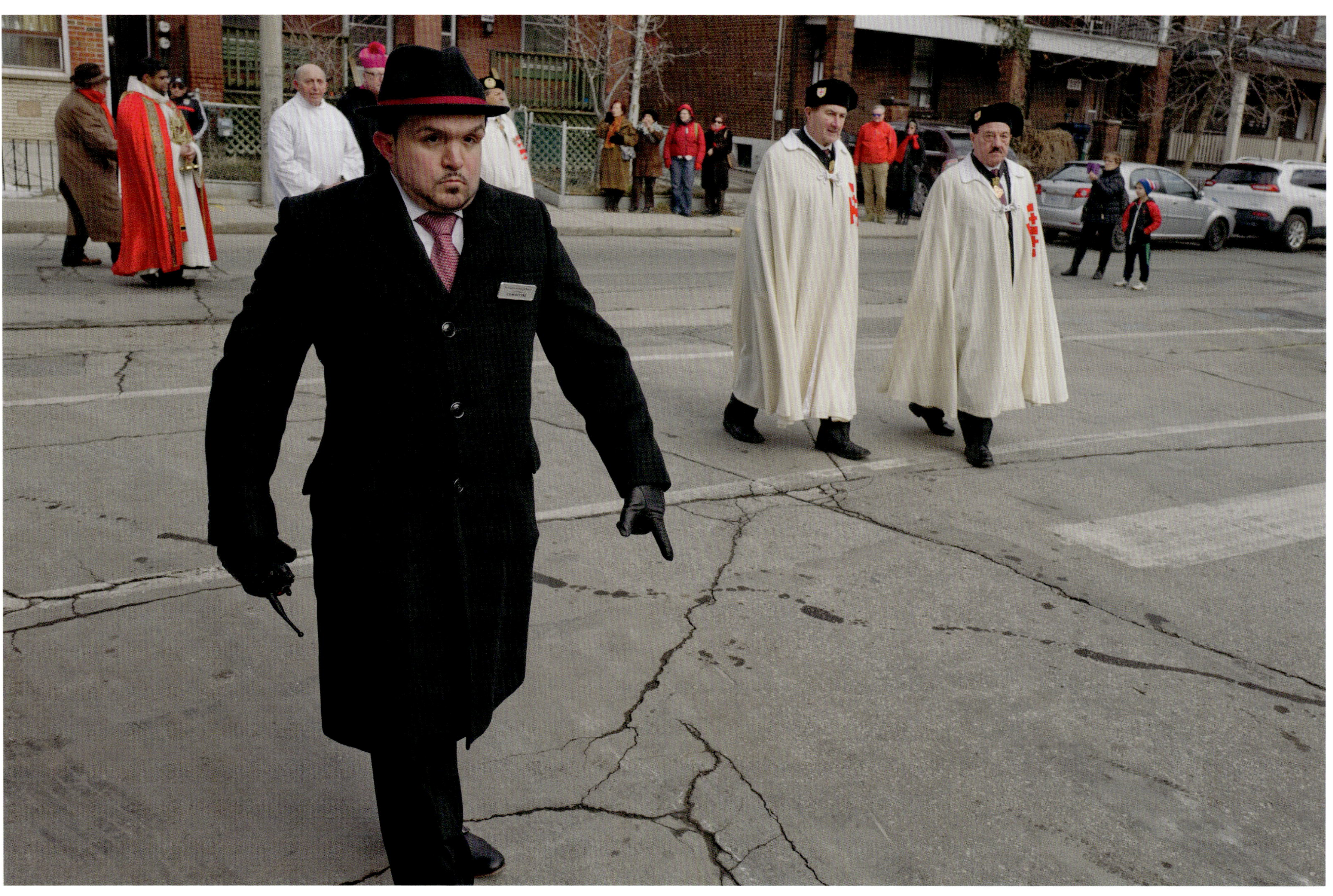

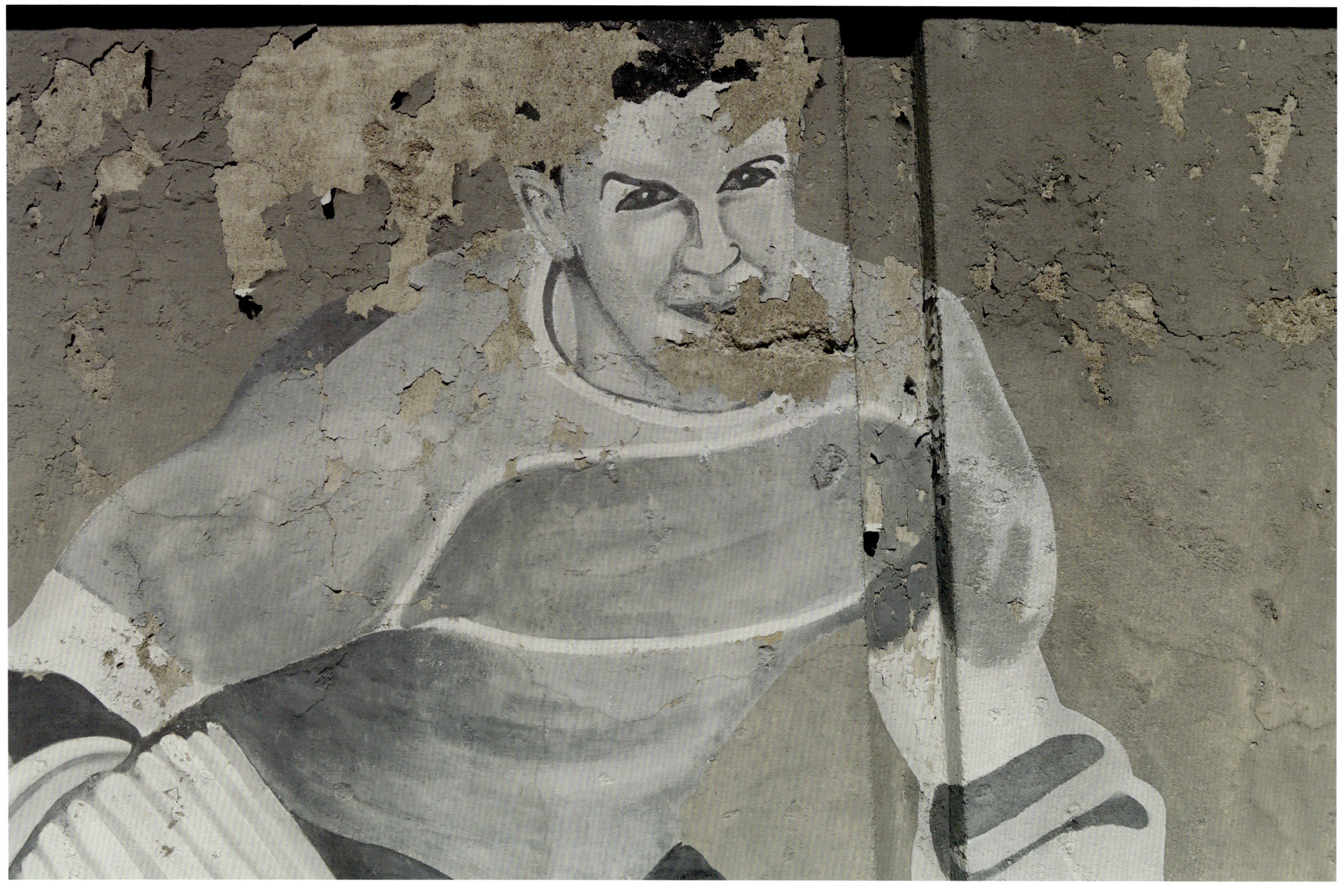

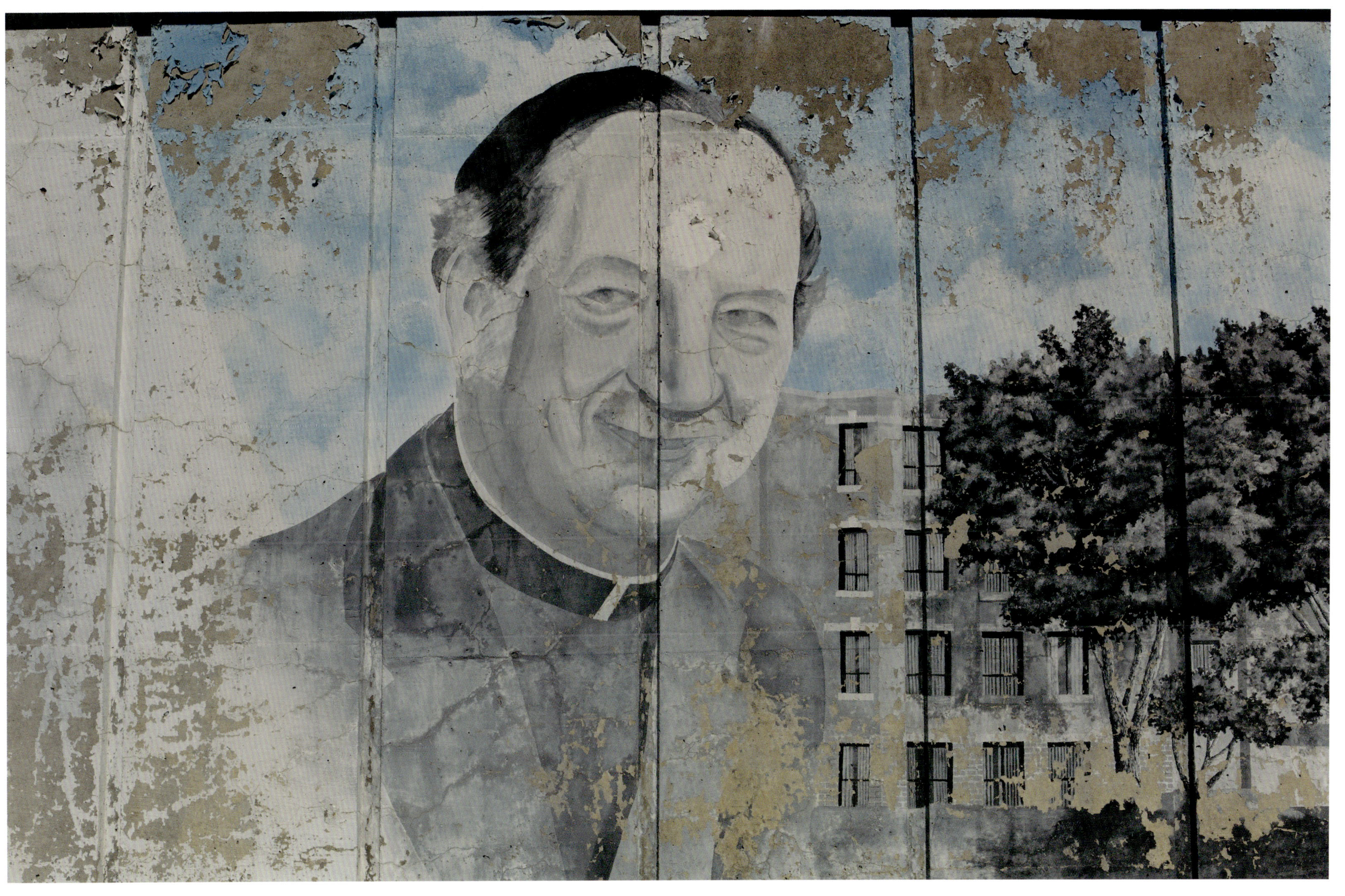

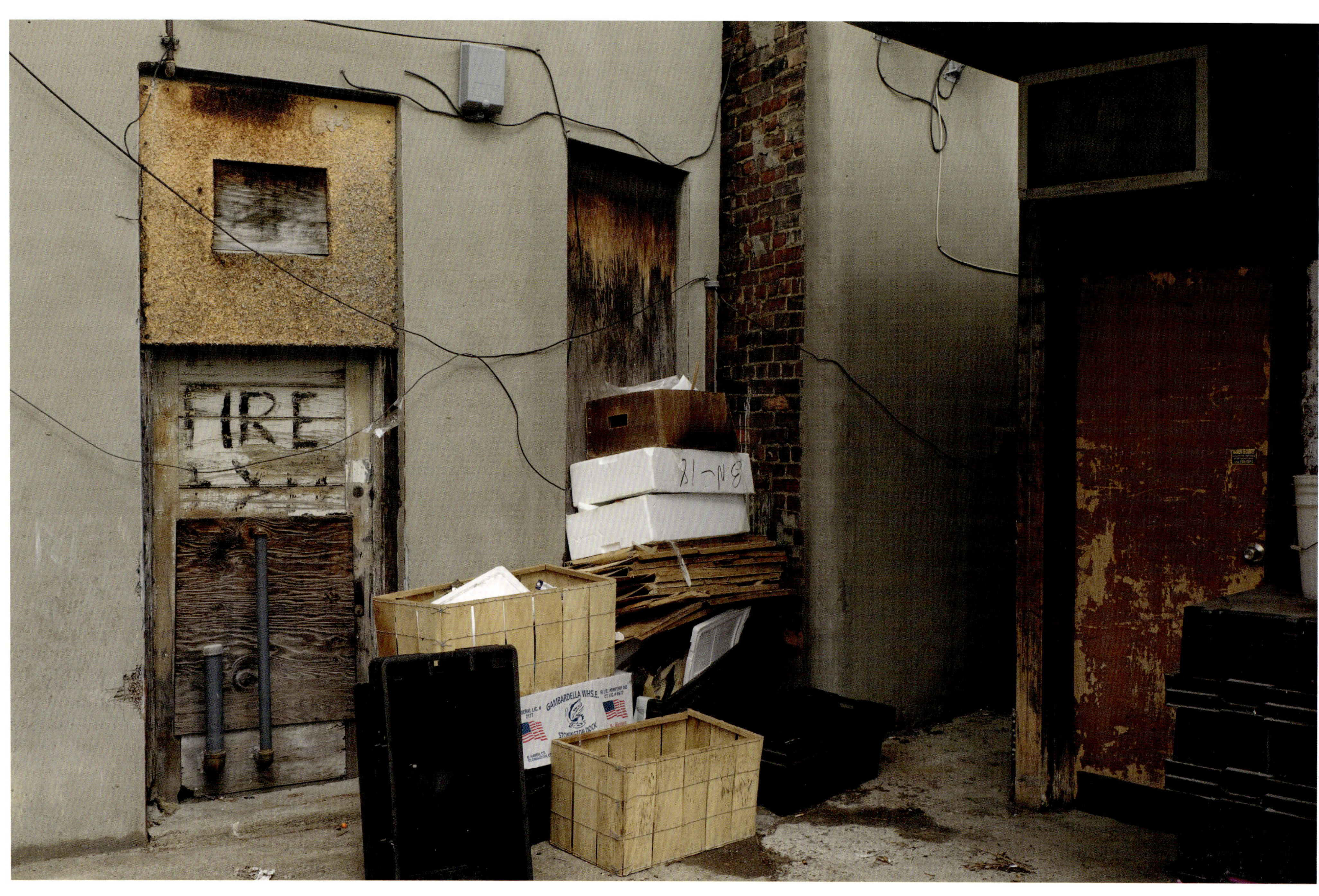
FIRE
GAMBARDELLA WHS.E

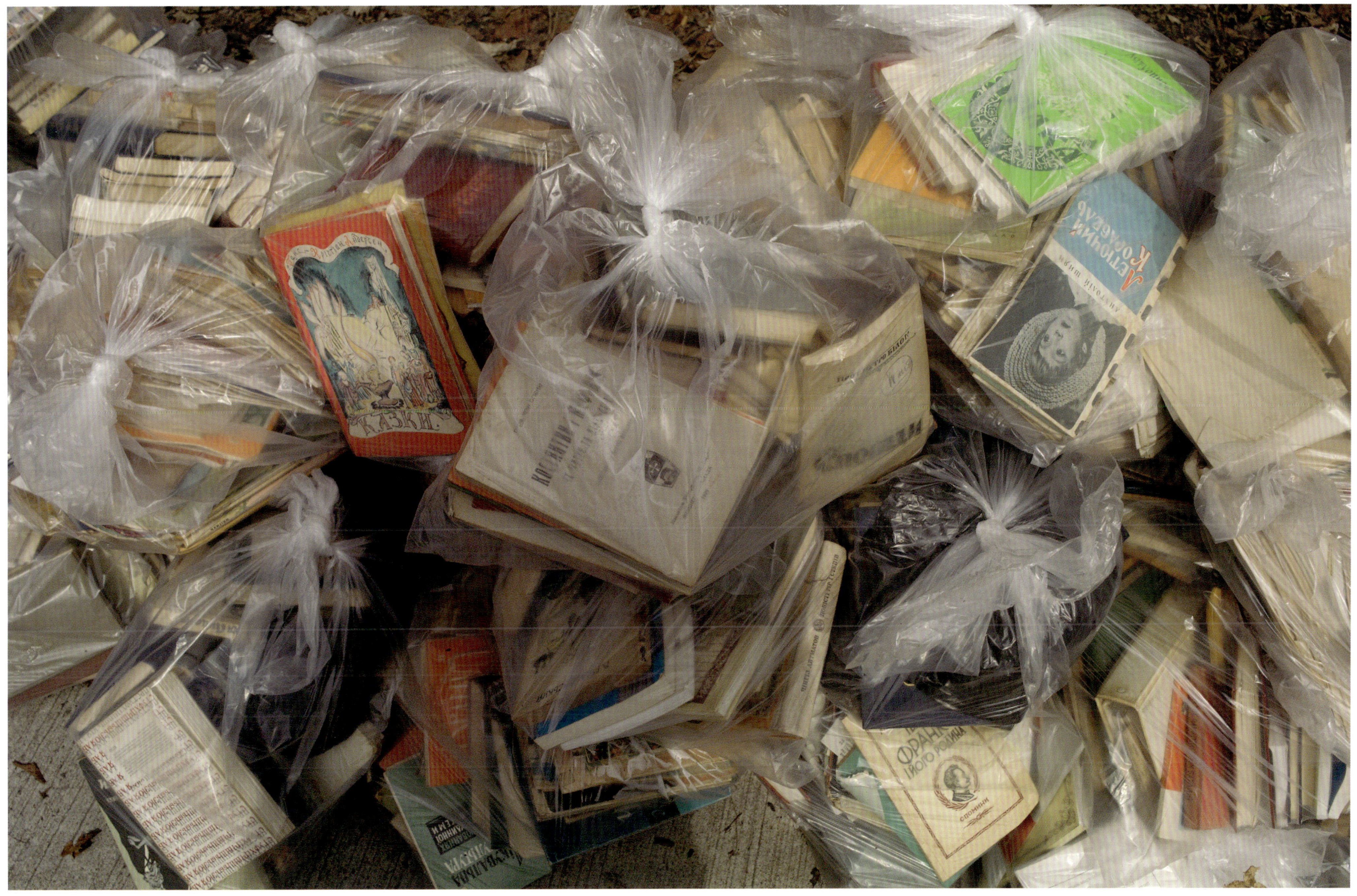
КАЗКИ

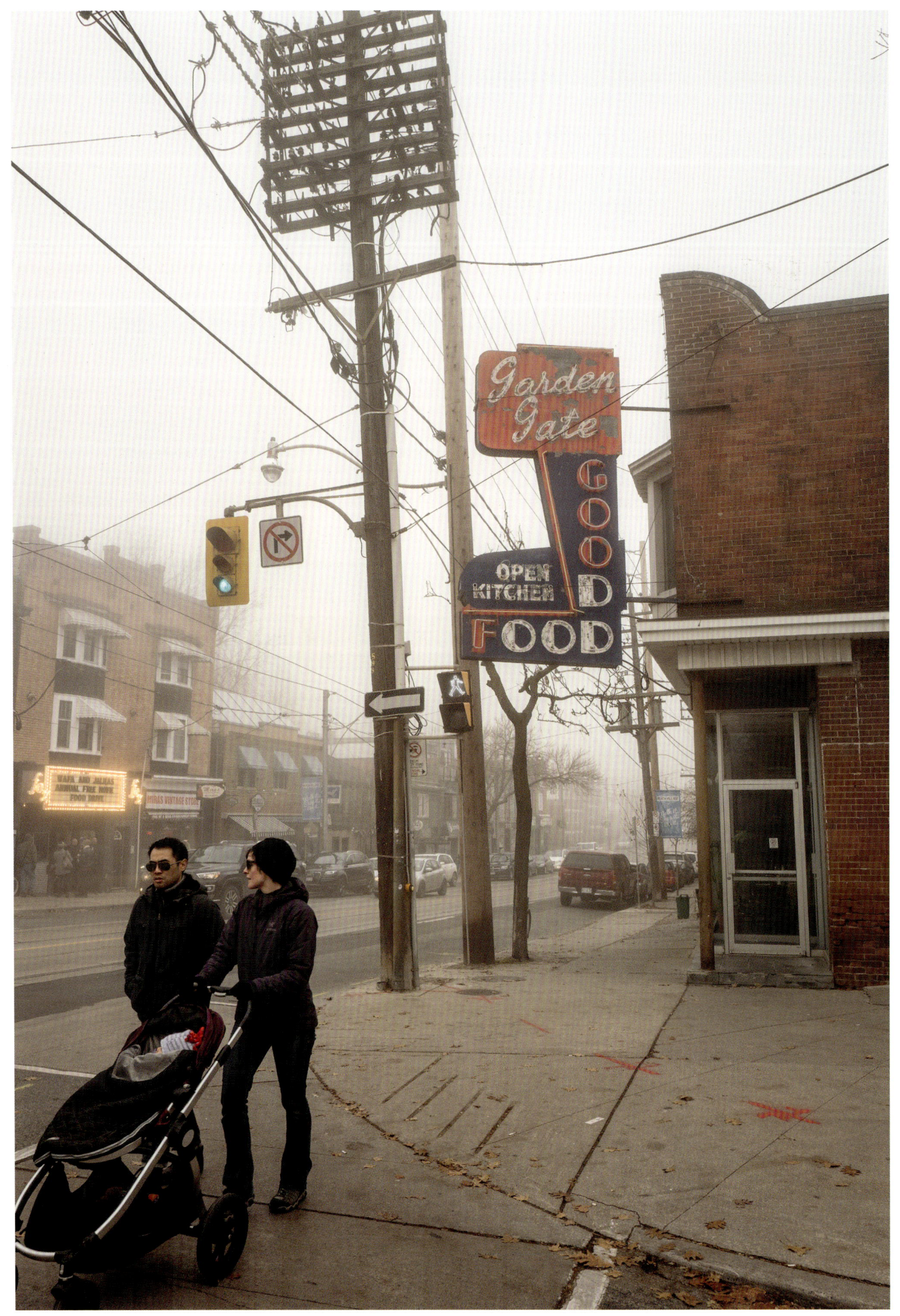
Garden Gate
GOOD
OPEN KITCHEN
FOOD

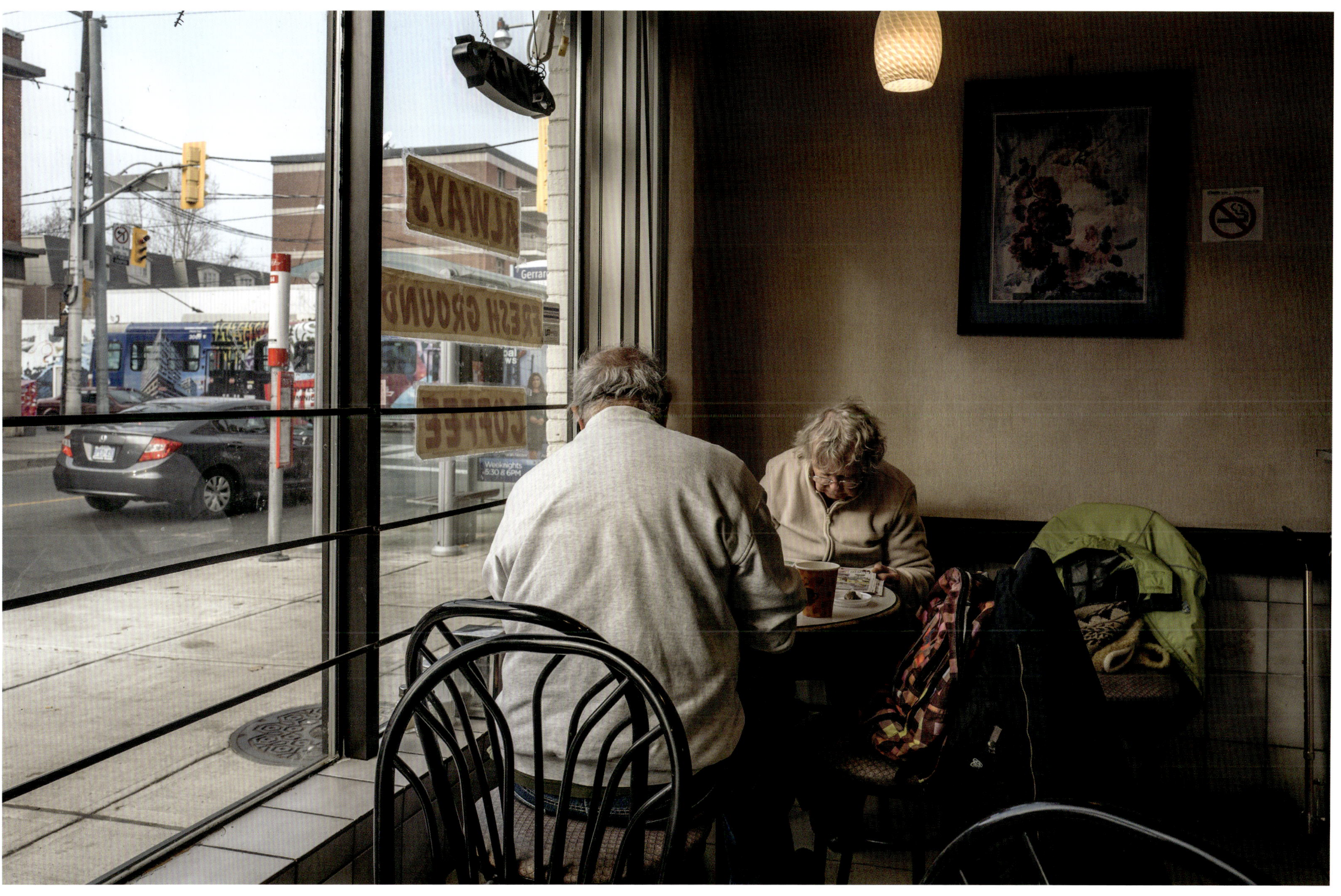
ALWAYS
COFFEE
Weeknights

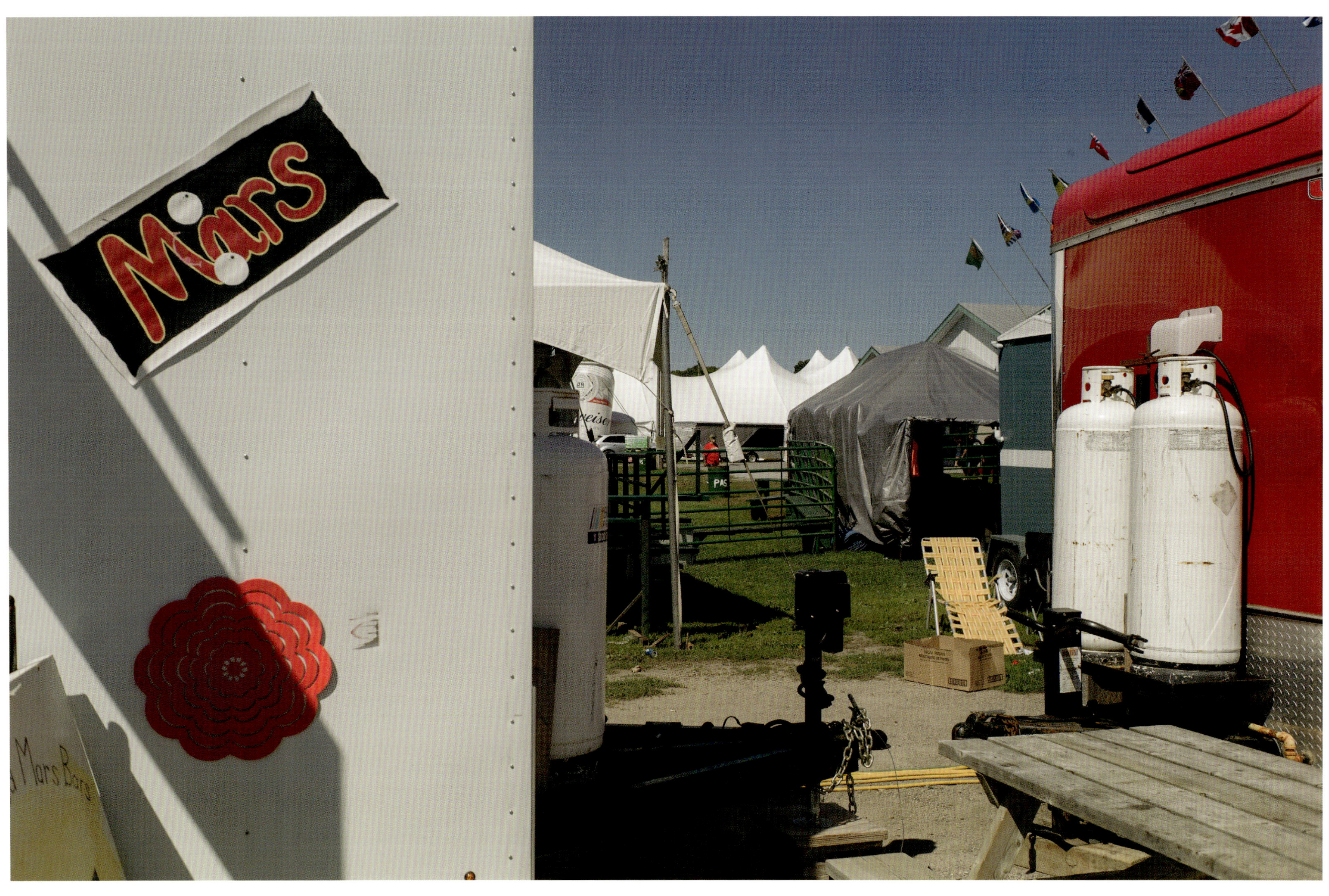
Mars
Mars Bars

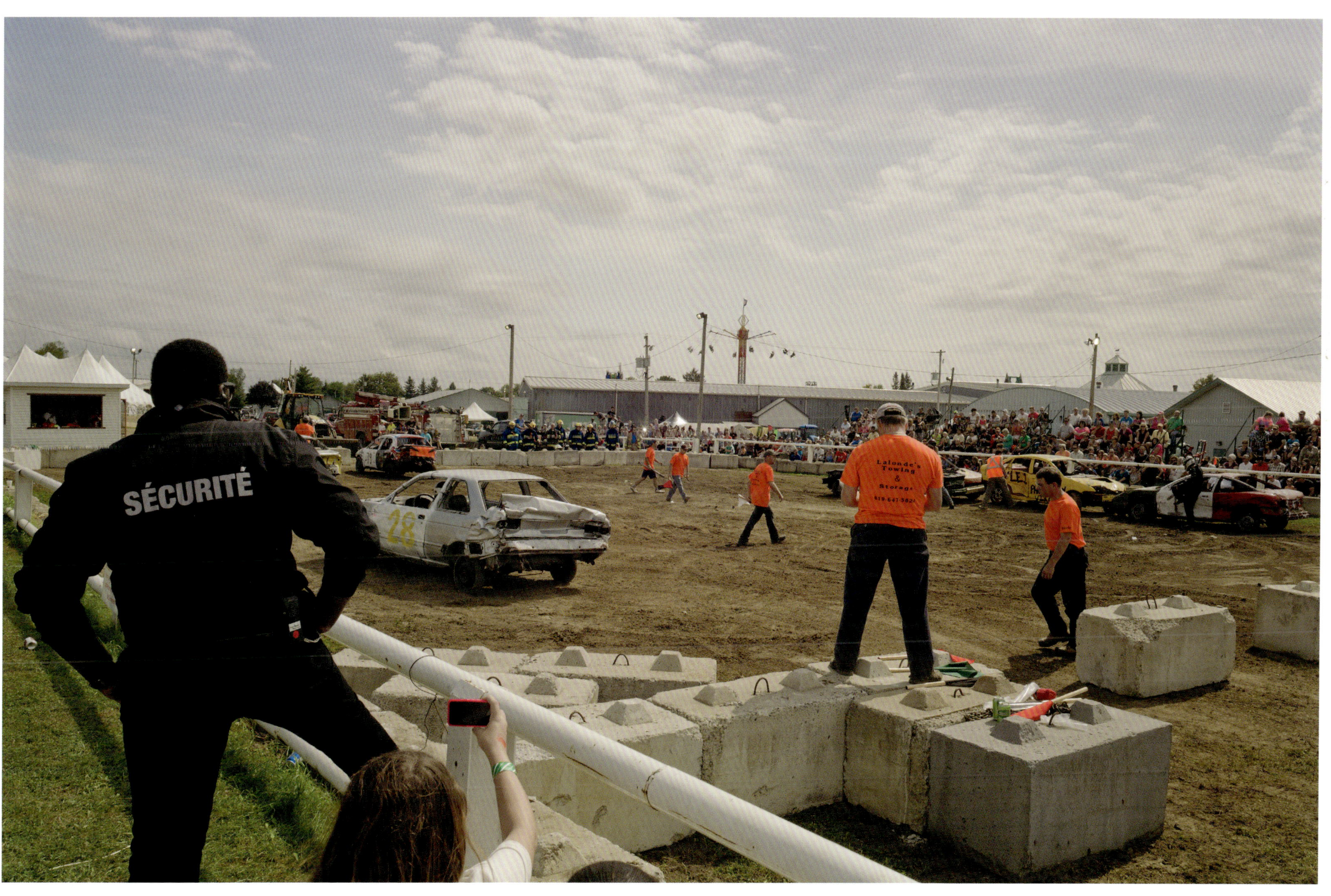
SÉCURITÉ

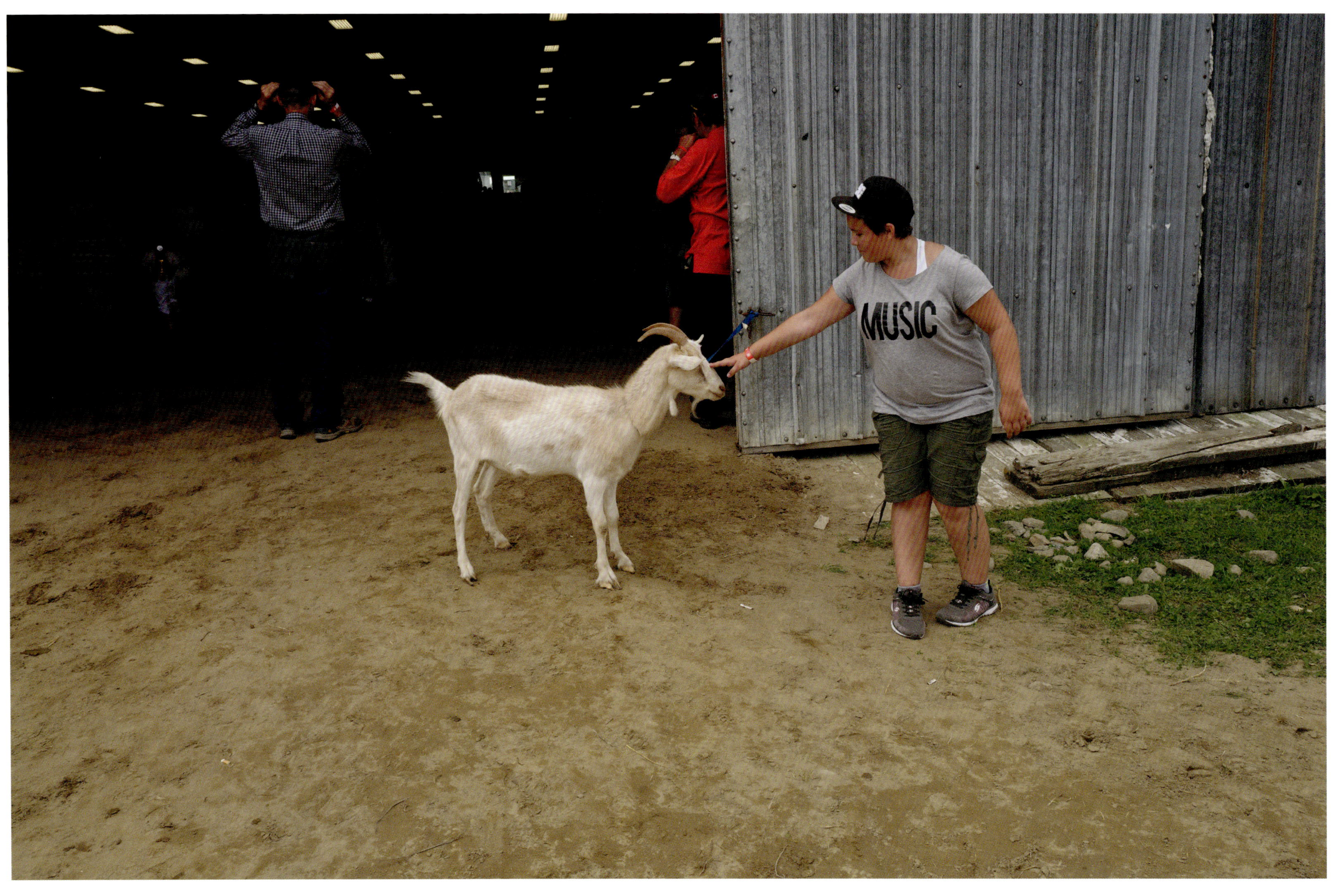
MUSIC

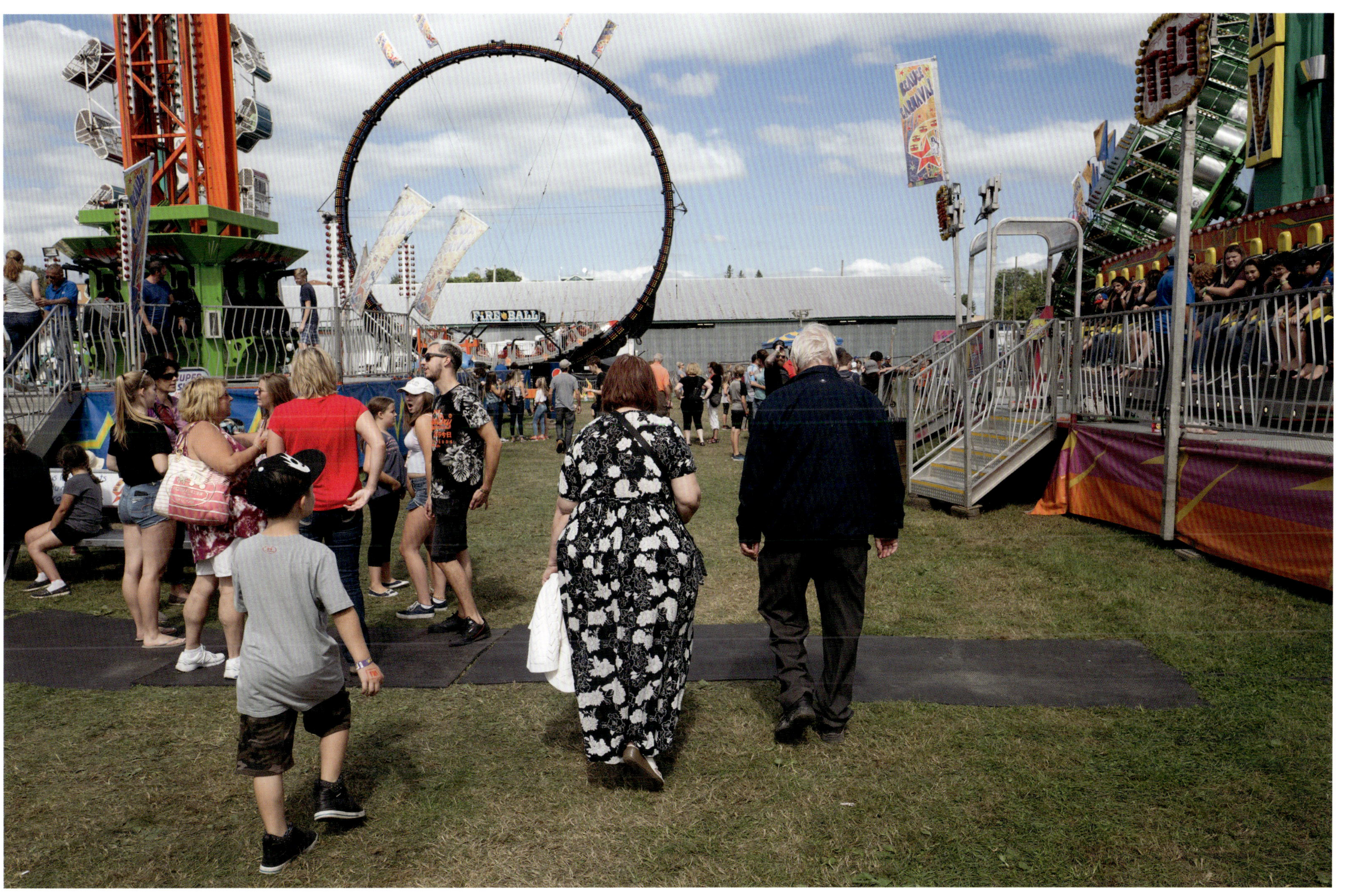
FIRE BALL

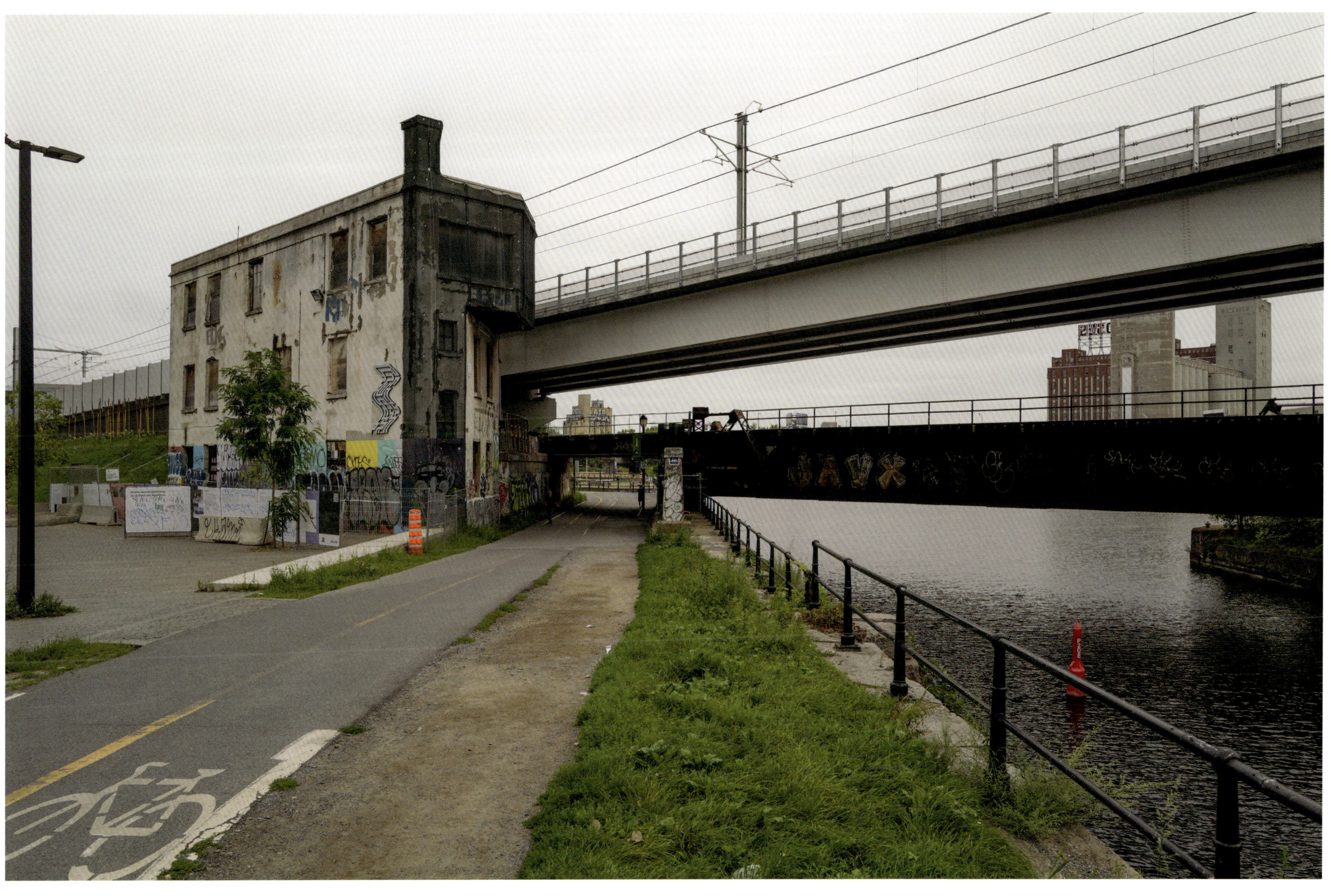

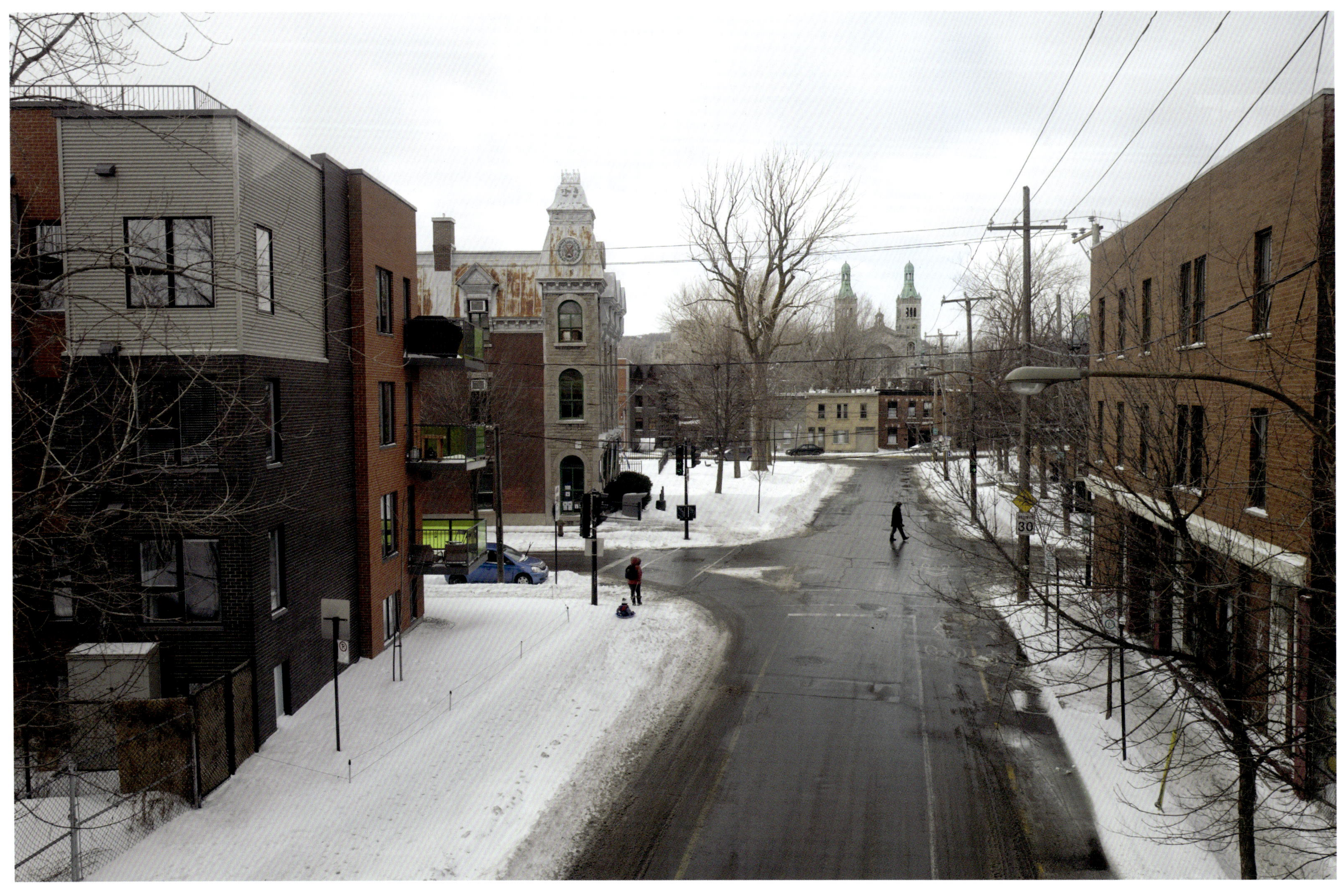
30

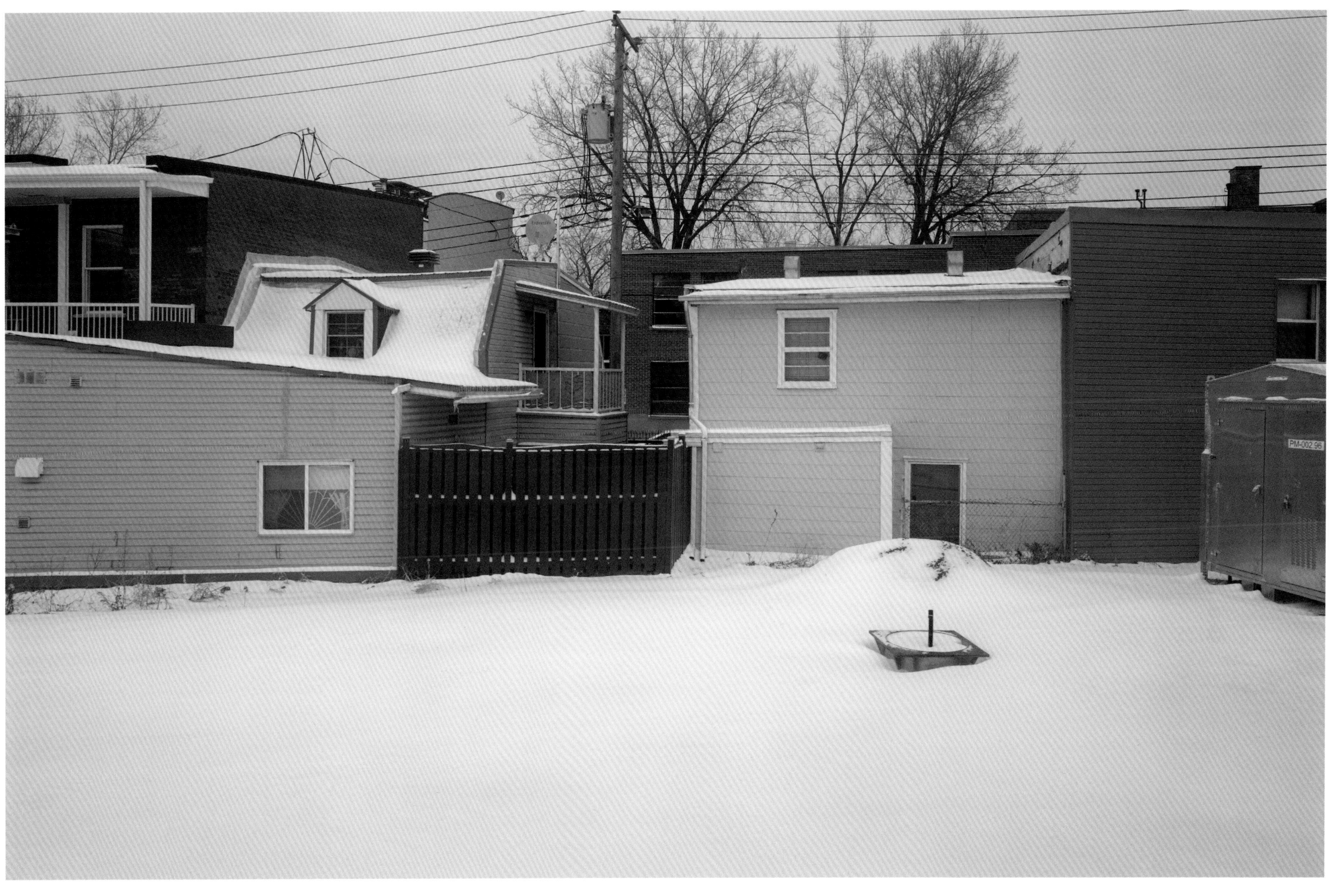
PM-002 96

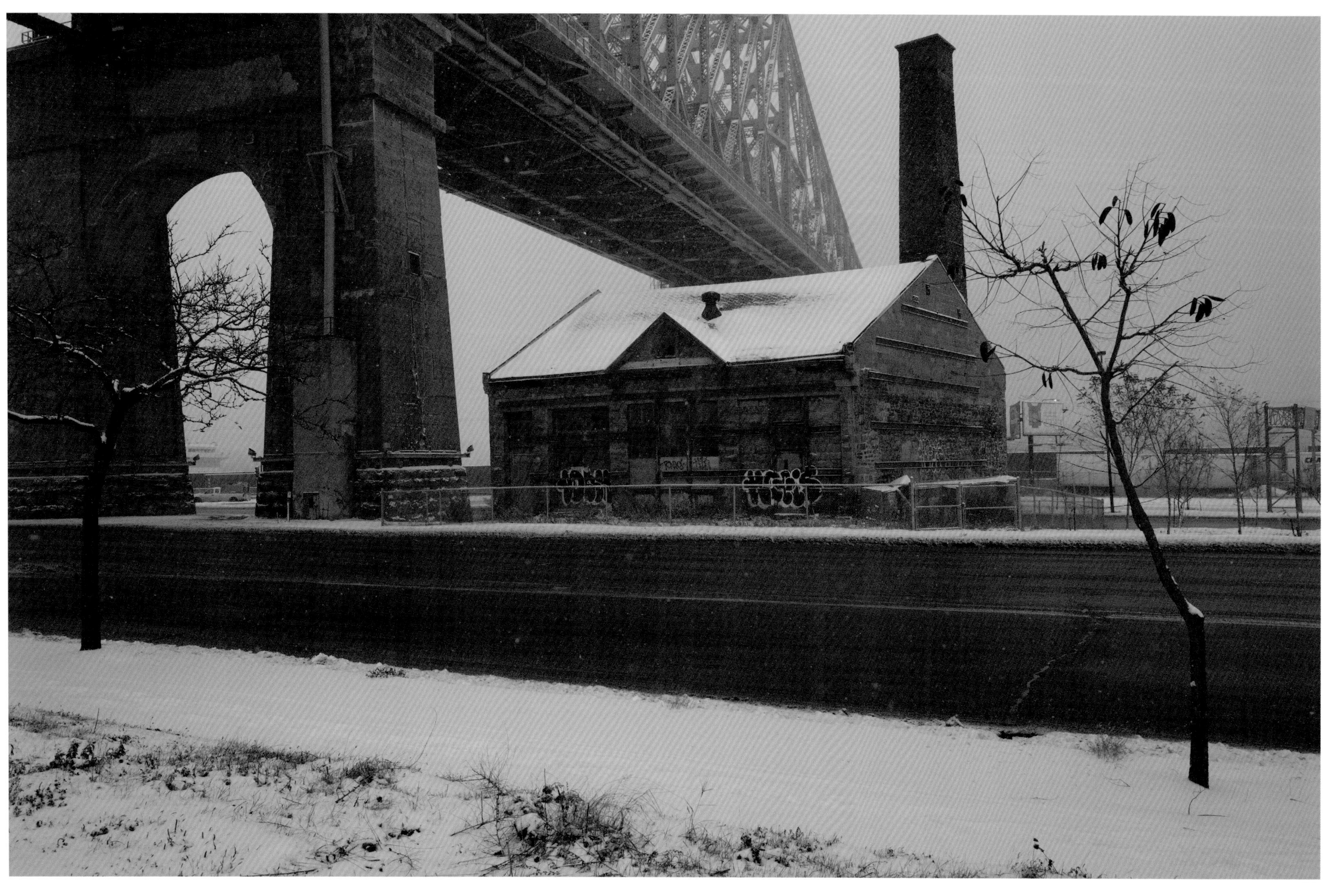

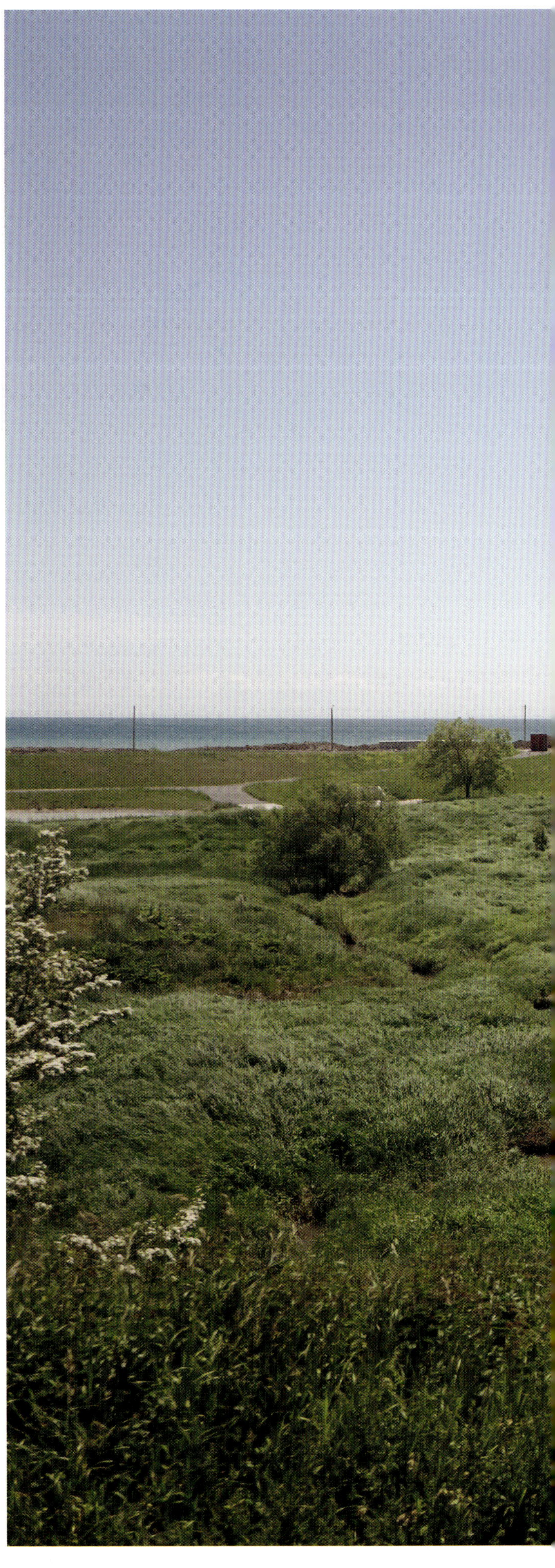

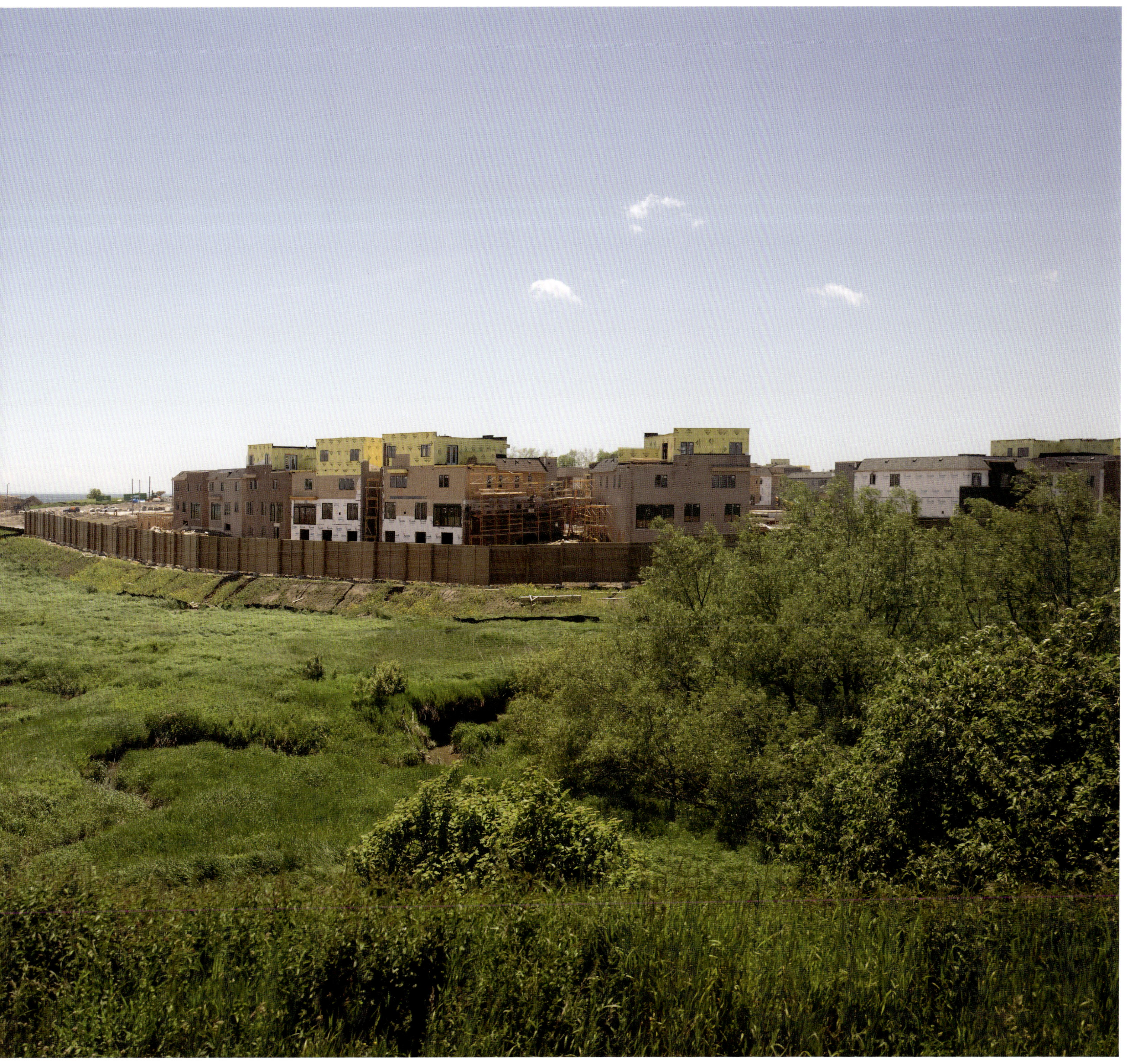

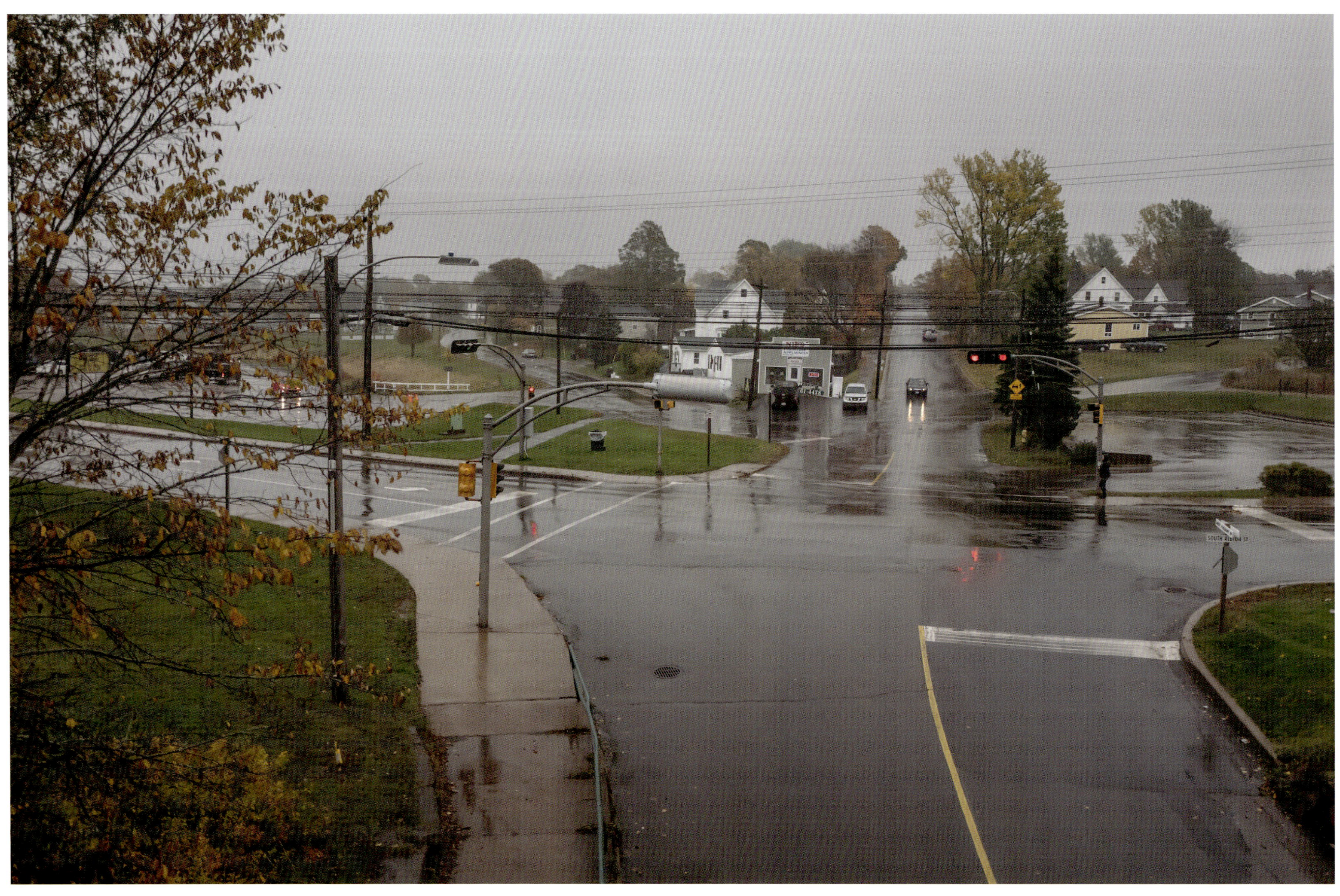

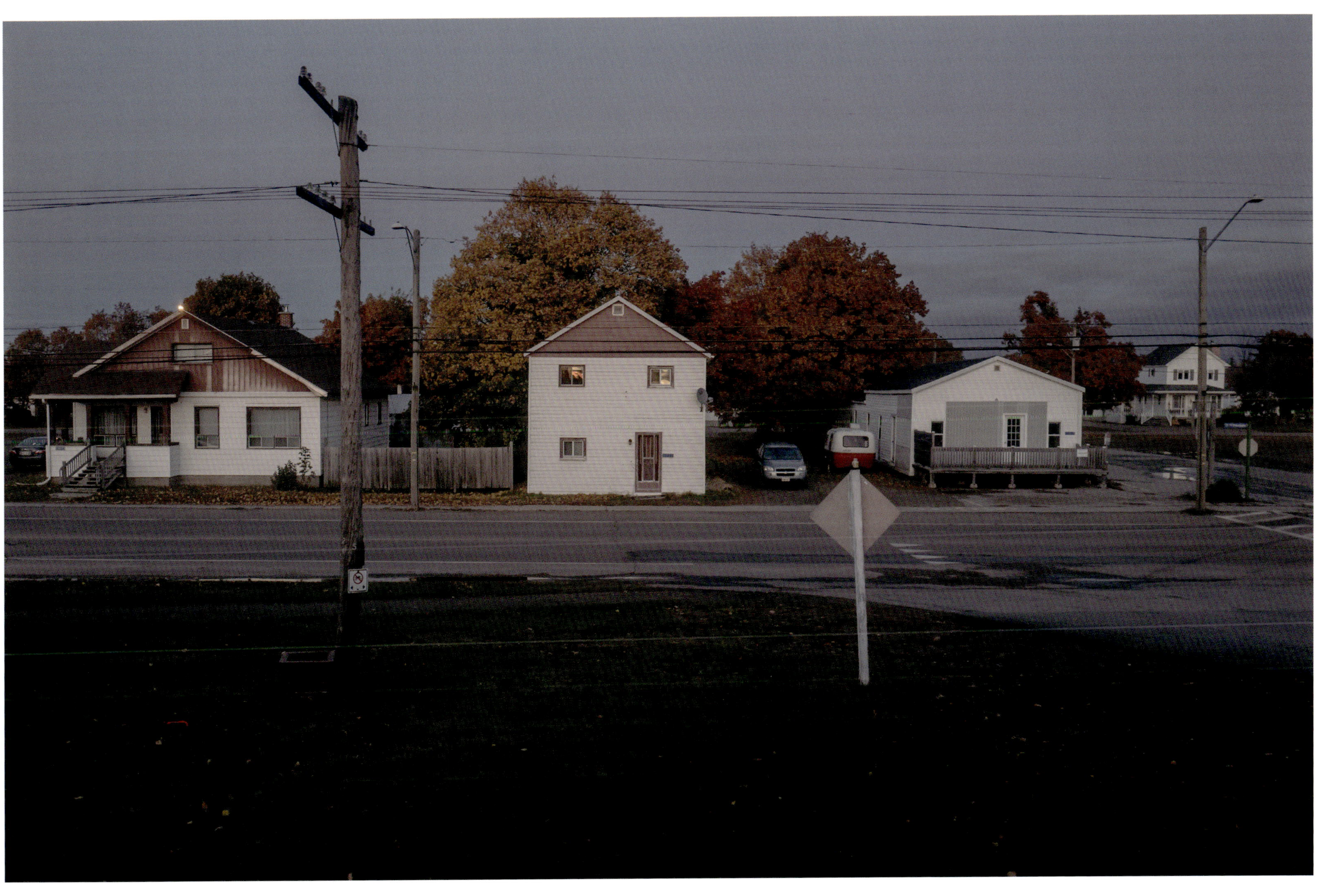

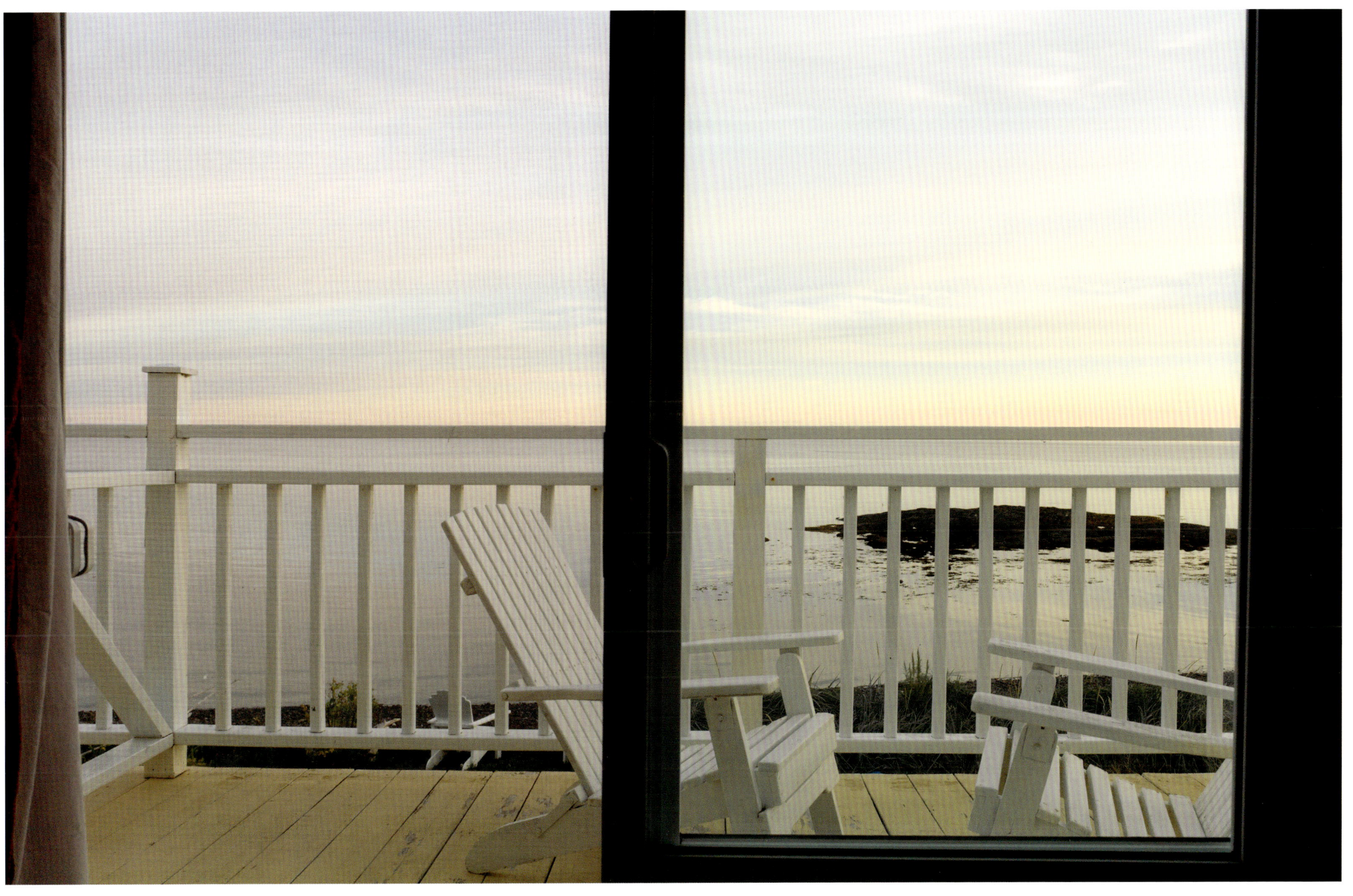

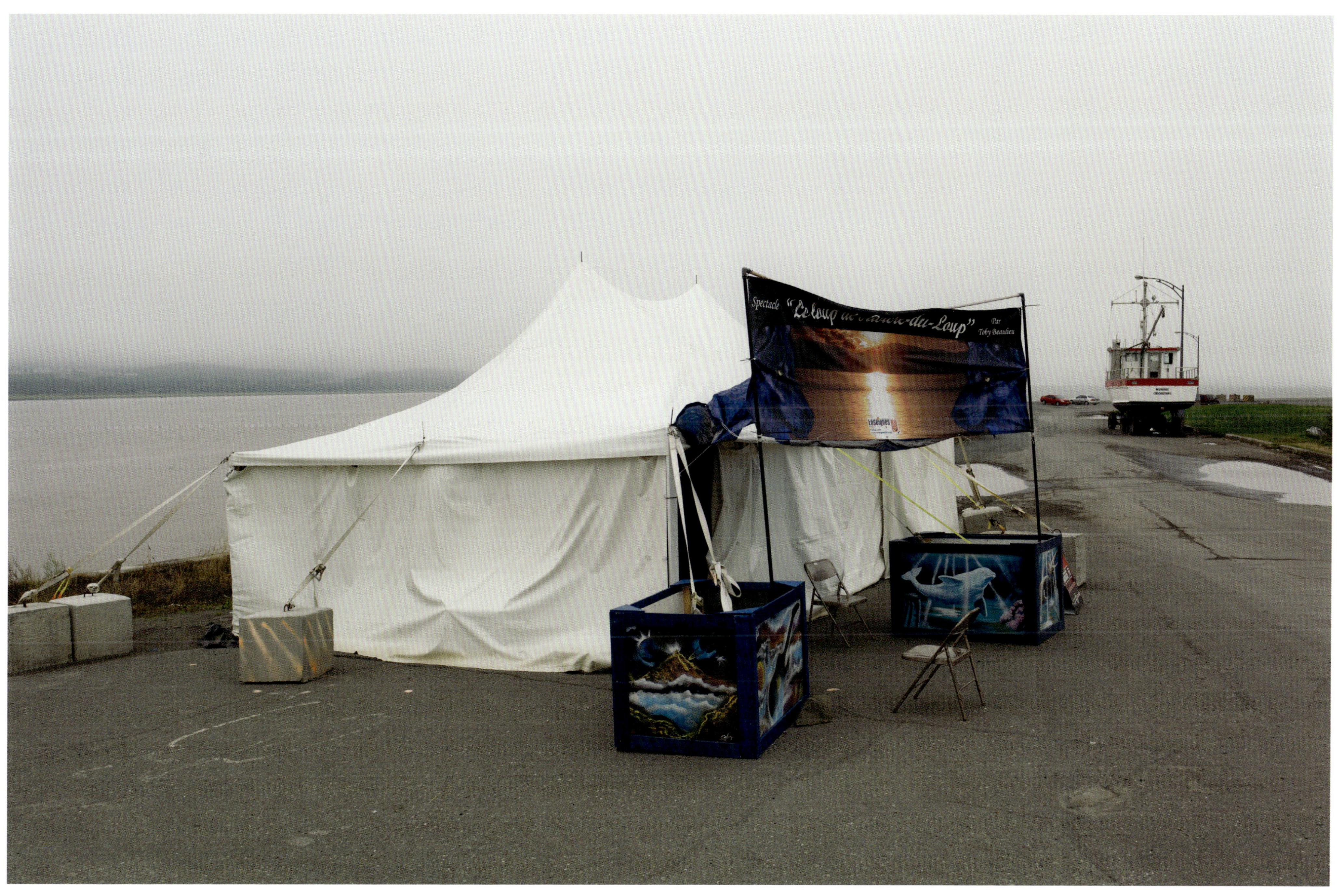
Spectacle
Le loup
du-Loup"
Par
Toby Beaulieu

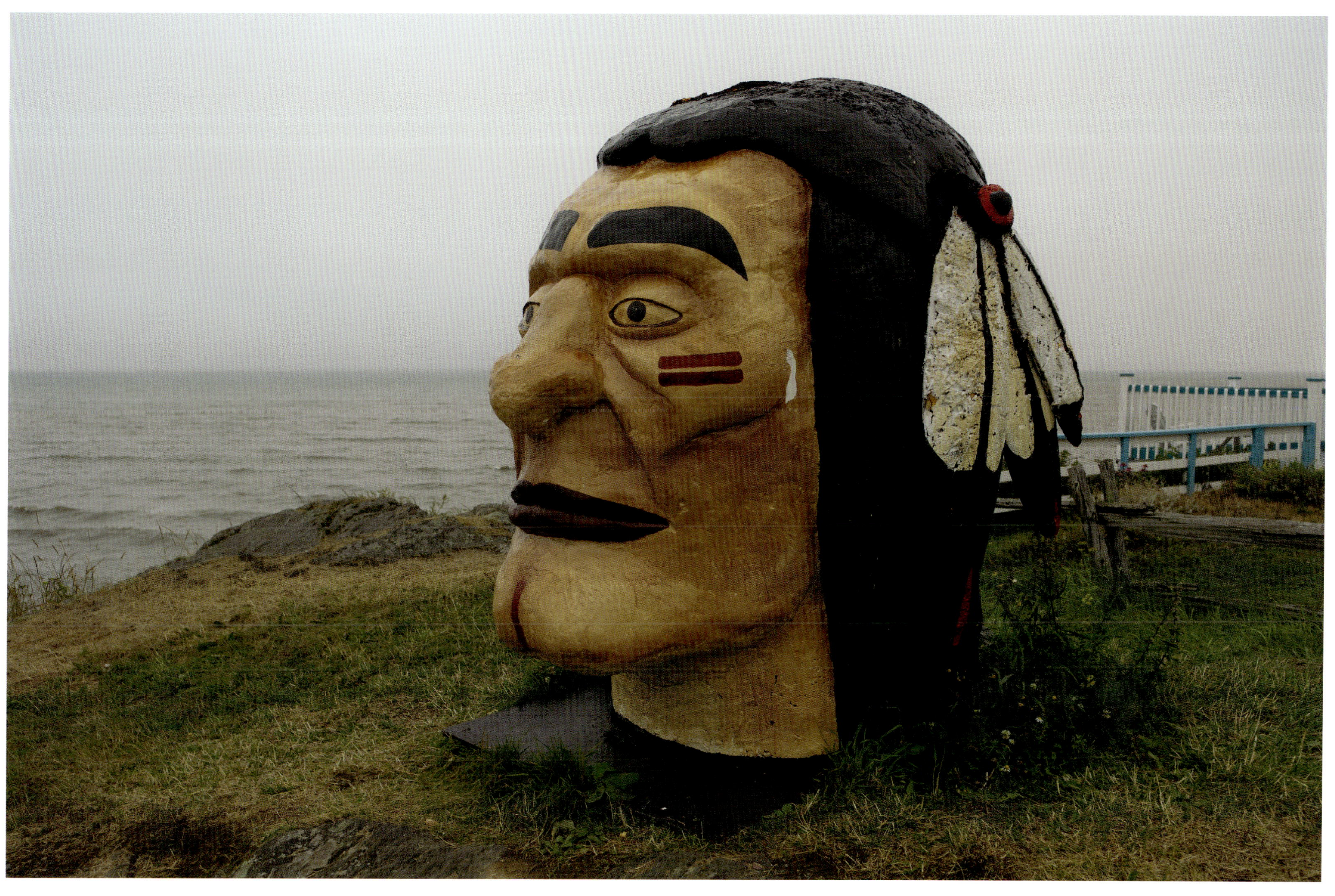

A CONVERSATION WITH GEOFFREY JAMES

Photographer Geoffrey James discusses *Canadian Photographs* with Peter Galassi, former chief curator of photography at the Museum of Modern Art (MoMA).

PETER GALASSI *Canadian Photographs* is quite a departure. Those familiar with your earlier work (which I'll touch on later) may want to learn how it came about.

GEOFFREY JAMES The book had its genesis in 2010, although at that time I had no idea it would be a book; I was simply exploring themes that interested me. That year, I bought a professional digital camera: a Leica rangefinder that felt in the hand just like the original 35 mm Leica. Before that, my projects had been done with much larger cameras: a very primitive Kodak panoramic camera for which film was no longer made and an 8- × 10-inch view camera. Both these tripod-mounted machines slowed me down in many ways and discouraged my dealing with flux. I found the digital world liberating because it relieved me of a lot of darkroom work, and the hand-held cameras allowed me to photograph anything I could see, including a landscape flashing by a train window.

PG I know that you arrived at the title reluctantly, but the book does seem to address Canada as a nation. It certainly covers a lot of territory, metaphorically as well as geographically.

GJ *Canadian Photographs* shamelessly borrows its title from *American Photographs*, Walker Evans's groundbreaking 1938 book. The title, with its ambiguity, solved a lot of problems for me, and it was also a way of tipping my hat. As Dizzy Gillespie said of Louis Armstrong: "No him, no me." I didn't try to represent the whole of the country, even though I have over time visited every province and most of the eastern Arctic. The book is not a geography lesson, although I did try to spread my net as widely as possible. I also wouldn't presume to try to deal with the "problem" of Canadian identity.

PG I'd never accuse you of that! But I do think that the range of the locations and subjects adds up to a very rich exploration of Canada, where you have lived very happily since 1966, when you turned 24.

GJ I came from England via the US, where I had worked as a reporter in Philadelphia. When I immigrated to Canada, I was given my permanent resident card, which included the instant right to vote, at the train stop at the Canadian border. The British were absurdly privileged at the time.

At the Canadian edition of *TIME* magazine, where I worked for seven years, I did a lot of cultural writing and travelled quite a bit in Canada. When the Canadian edition was closed, I was offered a job running the Visual Arts, Film and Video section of the Canada Council for the Arts. To this day, I don't know why they would have asked a journalist, but it was a very interesting job—a privilege really—where for seven years I advocated for artists, chaired juries, and travelled around the country and all over the world. I got an education in the arts and perhaps came to the realization that it was possible to have a life as a photographer. I should say that photography held no interest for me when I was young.

PG Shall we dive into the pictures? Page 5: We are in the Fraser Valley, British Columbia—the far shore of the country if one starts in the East, as of course the European settlers did. We are also in a train, which doubtless is how we got here, and through the window, we get a glimpse of Canada's fabled natural landscape. It's a lovely picture; the book is full of pleasures for the eyes. But the next picture makes no apologies about targeting the mind as well. Page 7: We are peering into Montreal's Sir George-Étienne Cartier national historic site, which at one point was the home of Sir George, known as the "Father of Confederation." The picture introduces the themes of both history and the dual culture inherited from the French and British settlers. In doing so, it suggests—indeed demands—that the pictures be read not just visually but symbolically. Moreover, quite a few pictures, including this one, contain messages to be read—literally.

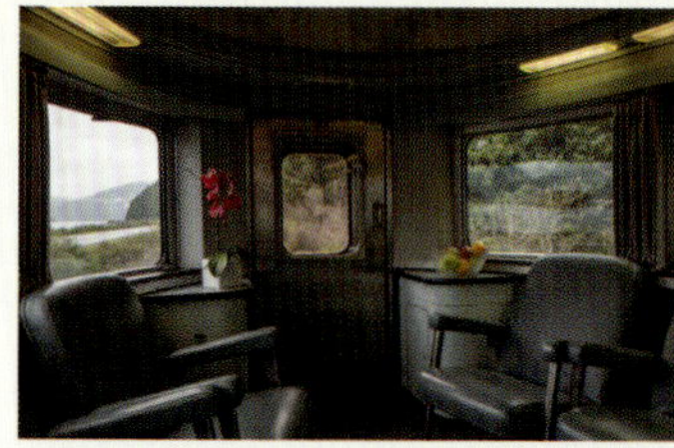
P. 5

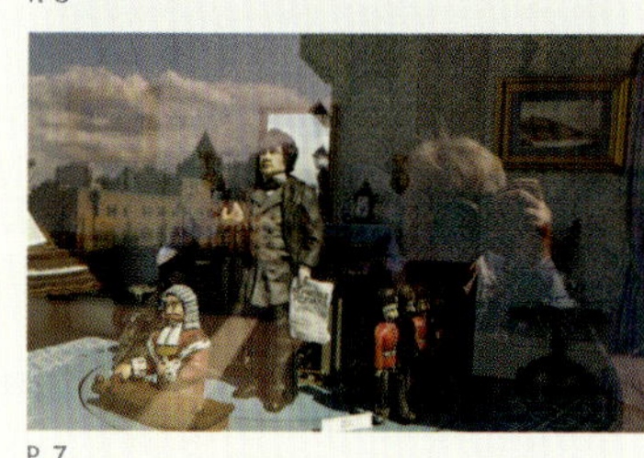
P. 7

GJ Yes. As I worked on the project, I found myself allowing words in photographs to tell part of the story. About a third of the images contain some kind of text. There can be an inbuilt irony here, but as Renata Adler once said, irony may be the sanest response to modern life.

PG That distinction is a prominent theme in the book. A billboard of billowing clouds against a clear blue sky in Calgary (page 86); Saudi National Day in Toronto, with men in traditional dress in front of a giant photograph of a lily-white crowd enthusiastically making photographs (page 84); and the next-to-last picture, in which a sagging synthetic image of a glorious sunset is propped up in front of a gloomy fog-filled vista (page 123). The term "representation" may be rather shopworn, but the difference between the picture and what it describes is fundamental to the art of photography. I would say that you have taken a creative step further in this book by insisting that representation is inescapably *a part* of our modern reality. The ubiquity of photographs in the urban landscape is a leitmotif. Another motif that makes the book feel very much up to date is those devices we persist in

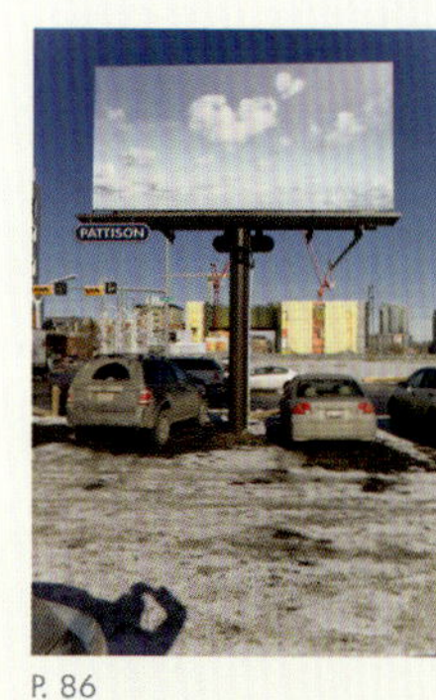
P. 86

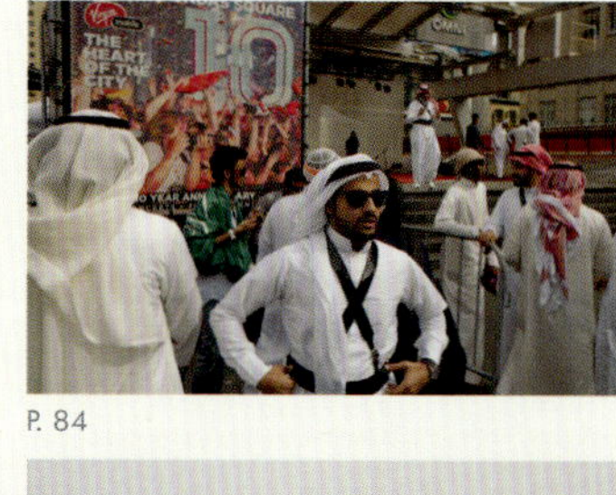
P. 84

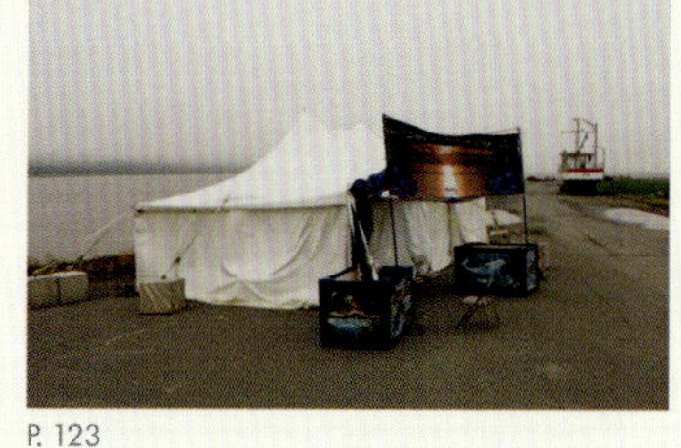
P. 123

calling “phones,” though they are also cameras and so much more (as seen on pages 30, 40, 42, and many more). Another deft contemporary touch is the four-wheeled carry-on (page 35), not to mention the joggers (pages 37 and 58).

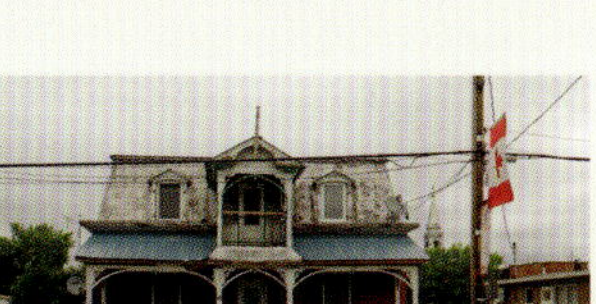
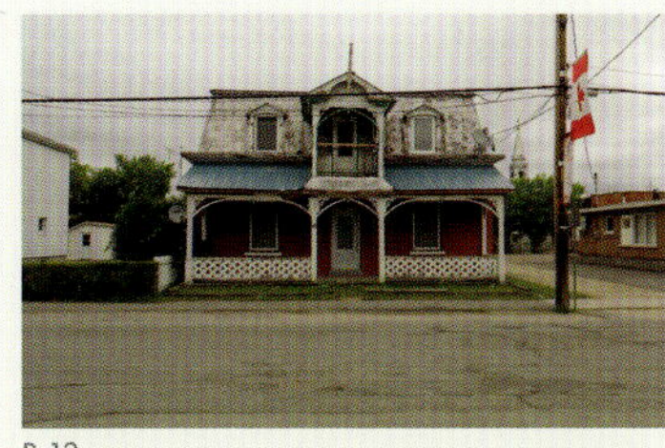
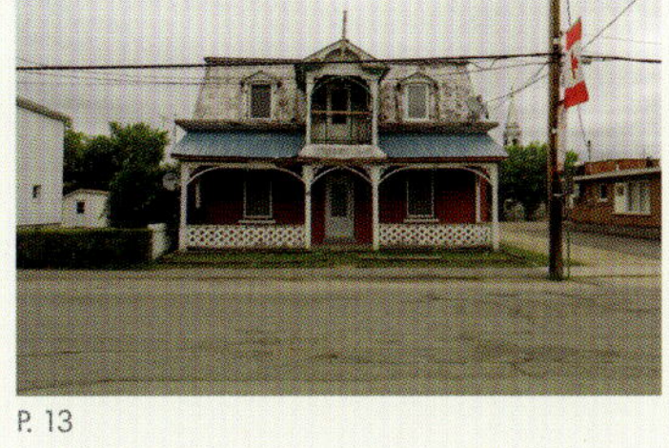
P. 13

Let’s return to the sequence that begins at page 13, a picture of a handsome old house that has seen better days. There is a sense of respect and affection for this homely survivor in your handling of it, from the frontality of the image and the reserved viewpoint from across the street—which gives the building room to breathe in its own surroundings—to the proud display of the flag and the steeple in the distance. That same sense pervades a number of other pictures as well: pages 19, 21, 32, and 71 (in the last, God seems to be lighting our way to the door of a dive bar), as well as 90–91.

GJ I have a weakness for places like the mining town of Sudbury, Ontario, or the prairie capital of Winnipeg, Manitoba, whose pre-1913 Exchange District has a bracing, mercantile confidence. Small towns seem to be under stress across the country, and our major cities are finding it very hard to accommodate Canada’s elevated number of new immigrants, a policy designed primarily to keep the economy going in a country with an aging population.

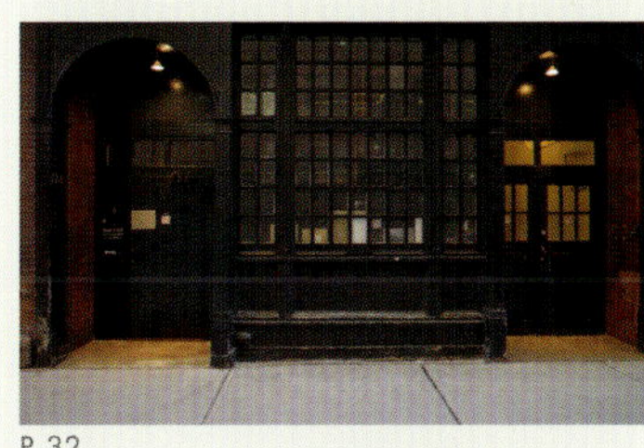
P. 32

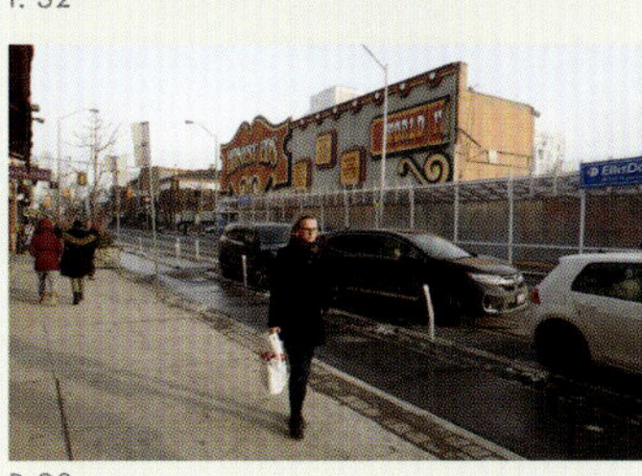
P. 80

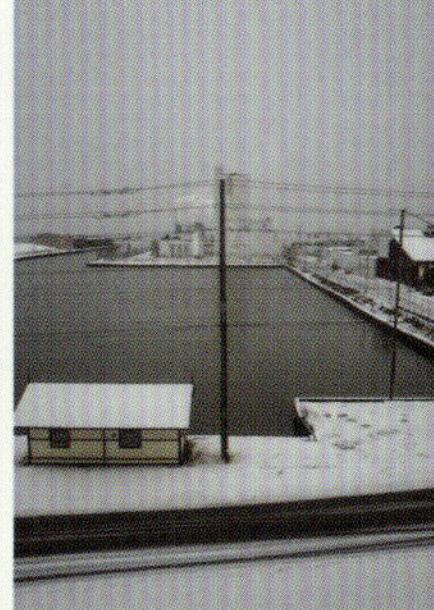
P. 61

In *Canadian Photographs*, I am interested in the physical traces of history, with things that survive or are about to disappear, and with the violent changes in scale that are happening in our cities as elsewhere. This transformation of the built environment has made me pay attention to some of the more modest, ephemeral elements of the landscape and place value on the humble and the mundane. The Dickensian side door of the legendary Massey Hall (page 32) disappeared in a renovation. The burger joint at Kaladar (page 14) and the blueberry stand at Madoc (page 15) are both gone, as are Honest Ed’s emporium in Toronto (page 80) and the venerable paint store in Vancouver’s East Hastings (page 38), but the smoke shop at the Alderville First Nation’s reserve (page 63) is doing fine, I am happy to say.

Sometimes, the lessons of history are apparent only after the fact. The pristine basin at the mouth of the Ganaraska River at Port Hope (page 61) turns out to be the principal site for the production of uranium used in the Manhattan Project, leaving behind a legacy of contamination that calls for a $1.28 billion cleanup.

PG Violent changes, in scale and just about everything else, do get a lot of attention—and not much applause. New architecture is awkward, anodyne, or garish (pages 27–30, 59, 87, and 96–97), and cheap commercial crap, be it shiny or tawdry, has all but swallowed up the country (pages 14, 64–65, 80–81, and 89). Meanwhile, many older buildings are falling apart (pages 54–55, 66, and 71), and we are forever finding ourselves in some sort of no man's land, which is not always a parking lot (pages 45, 51, 58, 68, 69, 82, 86–87, and 116).

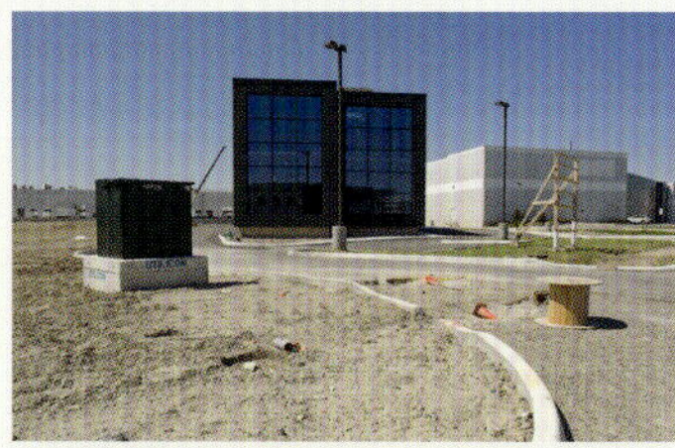
P. 28

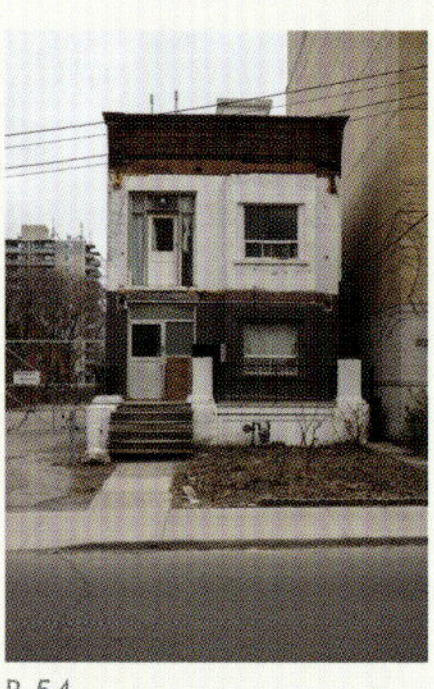
P. 54

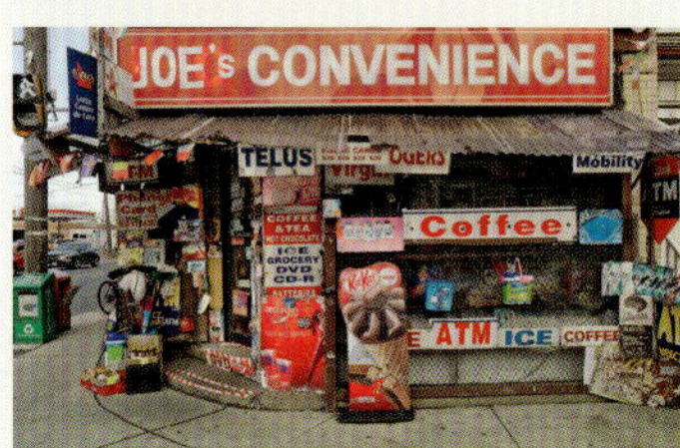

P. 64

GJ One of the themes that interested me as I worked on this book was the "905" region. Like many suburbs, it is low density, developer driven, and automobile dependent, but the 905 is also home to many transnational communities with one foot in the old country: Sikhs, Chinese, even a single persecuted Muslim sect from Pakistan. Unlike Chinatown or Little Italy, which over time have been woven into the fabric of the city, the 905 has increasingly grown in this self-segregated, region-specific way.

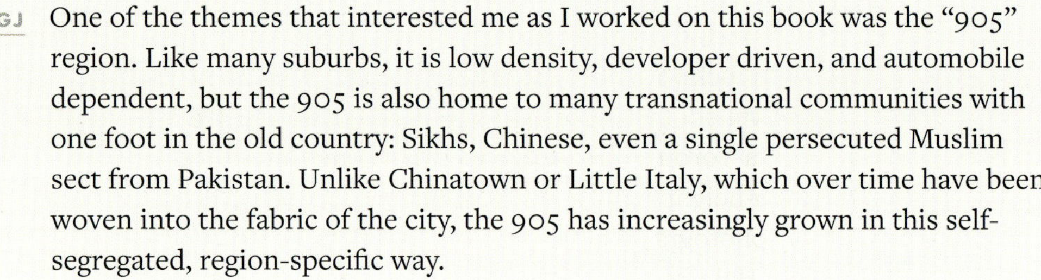

In planning terms, one central error I see with the 905 is that the soil there is extraordinarily fertile: about half the Grade 1 arable land in Canada is visible from the top of Toronto's CN Tower. You can see this in *Downsview 2018* (page 24). In the background is a huge mound of dark soil that looks like it could be bagged and sold. The site is in mid-development with new "urban towns," as they are called, under construction. But the bigger story is the collapse of any meaningful development on what was a former air base. At the turn of the century, an international competition that attracted nearly 200 architects was won by Rem Koolhaas. He proposed a visionary scheme for Downsview called "Tree City," with a matrix of tree clusters covering 25 percent of the 158-hectare site. But the project died from bureaucratic inertia.

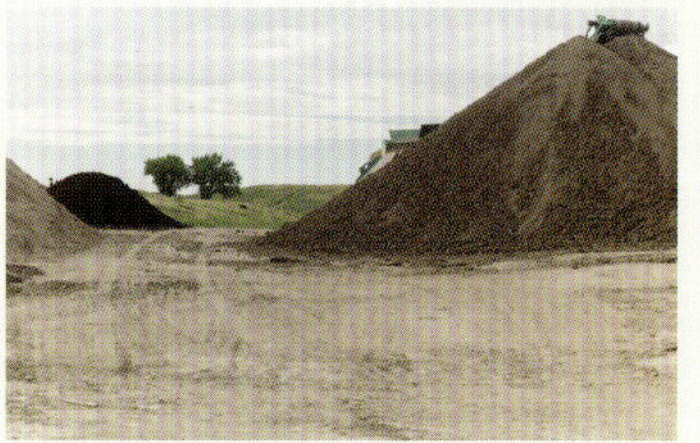
P. 24

PG If your book casts a critical eye on development and new architecture, your view of Canada's vaunted natural beauty is absolutely devastating. Beginning with the first picture and thereafter repeatedly, we get a glimpse of nature in the distance (pages 5, 37, 45, and 66). The unambiguous message is that in Canada untouched nature is forever out of reach. Alternatively, nature is under attack (pages 23 and 116) or accessible only through degraded representations (pages 47 and 123). In the entire book, the only images of pristine nature are cheap reproductions tacked up in a prison cell (page 95).

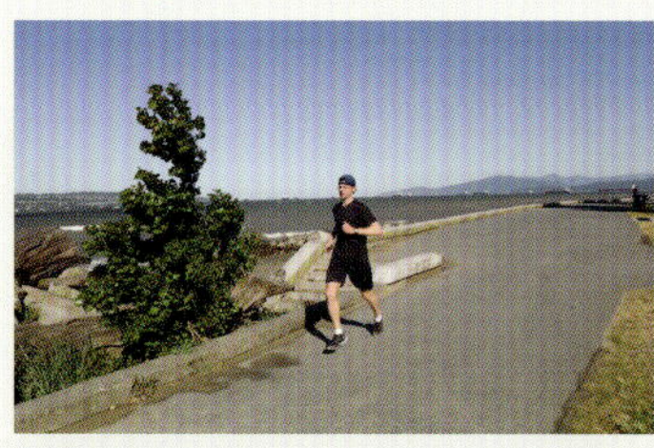
P. 37

P. 23

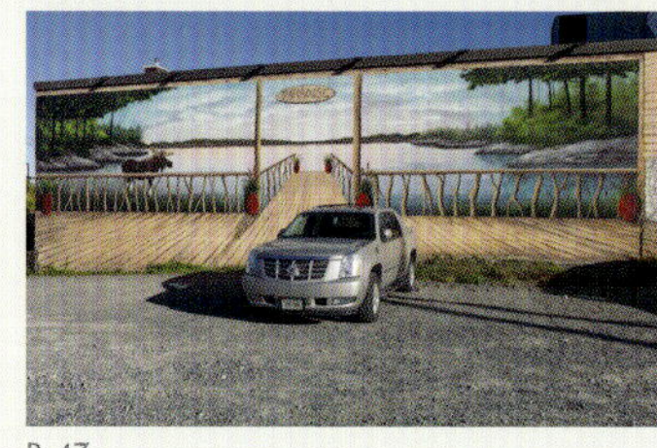
P. 47

P. 95

Another talisman of Canadian identity—winter sports—is reduced to an ad for athletic apparel on Toronto's Dundas Street (page 31), and the pride of French Canadian hockey, Maurice Richard, is literally crumbling away in Sudbury (page 100). Opposite him and suffering the same fate is a man of the

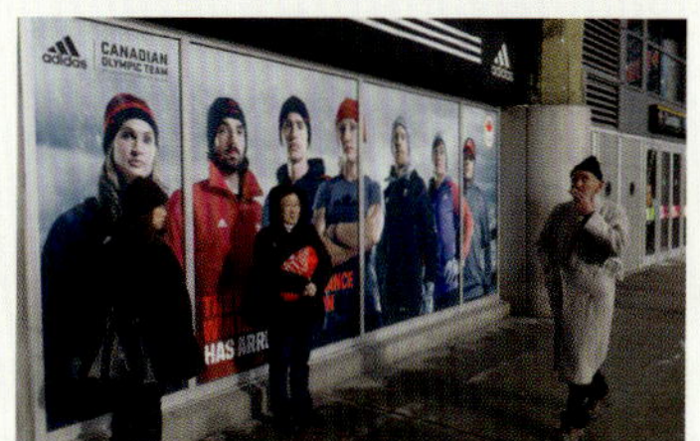

P. 31

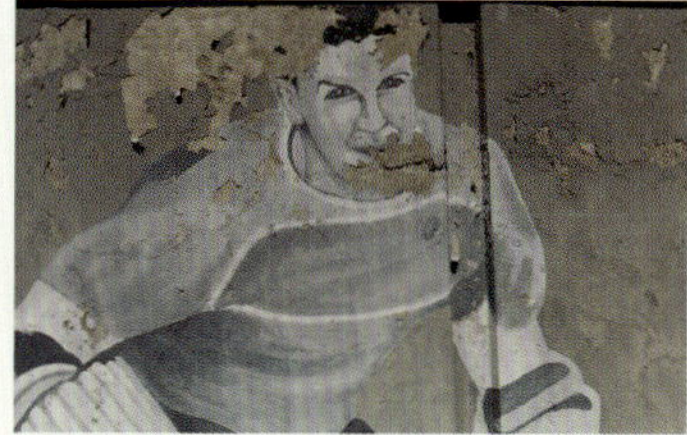
P. 100

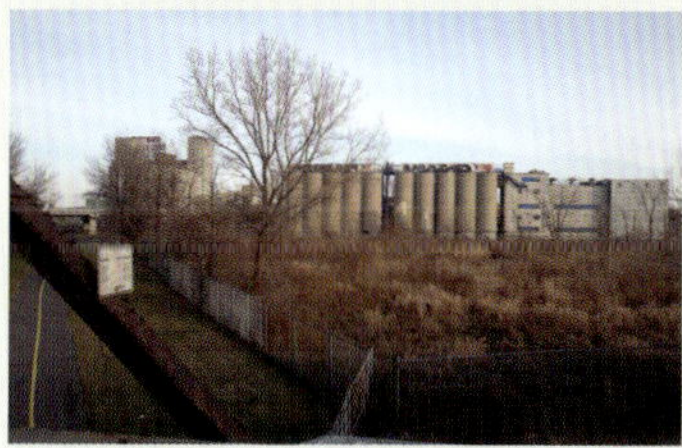
P. 49

cloth no doubt more familiar to French Canadians than to me (page 101), so perhaps religion is faring no better than hockey.

On the other hand, the railroad seems to be a reassuring presence. Tracks and bridges appear frequently, and quite a few pictures were made from the train. Of course, the railway played a key role in unifying the large country, and the image of grain elevators (page 49) reminds us that the train carries a great deal of Canadian grain and other resources across the continent to the ships waiting off Vancouver (page 37).

GJ I have never had much luck with road trips, so I simply made photographs wherever I lived or travelled. I also started photographing from train windows in the Montreal-Ottawa-Toronto corridor, which can sometimes produce a surprising equestrian-height view of the world. The process involved shooting many, many photographs. Eventually, I travelled across the country, from Prince Rupert to Halifax, a multi-tiered trip that took eight days. The train between Prince Rupert and Toronto—you can see the interior of the vintage railcar in the first image in this book (page 5)—is essentially a tourist experience. It stops for passengers to look at bears.

While the building of the railroad was crucial to the creation of Confederation, passenger rail is very much a second-class citizen in Canada. Since I arrived in 1966, there has been talk of a high-speed rail corridor between Quebec City and Windsor. But the single-track system still gives priority to freight trains. I should say that I have consciously avoided dealing with the untouched Canadian landscape, which is the way the country is often depicted. More interesting to me is how the land has been settled, often in a short-sighted, provisional way.

PG Let me turn at last to this book's considerable departure from your earlier work. (Readers who would like to get to know your work better will enjoy *Utopia/ Dystopia*, the handsome catalogue of your major retrospective at the National Gallery of Canada in 2008. In addition to the excellent plates, it includes a very informative chronology.)

The first departure has to do with craft. Nearly all your earlier work was in black-and-white. You first used colour film in 1998, in the context of your Toronto project, and *Inside Kingston Penitentiary* has a handful of colour photographs. You mentioned above that *Canadian Photographs* was shot with a digital Leica that you acquired in 2010—and of course colour is the default digital mode, just as black-and-white was for photography's first century.

GJ My work has changed a lot over the years. The project on Italian gardens, which took a decade to complete, came out of a childhood memory of visiting Hadrian's Villa outside Rome. My early work was all a bit innocent, especially since I insisted on using hopelessly obsolete equipment. When I had the retrospective at the National Gallery in 2008, I was a little worried that it might look like a group show. Since then, my subject matter has perhaps become even less ingratiating. My six-month foray into the Kingston Penitentiary in 2013 came from a belief that there had to be a historical record of this ancient prison. (It was shot using a colour and a monochrome Leica, so I had to commit to a camera on the spot.) It was not an easy project—the cultures of both the inmates and the guards were hard to penetrate. The resulting book was probably saved in the last two days, when I had access to the cells right after they were vacated, still full of the inmates' possessions and with walls whose writings revealed the realities of life there in ways that were deeply moving.

PG You have said that you first turned to colour film while working on Toronto to convey the "violent" colours and "vulgarity" of new building in the 905 region. *Canadian Photographs* depicts a fair amount of vulgarity as well, but it is an attribute of the subject matter, not the pictures themselves. That is, the pictures are in colour in the sense that the world is in colour, and in aesthetic terms, I regard that as an impressive achievement.

The other major departure in *Canadian Photographs* is the frequent appearance of people. Your earlier work explored the marks of humankind in the landscape, for better (Italian gardens or Frederick Law Olmsted's parks) and for worse (asbestos at Quebec's Thetford Mines or the fence along the US-Mexico border). But actual human beings have rarely appeared before now. For that reason alone, the people in these pictures invite scrutiny, and I believe they contribute a great deal to the book's bedrock equanimity.

Canadian Photographs presents an image of a multi-ethnic nation, and the people and text in the pictures display quite a range of racial, ethnic, religious, and other sorts of diversity. To my eye, the only person in the entire book who may fail to elicit our empathy is the fat cat striding by the Toronto Stock Exchange (page 33), and his status is reinforced by the contrast with the picture opposite him (page 32): the humble side door to Massey Hall, built by Hart Massey and completed in 1894, to make culture available to all. In one of my favourite pictures, an older Black man, a Sikh man, a woman who appears to be Asian, and a man who appears to be of white European descent are all obviously gathered for some shared occasion (page 72).

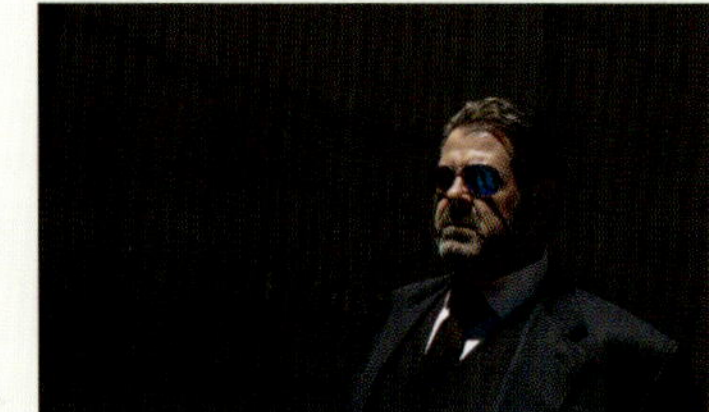

P. 33

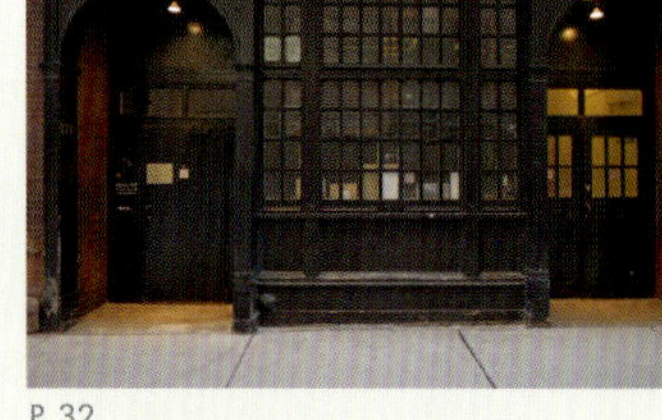

P. 32

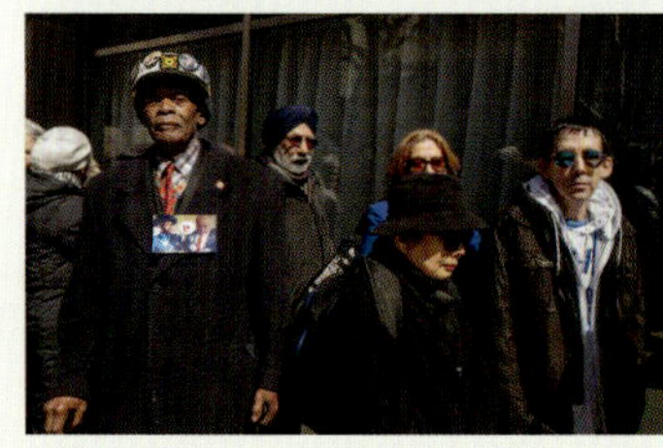

P. 72

GJ The people in that photograph were at Toronto City Hall in 2016 to mourn the death of Rob Ford, who appears in the photograph pinned to the Black man's lapel. As mayor from 2010 to 2014, Ford achieved a certain notoriety for his proclivity for crack cocaine and for dropping such phrases as "in one of my drunken stupors." Garrison Keillor said of Donald Trump that he was unfit for any public office other than Mayor of Toronto. At the time, I was the city's photo laureate; although I had no official duties, I felt I should record the presence of "Ford Nation" at his lying in state at City Hall. What struck me was the widespread expression of grief and real affection for Ford.

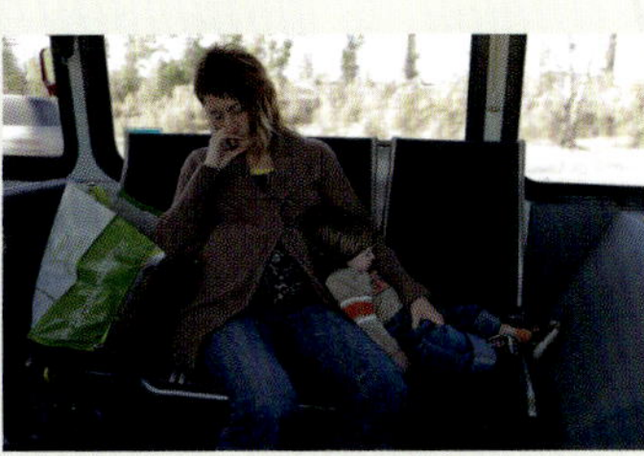

P. 75

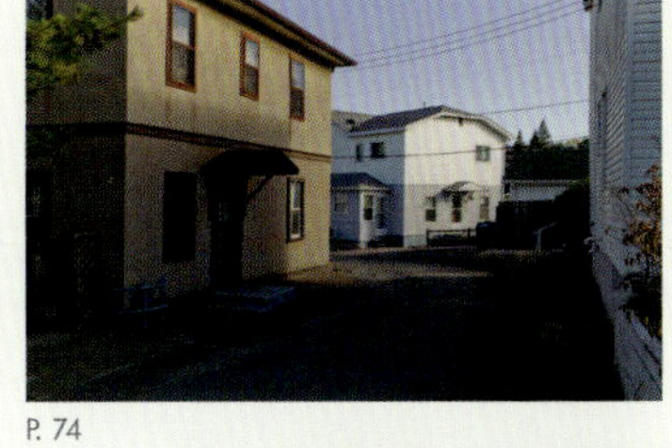

P. 74

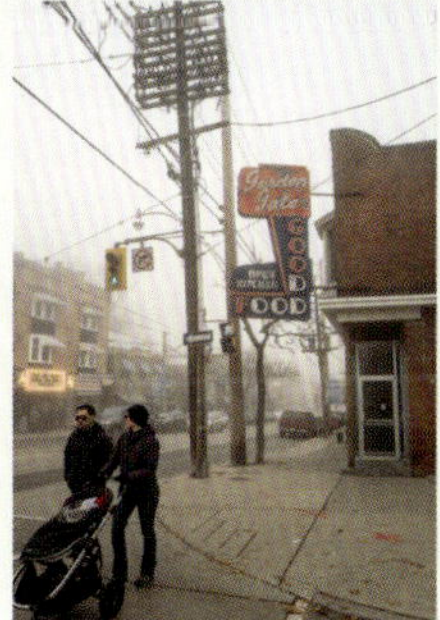

P. 104

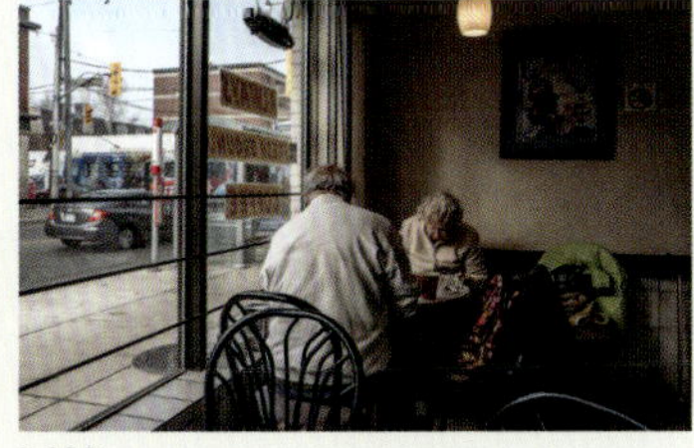

P. 105

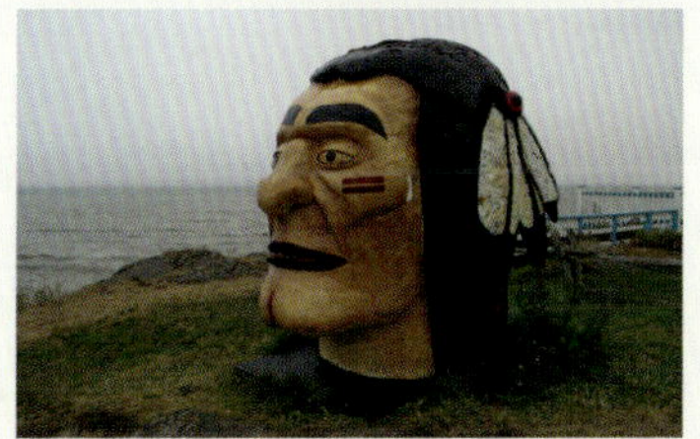

P. 125

PG Two pages later, a pair of pictures made in Copper Cliff, Ontario (pages 74–75), may be interpreted as a nod to the importance of the mining industry. They also strike me as among the tenderest pictures in the book: a pregnant mother and child opposite a few modest houses gently embraced by the sun. That tenderness carries over to page 78, a photo of an aging couple waiting for the train in Kingston. It resurfaces later in two more pictures of couples, one with an infant in a stroller, the other no longer young (pages 104–105).

The warmth of the couples nonetheless abides and resonates with two pairs of shots from the train, looking out at communities that might be good places to live (pages 112–113 and 118–119). The book concludes rather severely with two pictures, each isolated opposite a blank page: a pathetic arrangement that drives home the chasm between the myth and the reality of the Canadian natural landscape (page 123) and a blunt reminder of the fate of the people who first lived here (page 125).

Canadian Photographs does not pull its punches, but neither does it settle for easy judgments. That is a big part of why I think it is your best book to date.

Peter Galassi in conversation with Geoffrey James, winter 2024

SELECTED BOOKS AND CATALOGUES OF PHOTOGRAPHS BY GEOFFREY JAMES

Morbid Symptoms: Arcadia and the French Revolution (1986)

La Campagna Romana (1991)

The Italian Garden (1991)

Asbestos (1994)

Viewing Olmsted, with Robert Burley and Lee Friedlander (1996)

Running Fence (1999)

Paris (2001)

Place (2002)

Toronto (2006)

Utopia/Dystopia (2008)

Inside Kingston Penitentiary (2014)

LIST OF WORKS

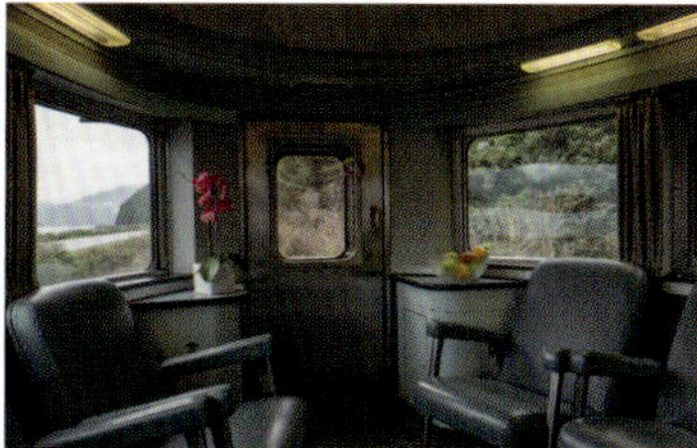

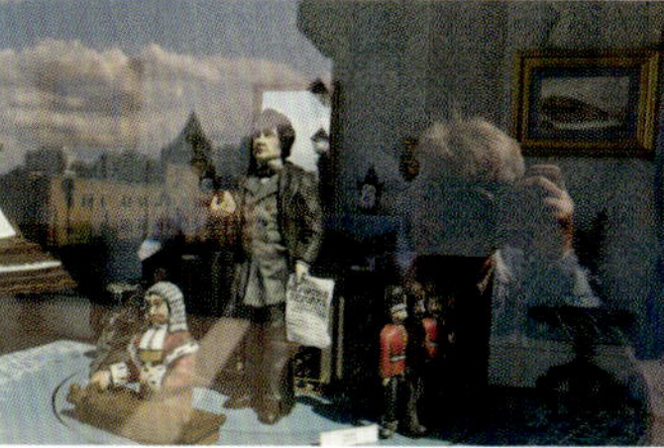

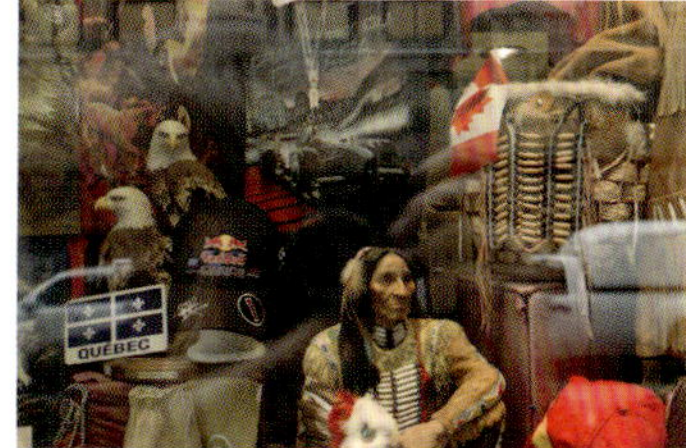

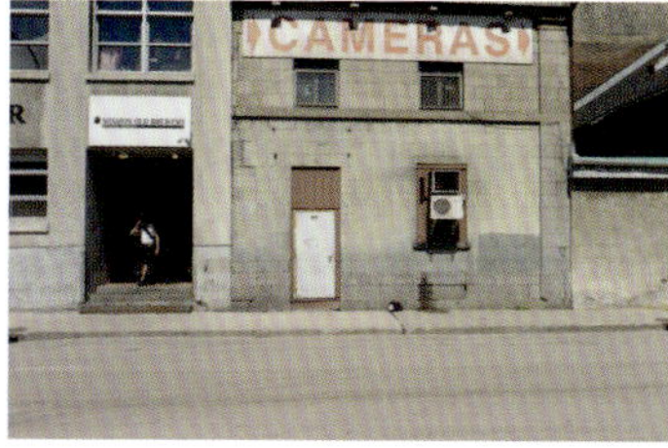

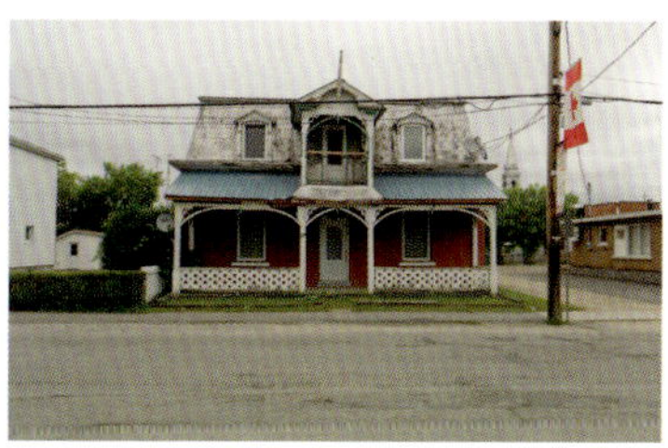

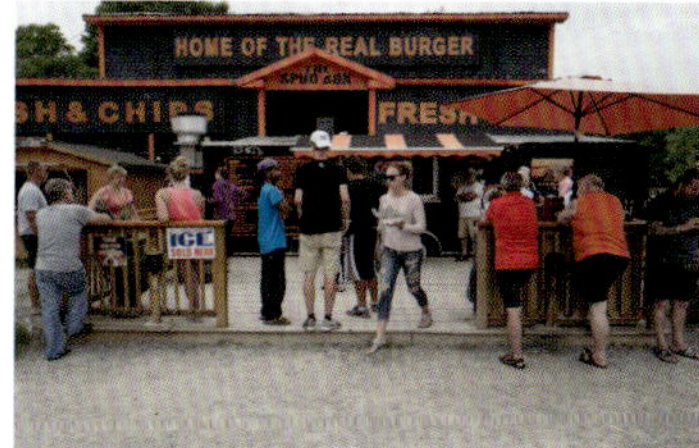

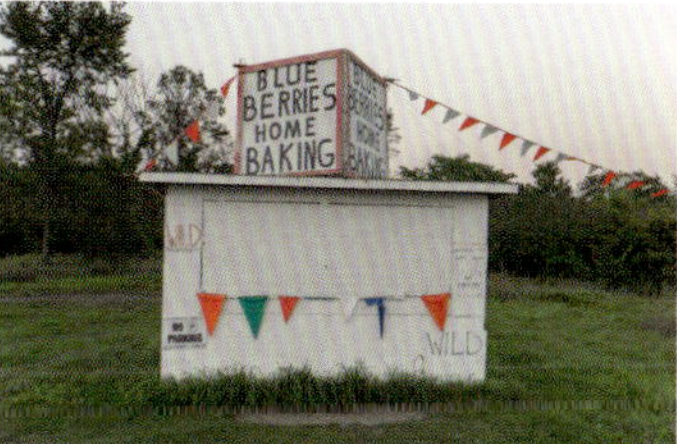

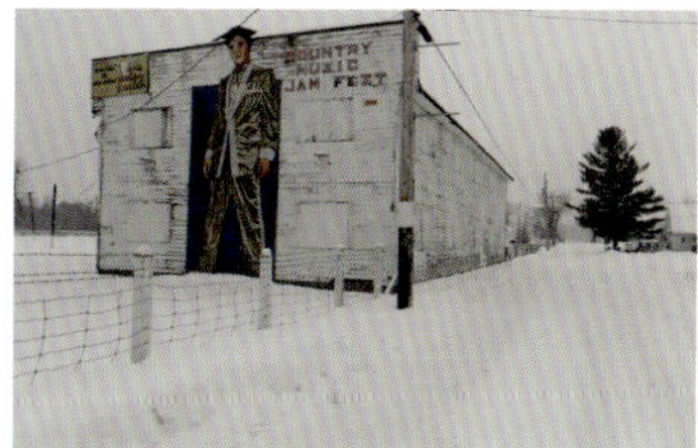

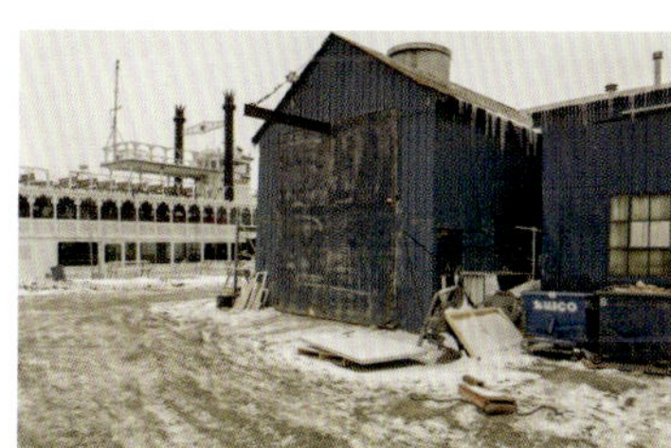

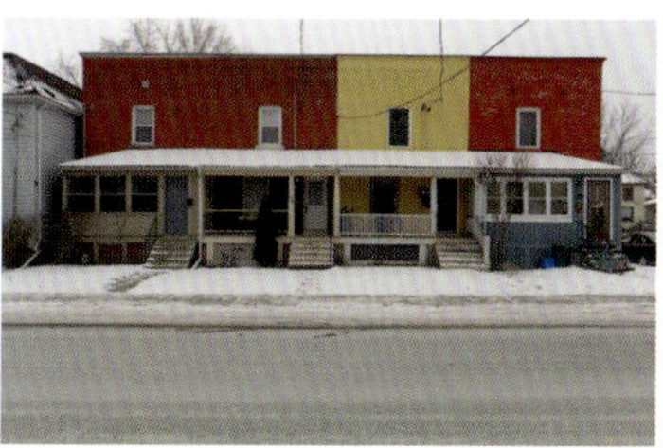

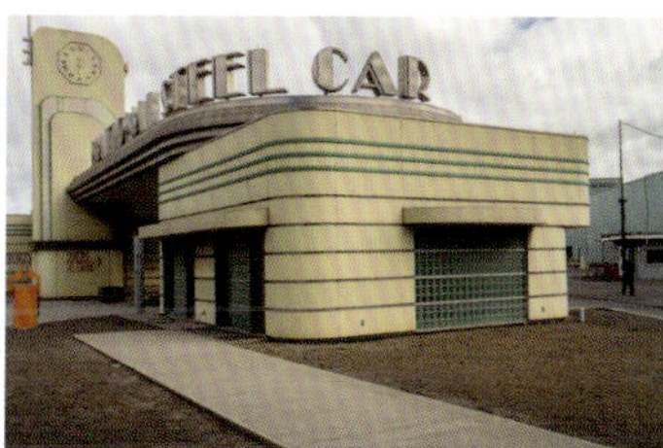

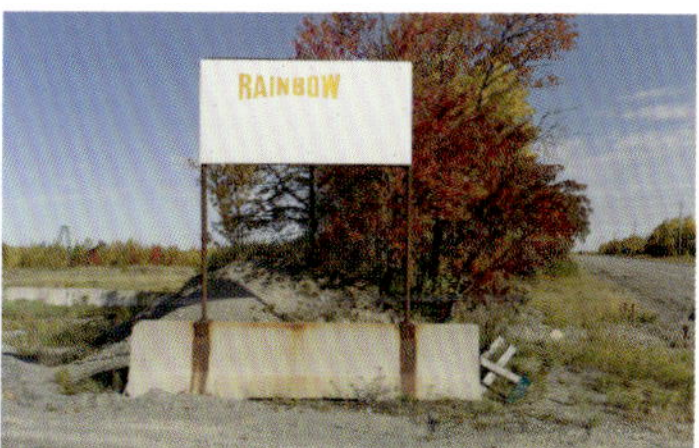

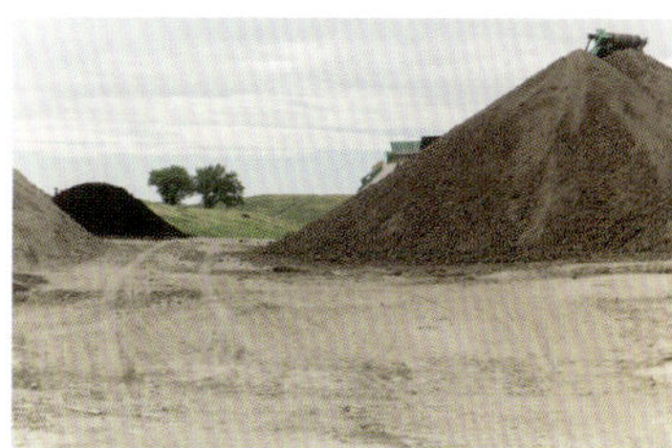

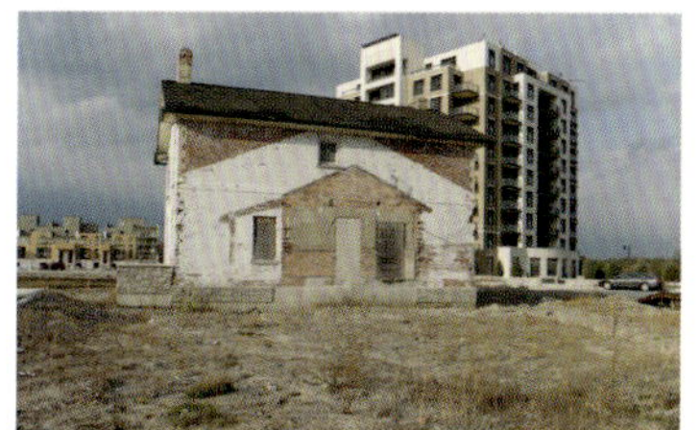

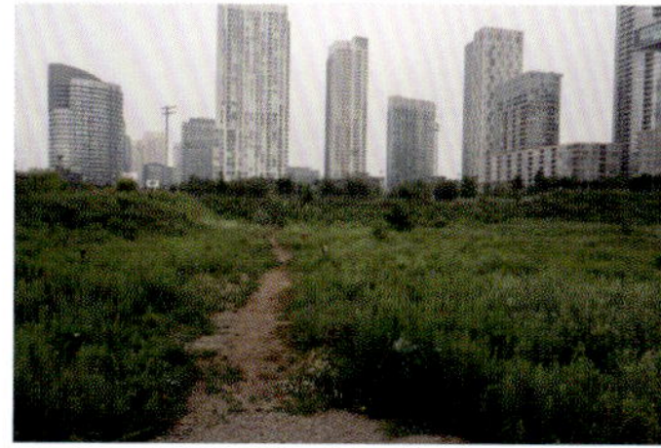

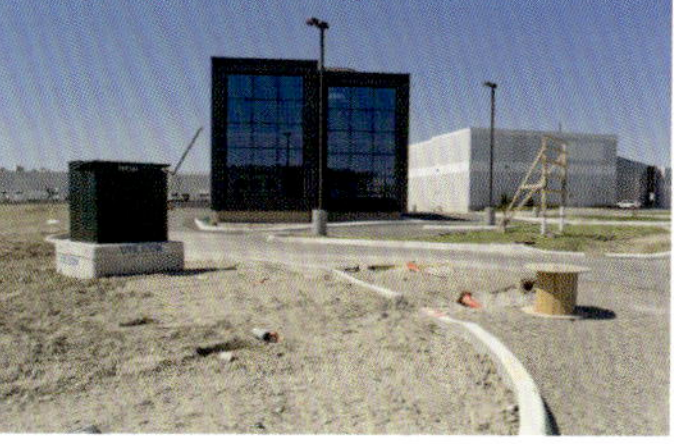

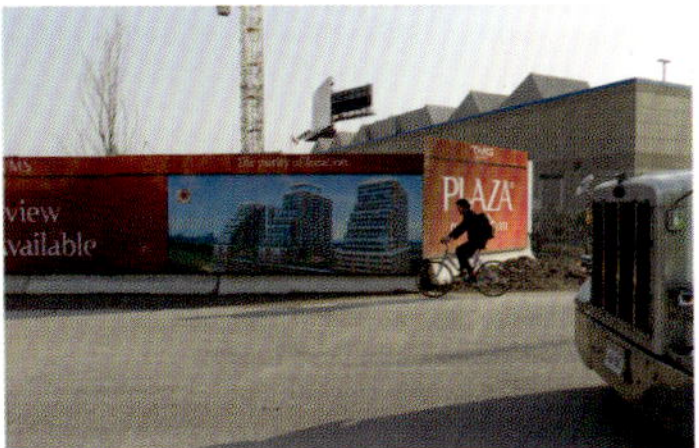

P. 29
Liberty Village, Toronto, ON, 2011

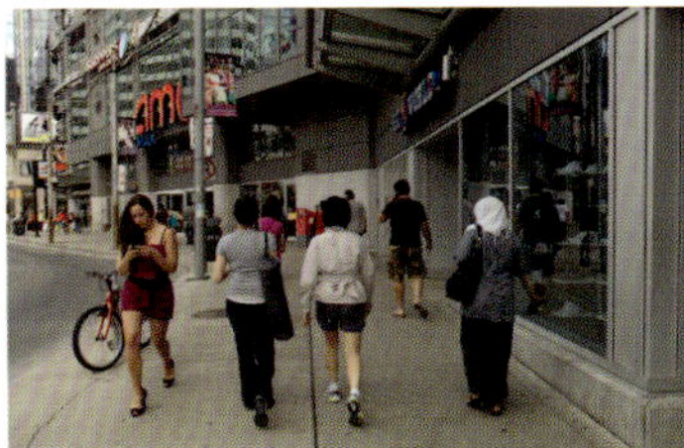

P. 30
Dundas Street, Toronto, ON, 2011

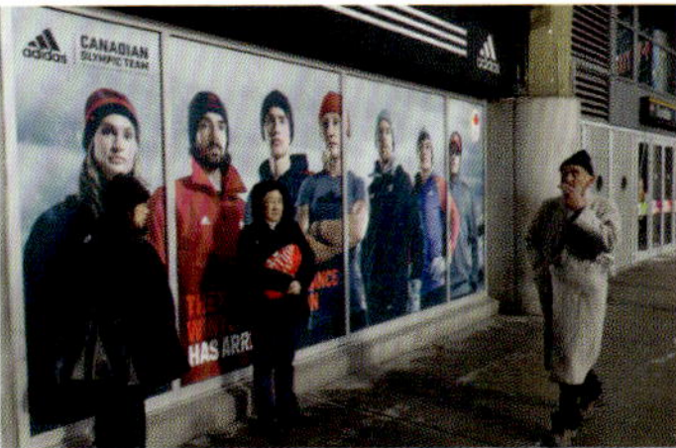

P. 31
Dundas Street, Toronto, ON, 2013

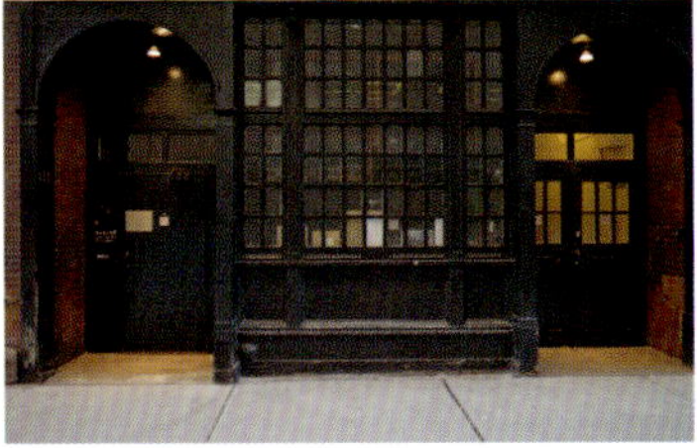

P. 32
Side door of Massey Hall, Toronto, ON, 2011

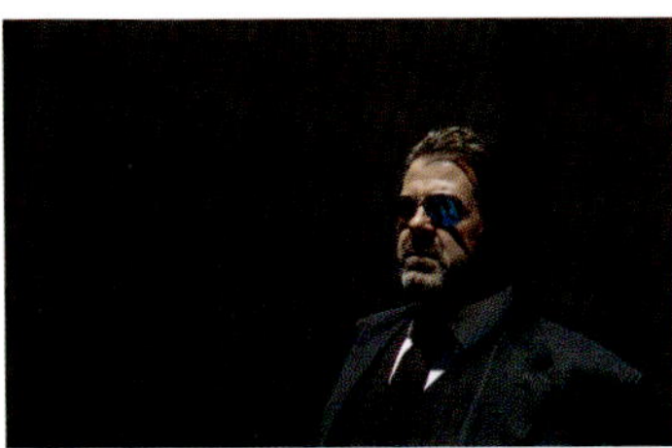

P. 33
Outside the Toronto Stock Exchange, Toronto, ON, 2018

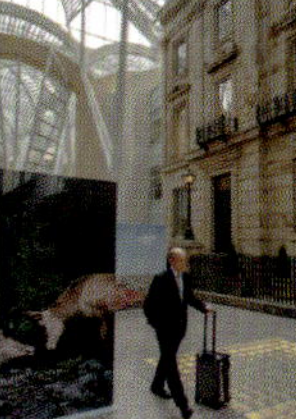

P. 35
Toronto, ON, 2019

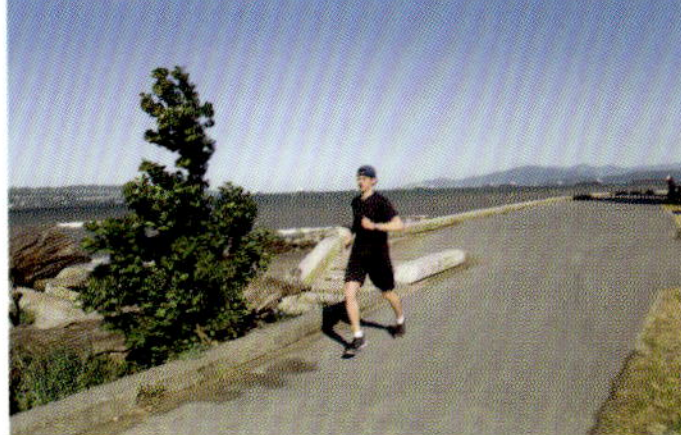

P. 37
English Bay Beach, Vancouver, BC, 2015

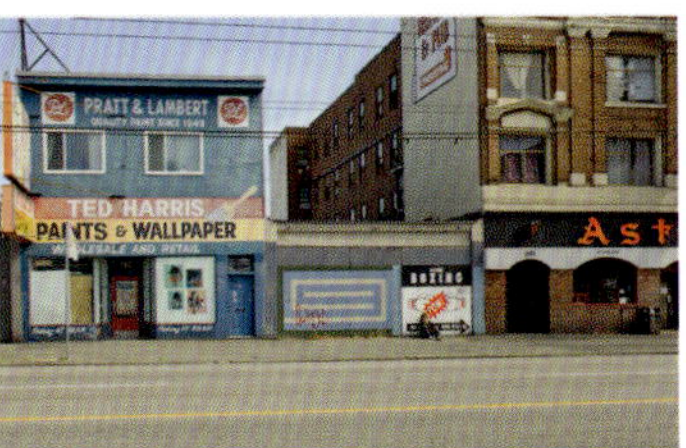

P. 38
East Hastings Street, Vancouver, BC, 2015

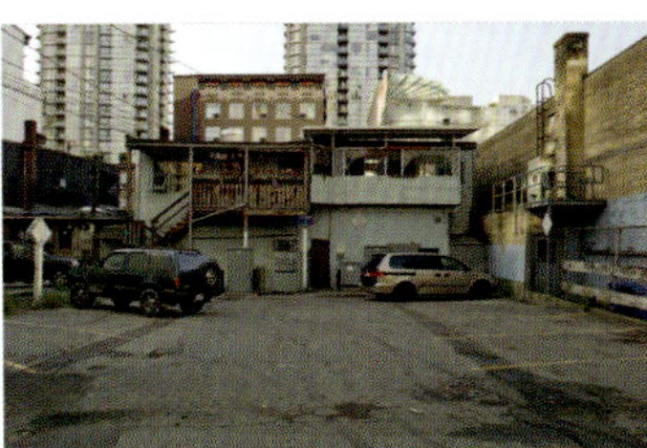

P. 39
Behind Granville Street, Vancouver, BC, 2015

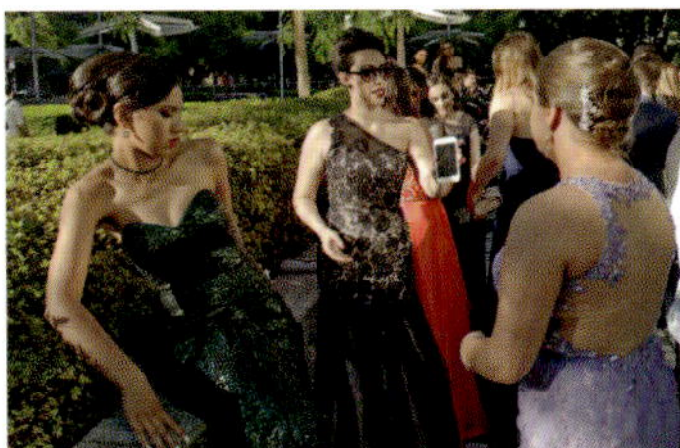

P. 40
Graduation, Notre Dame Regional Secondary School, Vancouver, BC, 2015

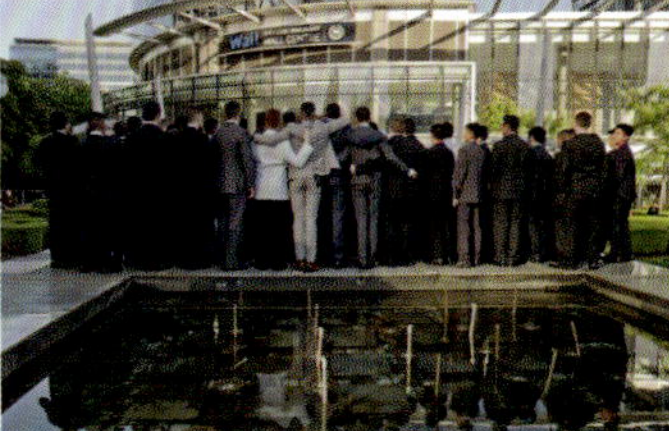

P. 41
Graduation, Notre Dame Regional Secondary School, Vancouver, BC, 2015

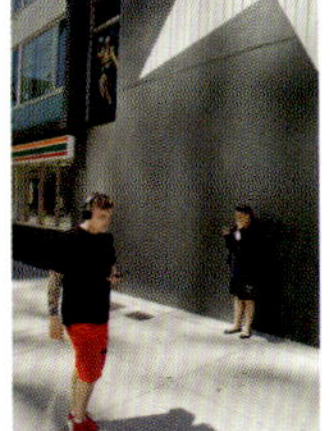

P. 42
Off Burrard Street, Vancouver, BC, 2015

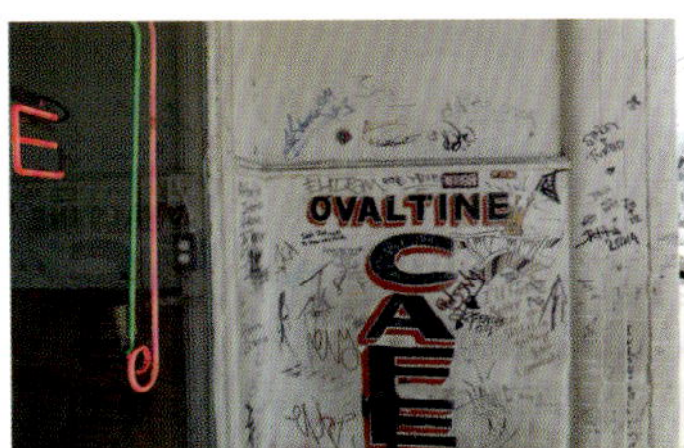

P. 43
Ovaltine Cafe, East Hastings Street, Vancouver, BC, 2017

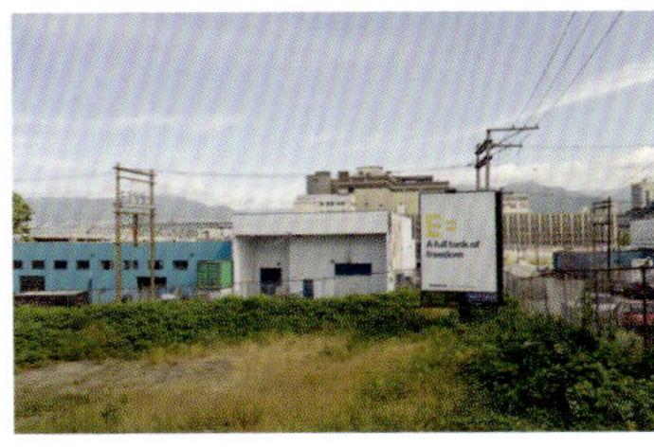

P. 45
East Hastings Street, Vancouver, BC, 2015

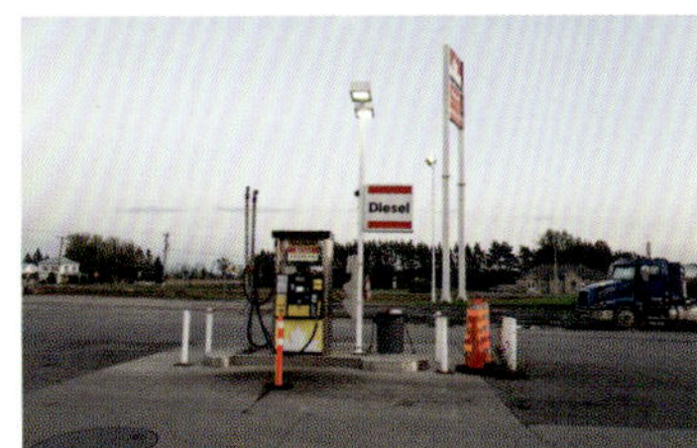

P. 46
Casselman exit, Highway 417, ON, 2017

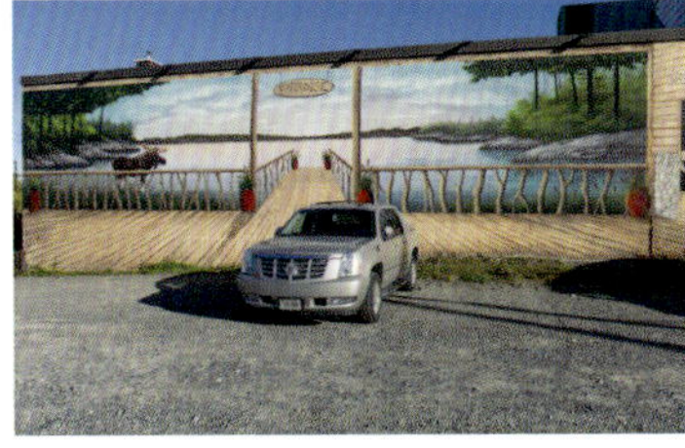

P. 47
Sudbury, ON, 2012

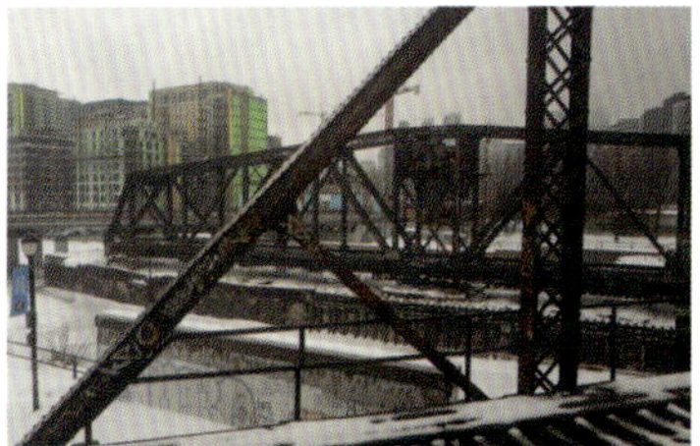

P. 48
From the train, Lachine Canal, Montreal, QC, 2018

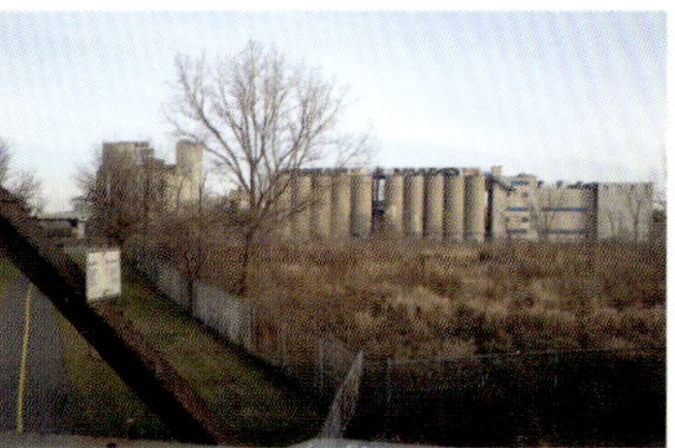

P. 49
From the train, Five Roses Flour, Montreal, QC, 2019

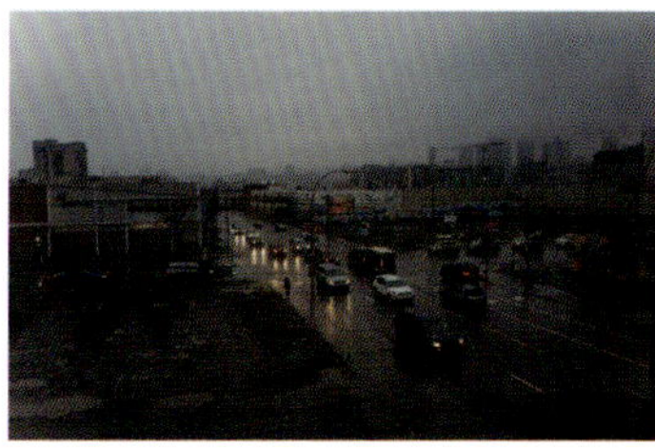

P. 51
From the train, Montreal, QC, 2016

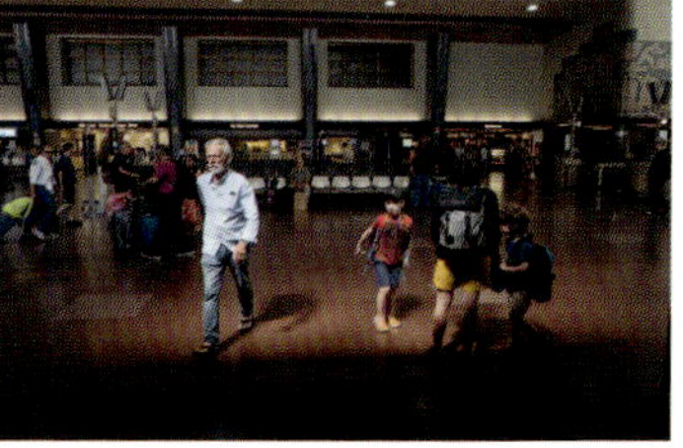

P. 52
Central Station, Montreal, QC, 2018

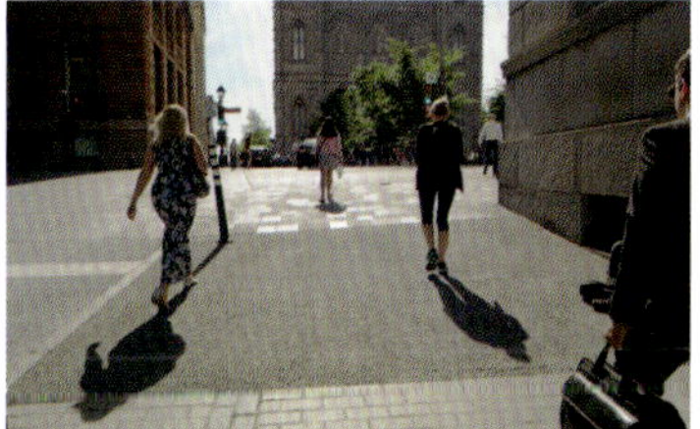

P. 53
Old Montreal, QC, 2014

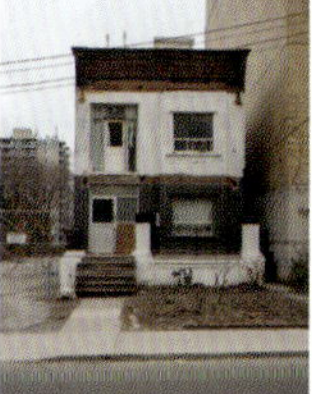

P. 54
Charles Street East, Toronto, ON, 2019

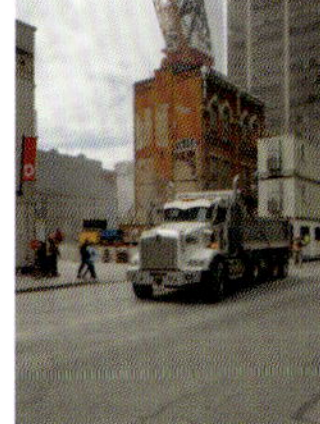

P. 55
Yonge Street, Toronto, ON, 2019

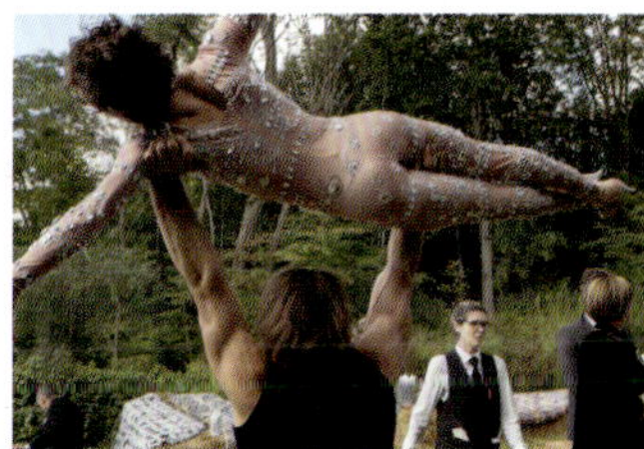

P. 56
Fête Champêtre, near Toronto, ON, 2018

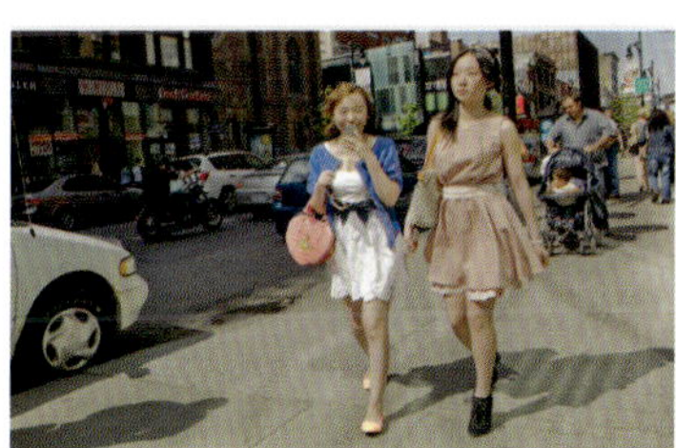

P. 57
Sainte-Catherine Street, Montreal, QC, 2013

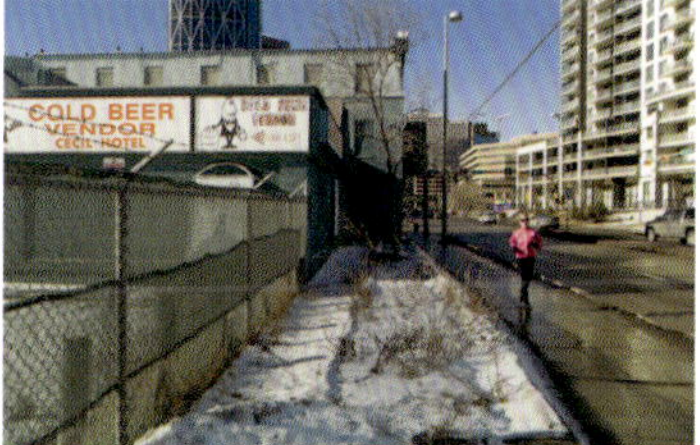

P. 58
Calgary, AB, 2015

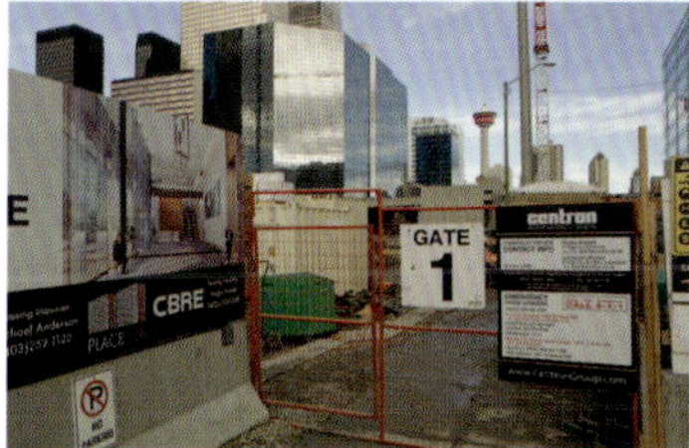

P. 59
Calgary, AB, 2015

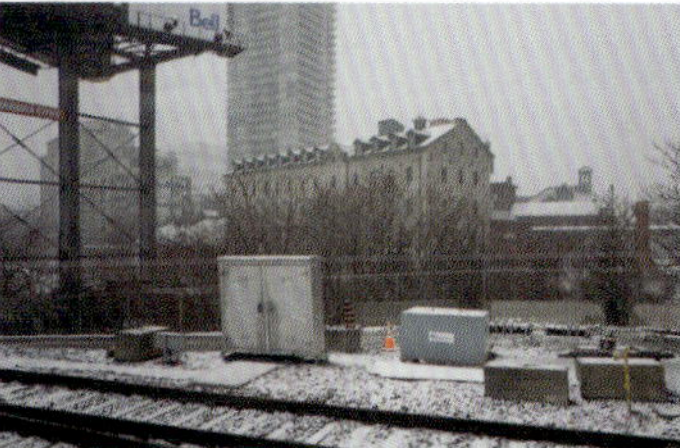

P. 60
From the train, the Distillery District, Toronto, ON, 2019

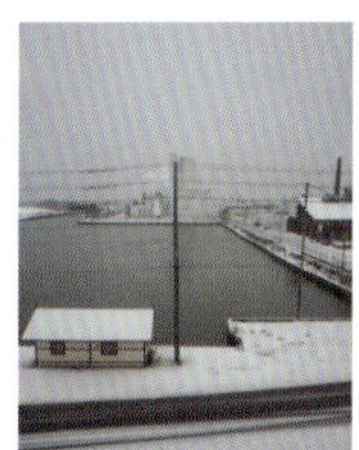

P. 61
From the train, uranium refinery, Port Hope, ON, 2017

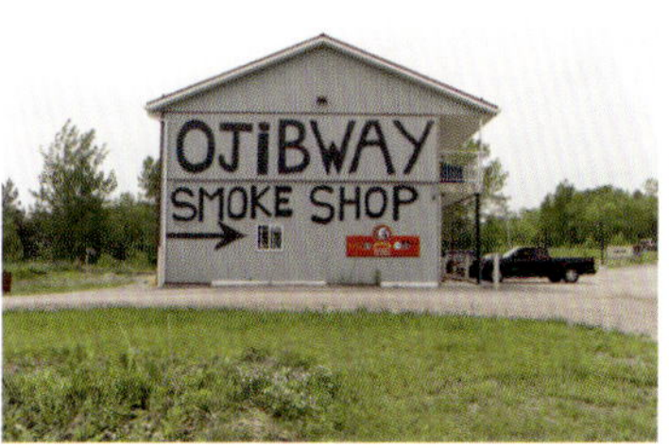

P. 63
Alderville First Nation's reserve, Roseneath, ON, 2011

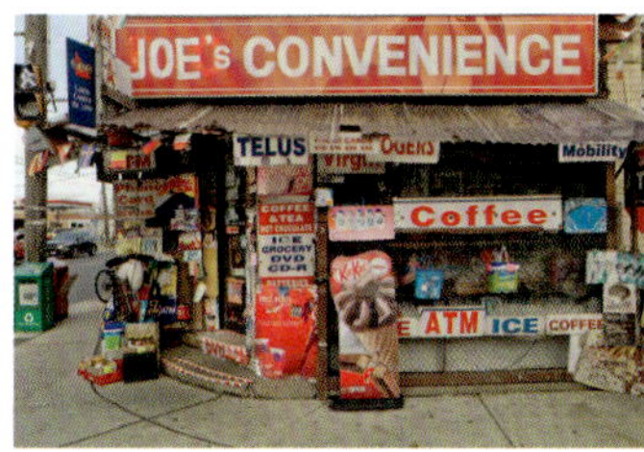

P. 64
Ossington Avenue, Toronto, ON, 2015

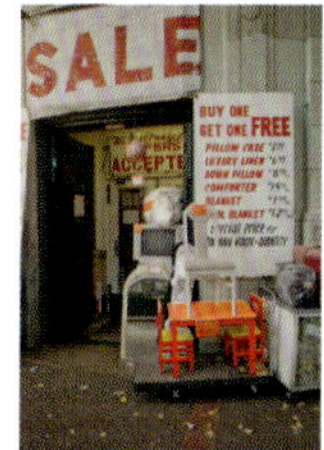

P. 65
West Hastings Street, Vancouver, BC, 2013

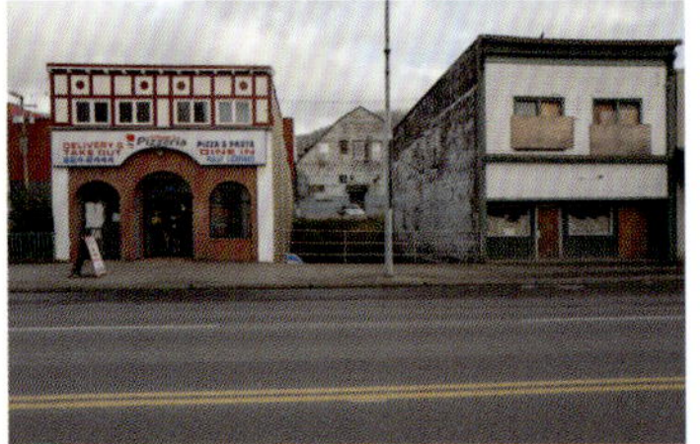

P. 66
Prince Rupert, BC, 2019

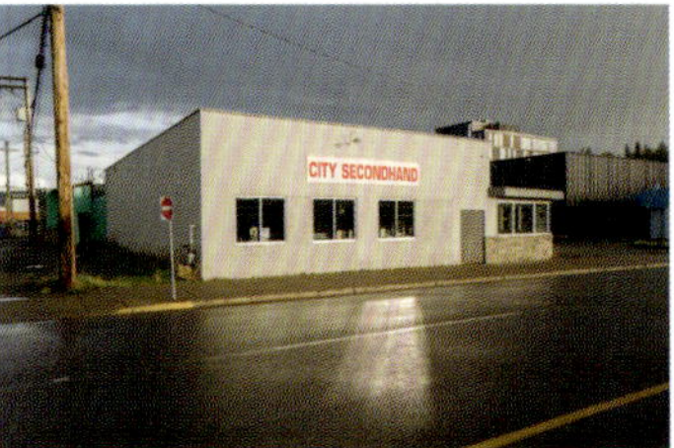

P. 67
Prince George, BC, 2019

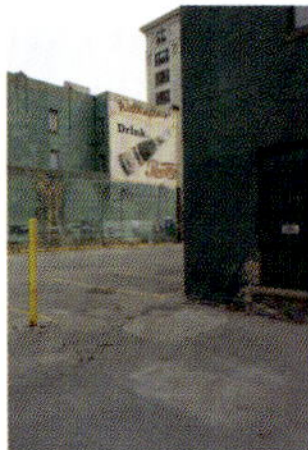

P. 68
Exchange District, Winnipeg, MB, 2017

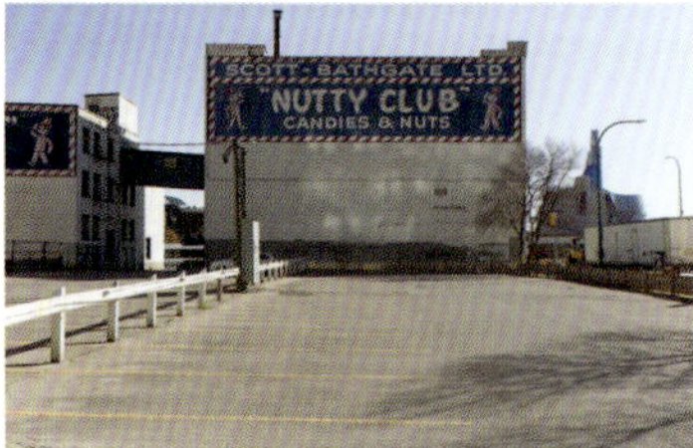

P. 69
Nutty Club and the Canadian Museum for Human Rights, Winnipeg, MB, 2017

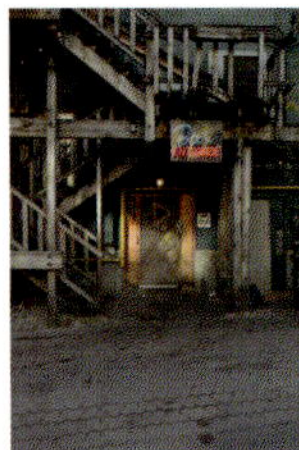

P. 71
Exchange District, Winnipeg, MB, 2017

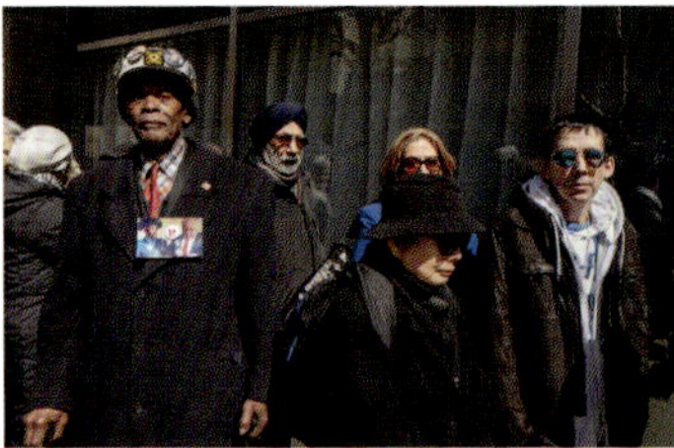

P. 72
Mourners for Mayor Rob Ford, City Hall, Toronto, ON, 2016

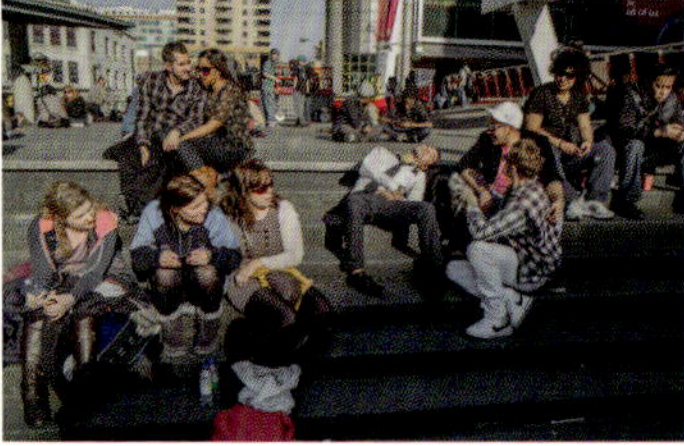

P. 73
The first warm day of the year, Dundas Square, Toronto, ON, 2012

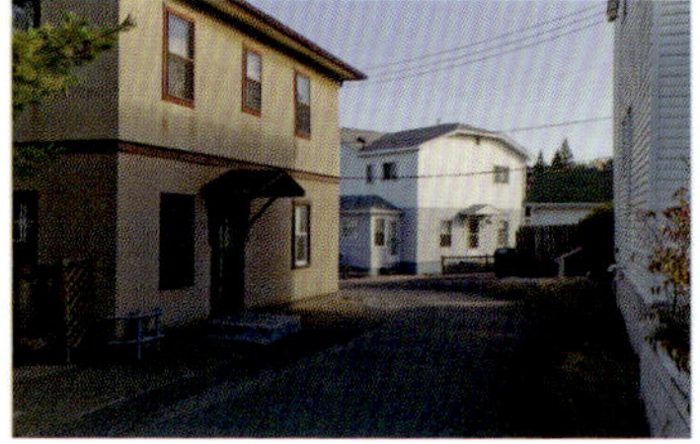

P. 74
Miners' houses, Copper Cliff, ON, 2012

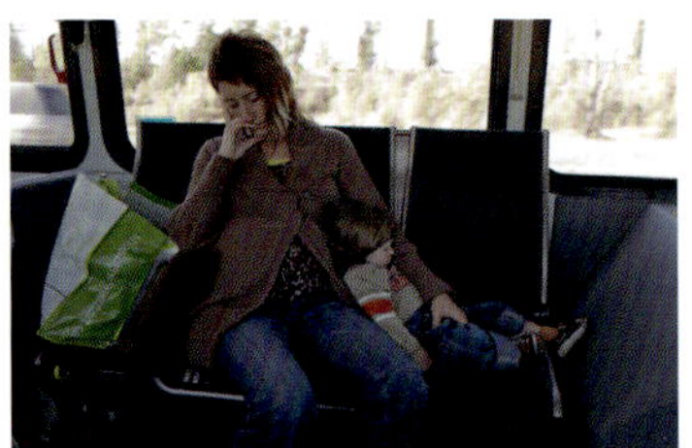

P. 75
On the Copper Cliff bus, Copper Cliff, ON, 2011

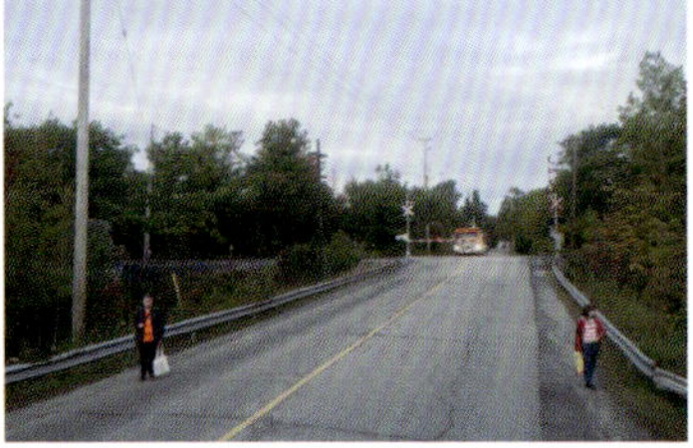

P. 77
From the train, near Washago, ON, 2019

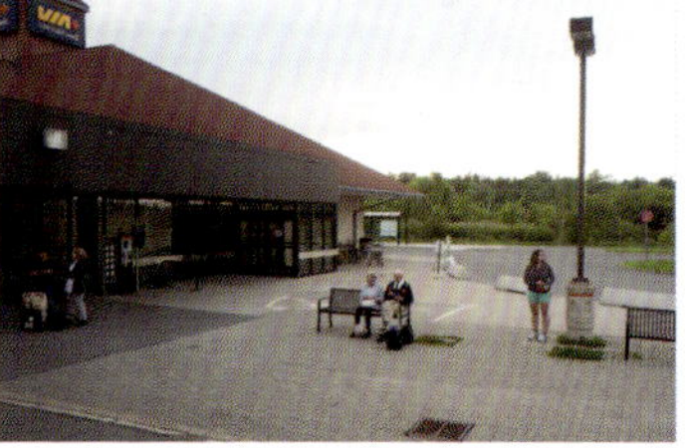

P. 78
From the train, Kingston, ON, 2019

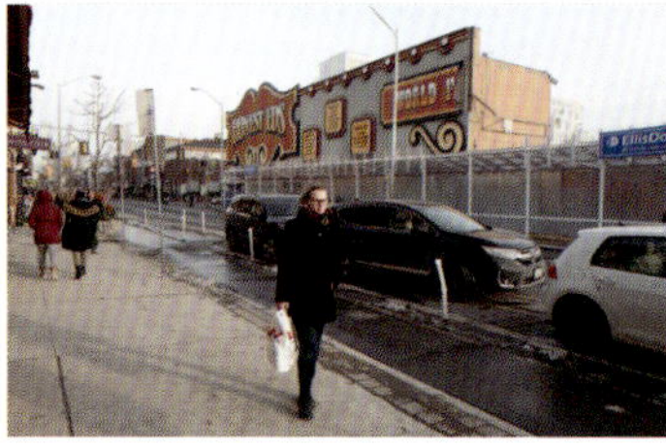

P. 80
The end of Honest Ed's, Bloor Street, Toronto, ON, 2018

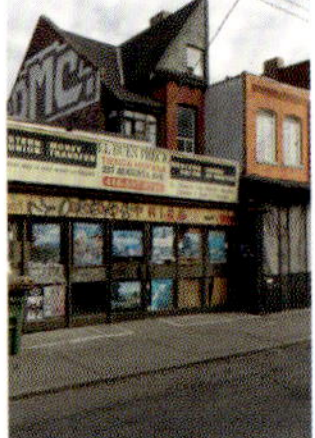

P. 81
Kensington Market, Toronto, ON, 2010

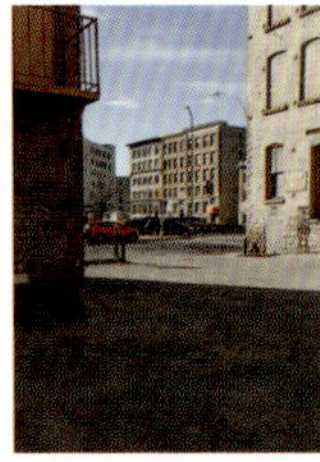

P. 82
Exchange District, Winnipeg, MB, 2012

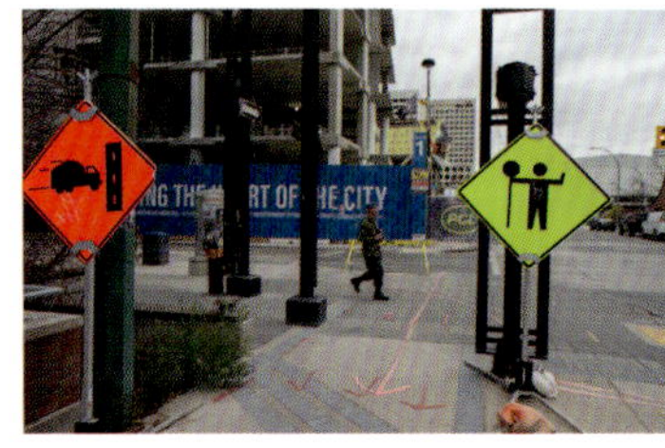

P. 83
Winnipeg, MB, 2017

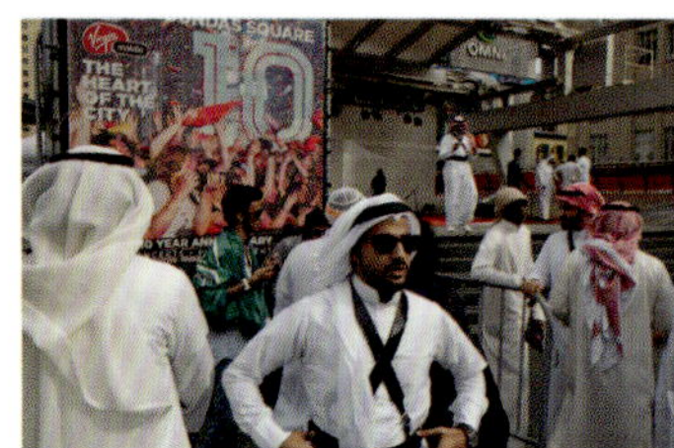

P. 84
Saudi National Day, Dundas Square, Toronto, ON, 2013

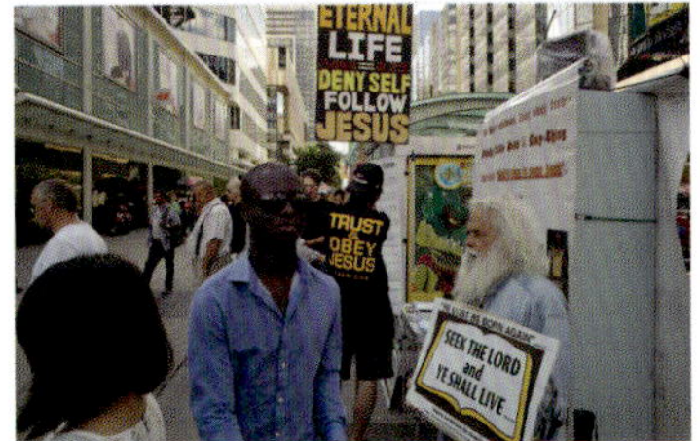

P. 85
Dundas Street, Toronto, ON, 2013

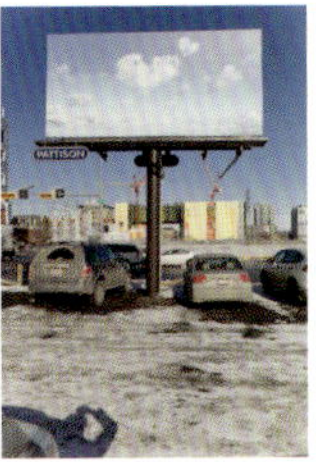

P. 86
Calgary, AB, 2015

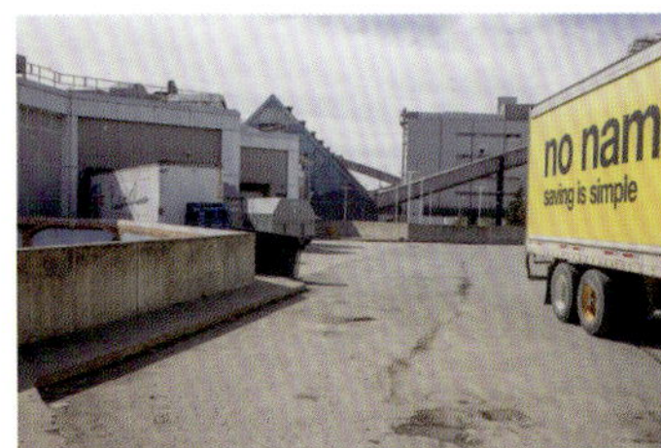

P. 87
Harbourfront, Toronto, ON, 2019

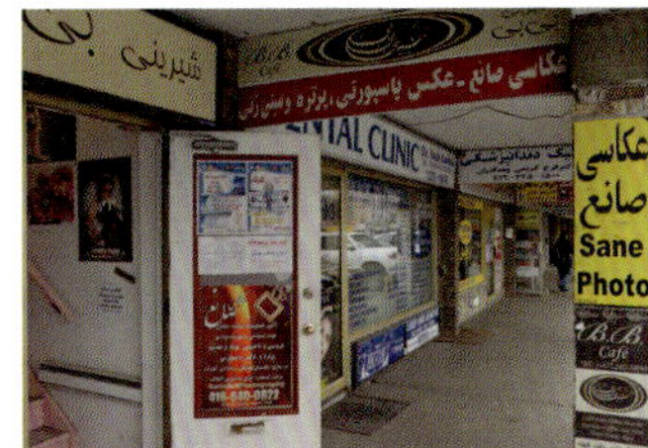

P. 89
Iranian Plaza, North York, ON, 2011

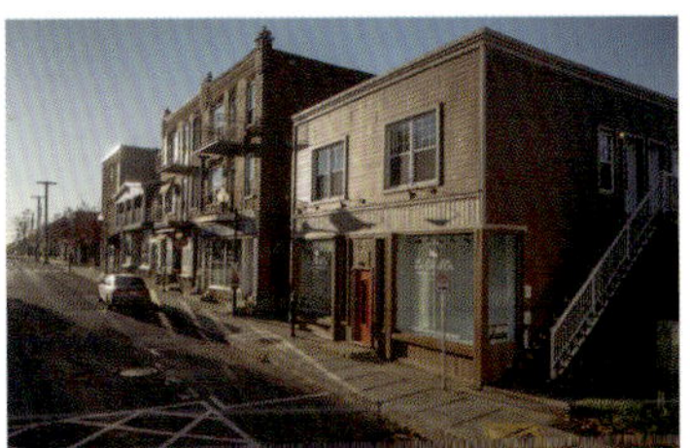

P. 90
From the train, Drummondville, QC, 2019

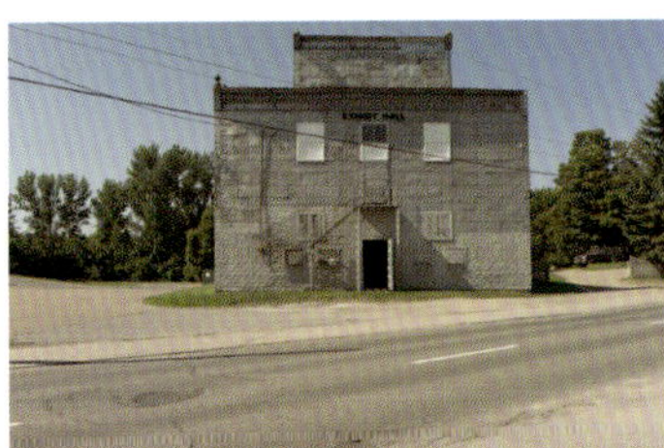

P. 91
Exhibit Hall, Renfrew, ON, 2011

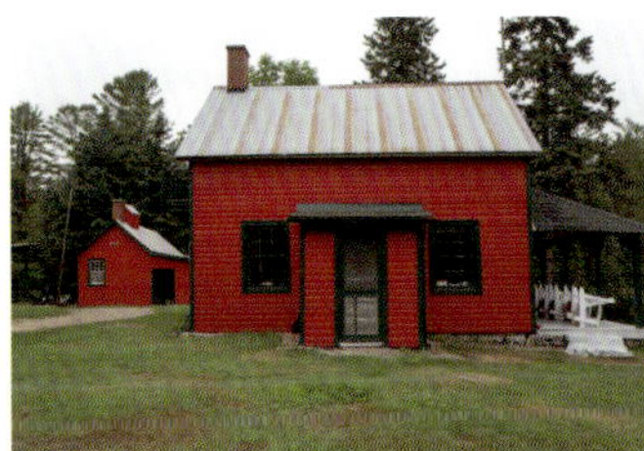

P. 92
Fishing club, Pontiac County, QC, 2016

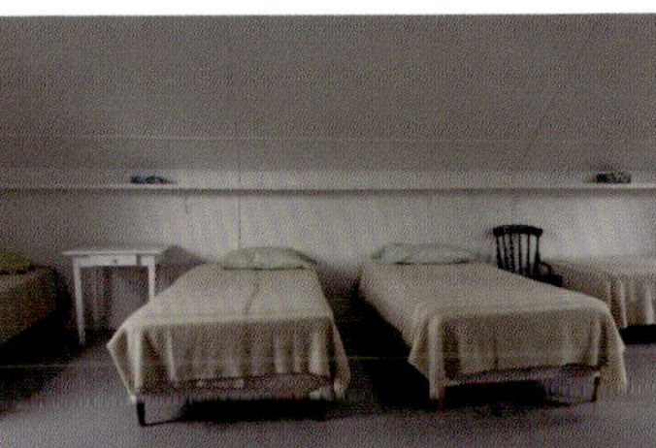

P. 93
Fishing club, Pontiac County, QC, 2016

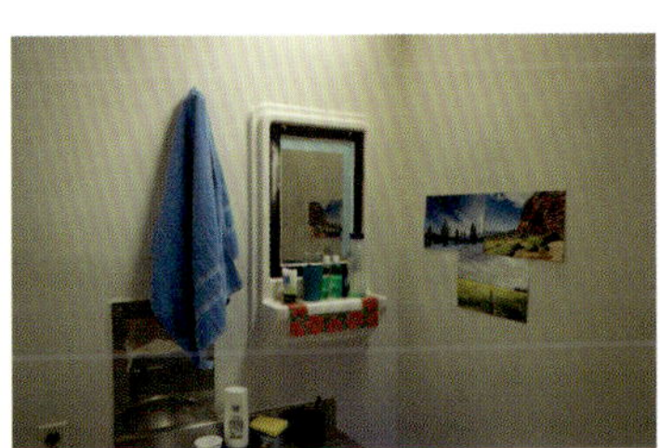

P. 95
Cell, Kingston Penitentiary, Kingston, ON, 2013

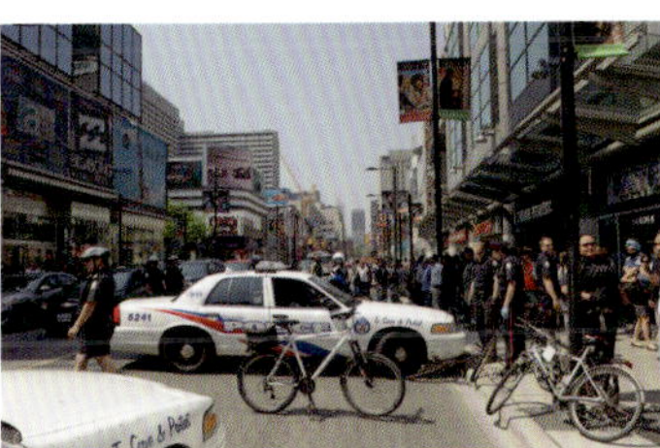

P. 96
After an arrest, Yonge Street, Toronto, ON, 2011

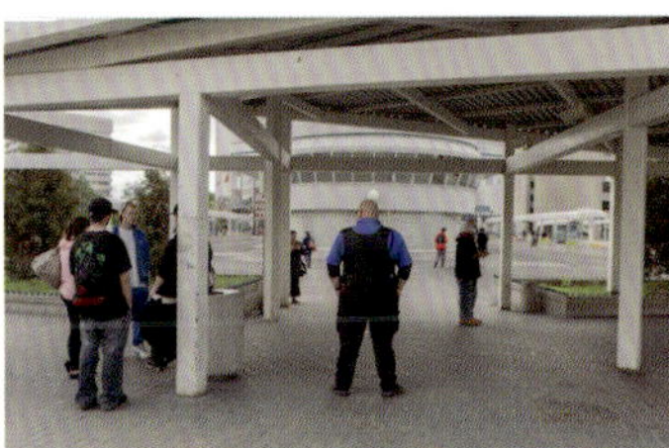

P. 97
Bus station, Sudbury, ON, 2011

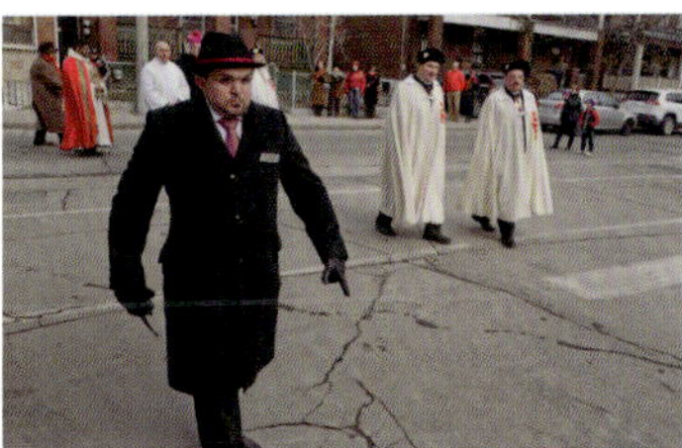

P. 98
Good Friday Procession, Little Italy, Toronto, ON, 2016

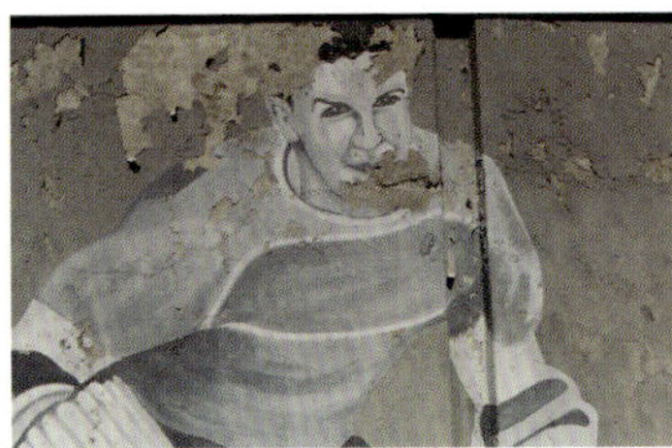

P. 100
Sudbury, ON, 2011

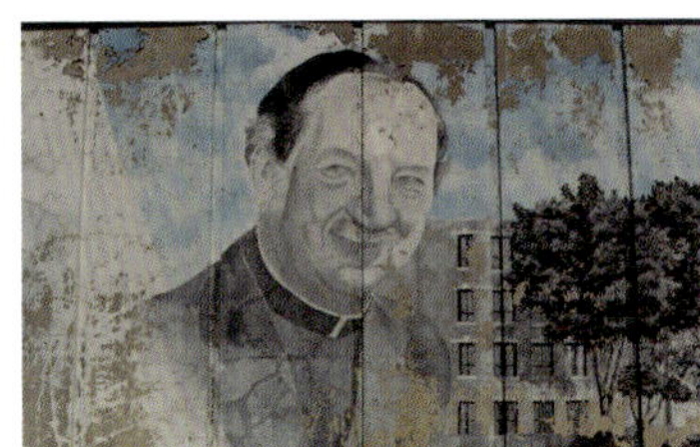

P. 101
Sudbury, ON, 2011

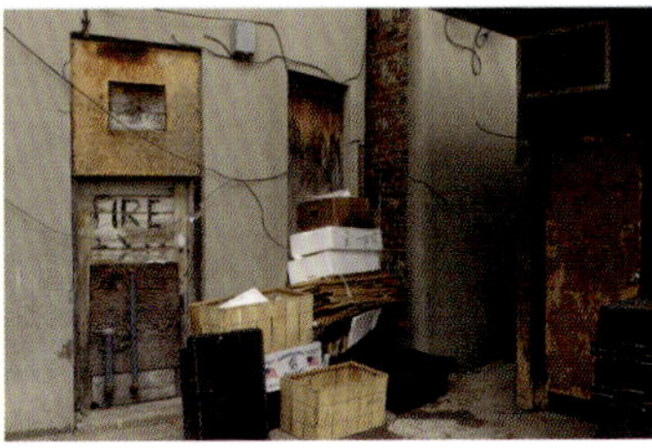

P. 102
Toronto, ON, 2012

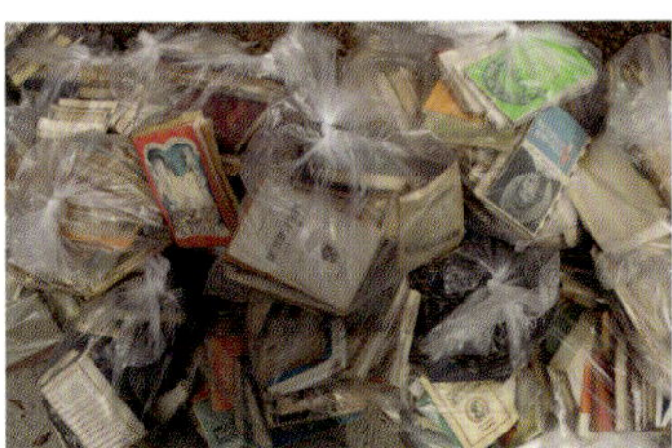

P. 103
Books for recycling, Trinity Bellwoods, Toronto, ON, 2014

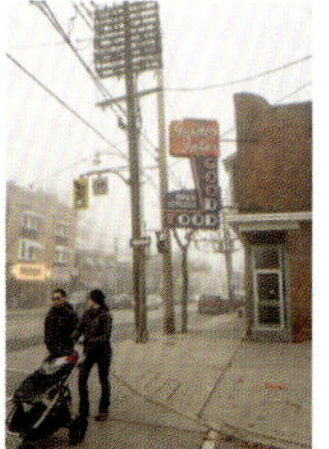
P. 104
Queen Street East, Toronto, ON, 2017

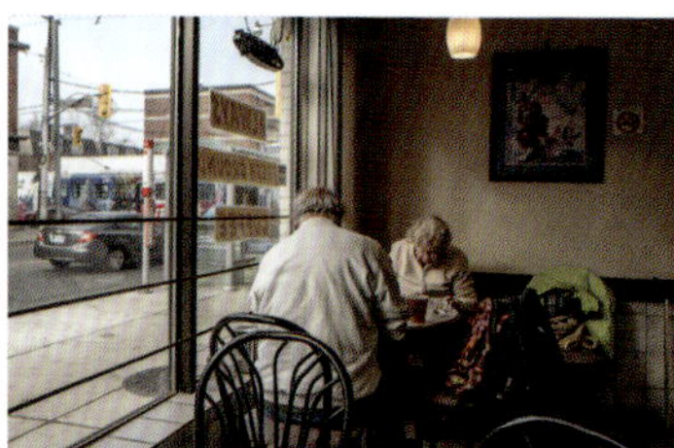
P. 105
Main Street, Toronto, ON, 2017

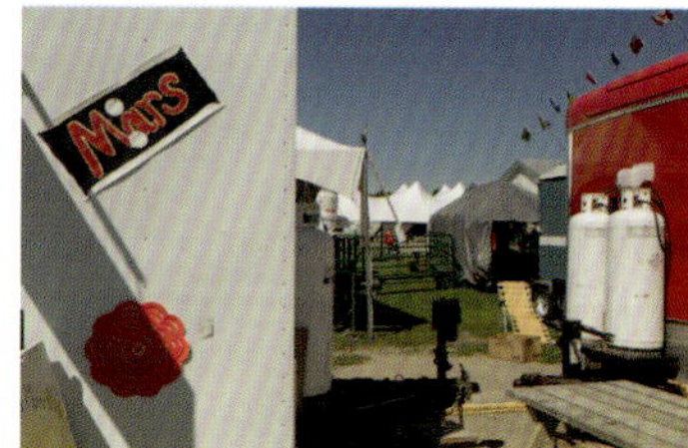
P. 106
Shawville, QC, 2018

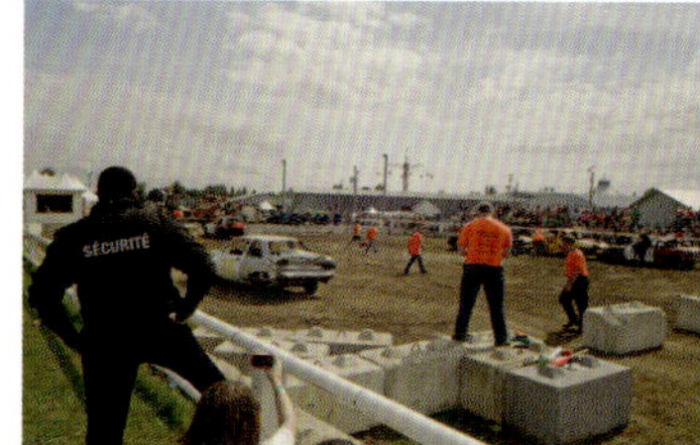
P. 107
Shawville, QC, 2013

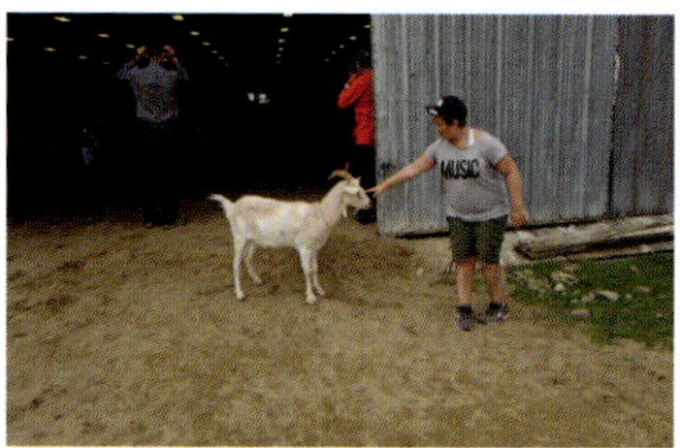
P. 108
Shawville, QC, 2015

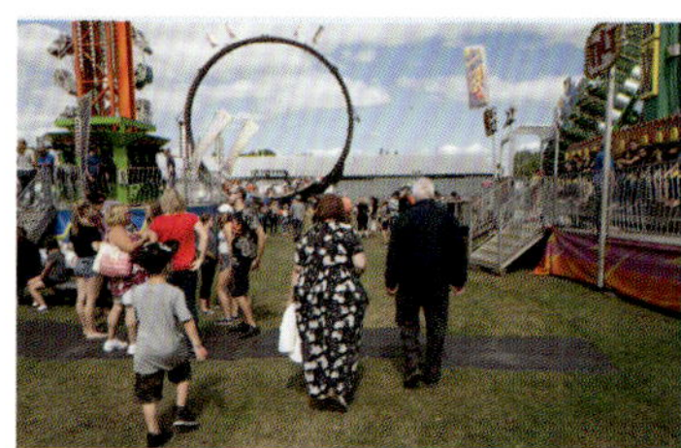
P. 109
Shawville, QC, 2018

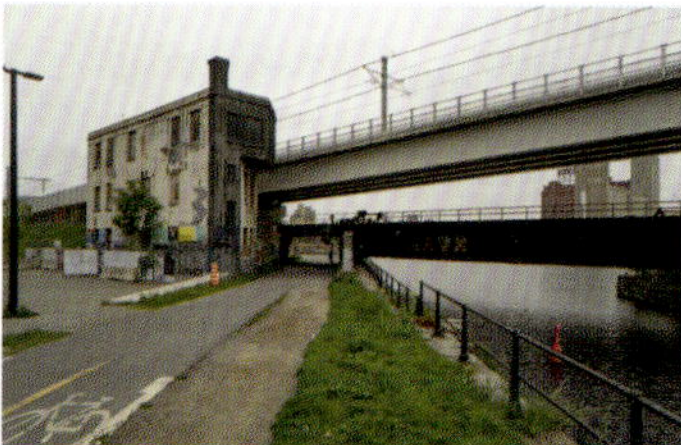
P. 111
Lachine Canal, Montreal, QC, 2023

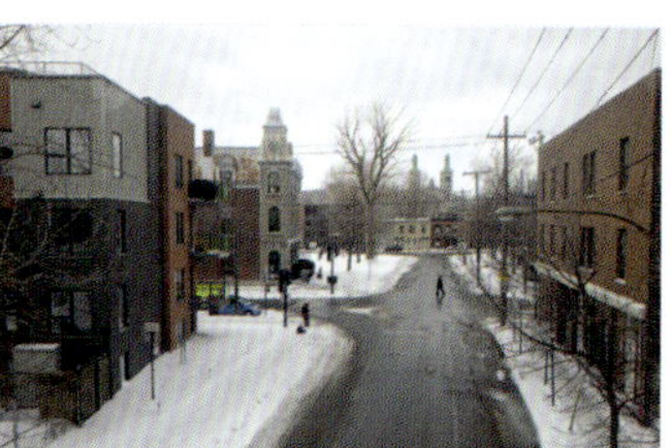
P. 112
From the train, Montreal, QC, 2016

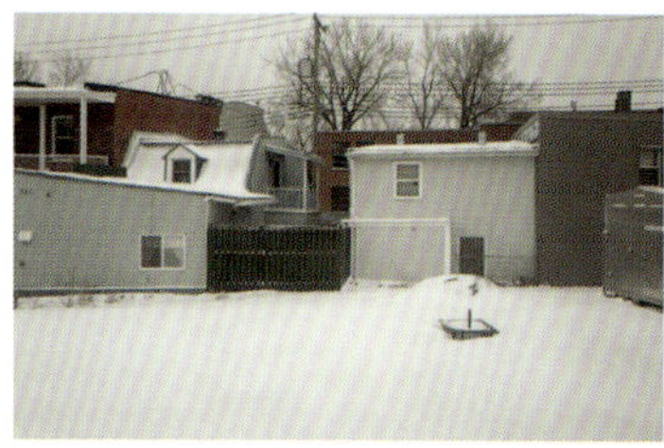
P. 113
From the train, Montreal, QC, 2019

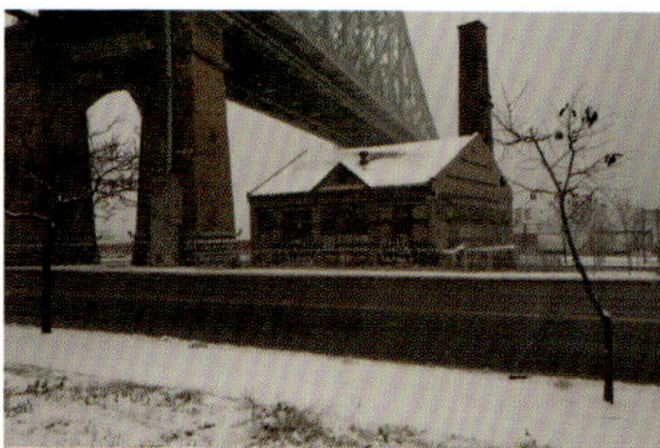
P. 114
Craig Pumping Station, Montreal, QC, 2018

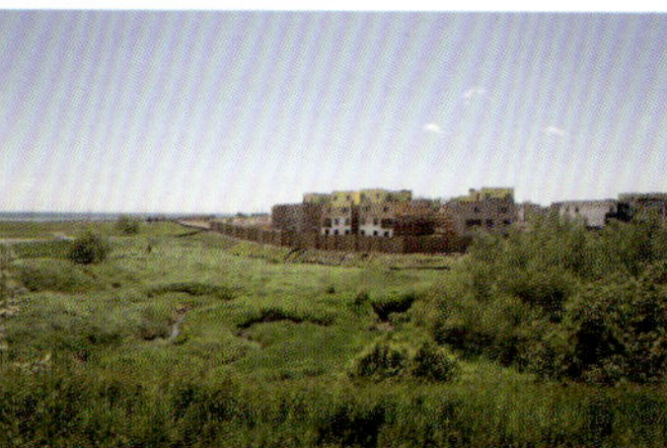
P. 116
From the train, Newcastle, ON, 2019

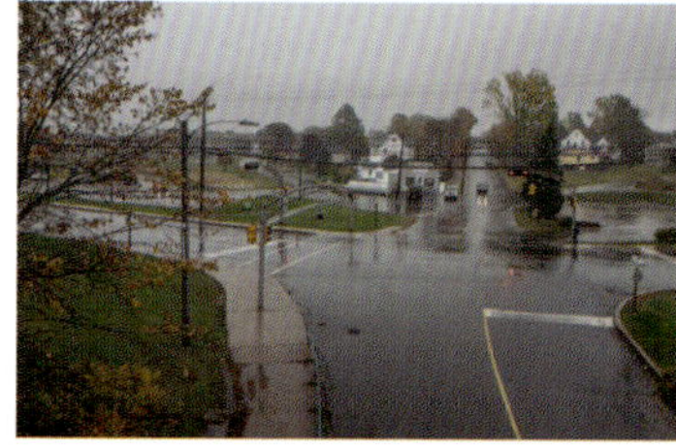
P. 118
From the train, Amherst, NS, 2019

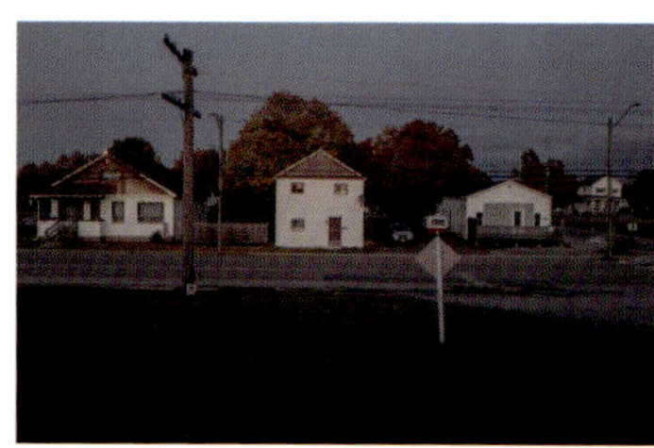
P. 119
From the train, Rogersville, NB, 2019

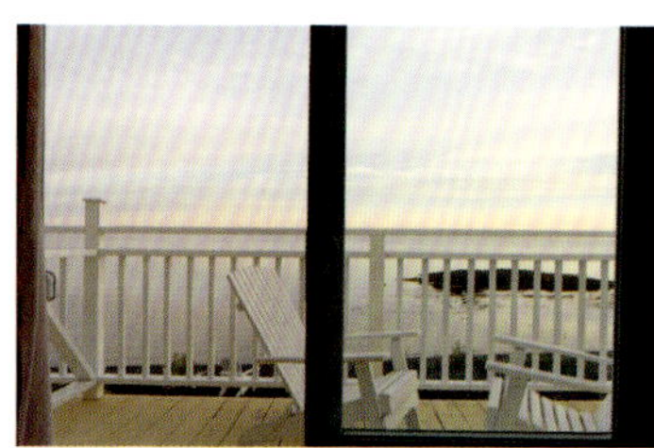
P. 121
Métis-sur-Mer, QC, 2012

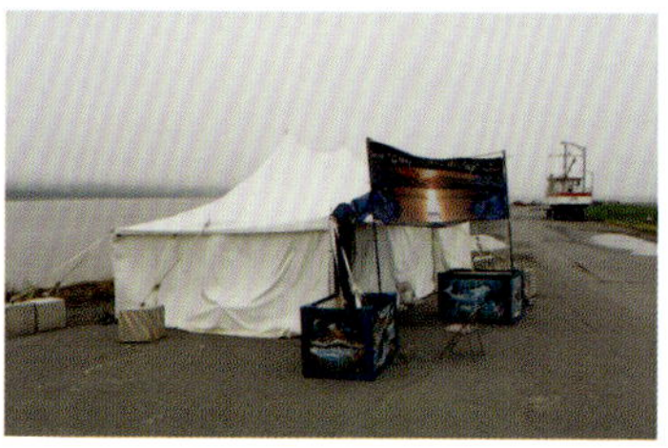
P. 123
Rivière-du-Loup, QC, 2012

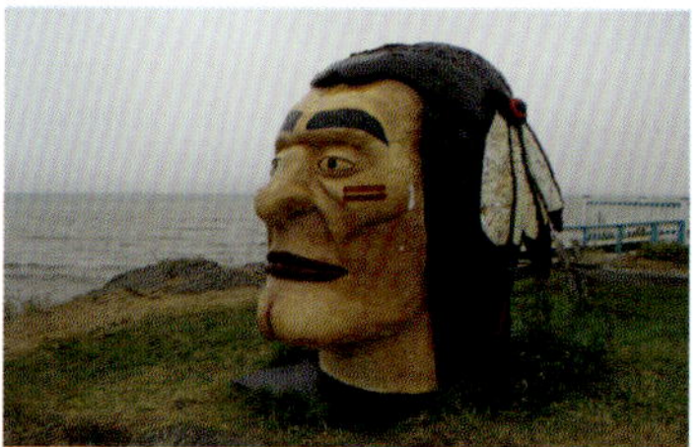
P. 125
Rivière-du-Loup, QC, 2012

ACKNOWLEDGEMENTS

FOR SUPPORT, sometimes practical, sometimes moral, I am grateful to the following: Atom Egoyan CC, Maia Sutnik, Robert Burley, Christian Lambert, Jan Allen, Susan Close, the Musagetes Foundation, Pierre Santoni of VIA Rail, Sarah Milroy, Phyllis Lambert, Ron Graham, David Christensen, Henri Robideau, Robert Fones, Yves Trépanier, Stephen Bulger, Andy Sylvester, Robert Walker, and David Cyrenne. A very special thanks to Peter Galassi for taking time from a busy writing schedule to look so closely and so carefully at the photographs that make up this book.

ABOUT PETER GALASSI

THE AMERICAN art historian Peter Galassi was chief curator of photography at the Museum of Modern Art (MoMA) from 1991 to 2011. Among the forty shows he mounted at the museum were solo exhibitions accompanied by major publications, including *Henri Cartier-Bresson: The Modern Century* (2010), *Jeff Wall* (2007), *Friedlander* (2005), *Andreas Gursky* (2001), *Aleksandr Rodchenko* (1998), and *Roy DeCarava: A Retrospective* (1996). Since retiring from the museum, he has also written *Robert Frank in America* (2014) and *Brassaï* (2018).

ABOUT GEOFFREY JAMES

GEOFFREY JAMES was born in Wales in 1942 and educated at Wellington College, Berkshire, and Wadham College, Oxford, where he edited the university magazine the *Isis*. Immigrating to Canada in 1966, he became a writer and editor with the Canadian edition of *TIME*. Self-taught as a photographer, he had his first exhibition in 1971 at Sir George Williams University in Montreal. James has produced or is the subject of more than a dozen books and monographs. His early work looked at the tradition of European garden-making and the oeuvre of Frederick Law Olmsted. More recent projects have considered the asbestos-mining landscape of Quebec, the US-Mexico border at Tijuana, as well as profiles of Lethbridge, Alberta; Paris, France; and Toronto, Ontario. His most recent book, *Inside Kingston Penitentiary*, covered the last six months of the prison's operational life. James has exhibited internationally, with solo museum shows at the Palazzo Braschi in Rome, the Royal Institute of British Architects in London, the Museum of Contemporary Art San Diego, the Americas Society in New York, the National Gallery of Canada, Architekturzentrum Wien, and UNESCO in Paris. His work is in the collections of MoMA, the San Francisco Museum of Modern Art, the Musée Carnavalet in Paris, and the Canadian Centre for Architecture. He is a Fellow of the John Simon Guggenheim Memorial Foundation and the Graham Foundation for Advanced Studies in the Fine Arts and is the recipient of the Gershon Iskowitz Prize and the Governor General's Award in Visual and Media Arts. He holds an honorary doctorate from St. John's College, University of Manitoba. Named as Toronto's first photo laureate, James now lives in Montreal. He is represented by the Stephen Bulger Gallery in Toronto.

For Jessica

24 25 26 27 28 5 4 3 2 1

Cataloguing data is available from Library and Archives Canada
ISBN 978-1-77327-253-5 (hbk.)

Design by Naomi MacDougall | DSGN Dept.

Editing by Steve Cameron
Copy editing by Marnie Lamb
Proofreading by Alison Strobel

FRONT COVER: *Miners' houses,* Copper Cliff, ON, 2012
BACK COVER: *Shawville Fair,* Shawville, QC, 2015

Printed and bound in China by Shenzhen Reliance Printing Co., Ltd.

Figure 1 Publishing Inc.
Vancouver BC Canada
www.figure1publishing.com

Figure 1 Publishing works in the traditional, unceded territory of the xʷməθkʷəy̓əm (Musqueam), Sḵwx̱wú7mesh (Squamish), and səlilwətaɬ (Tsleil-Waututh) peoples.